NEW YORK GIANTS

THE COMPLETE ILLUSTRATED HISTORY
REVISED EDITION

NEW YORK GIANTS

THE COMPLETE ILLUSTRATED HISTORY
REVISED EDITION

Lew Freedman

Foreword by Pat Summerall

MVP
BOOKS

On the front cover: (center) Eli Manning, 2012, photo by Ezra Shaw/Getty Images; (top right) Lawrence Taylor, 1981, photo by Nate Fine/Getty Images; (lower right) Giants' defense, 1958, photo by Robert Riger/Getty Images; (lower left) Giants defensive line, 2009, photo by Scott Cunningham/ Getty Images; (top left) David Tyree, 2008, photo by Drew Hallowell/Getty images

On the frontispiece: Osi Umenyiora (72) and Devin Thomas (15) celebrate after Super Bowl XLVI at Lucas Oil Stadium, February 5, 2012, photo by Al Pereira/Getty Images.

On the title page: MetLife Stadium, January 1, 2012, photo by Michael Heiman/Getty Images.

Right: Eli Manning, 2008, photo by Jeff Zelevansky/ Icon SMI/Corbis.

First published in 2009 by MVP Books, an imprint of MBI Publishing Company, 400 First Avenue North, Suite 300, Minneapolis, MN 55401 USA.

This second edition published 2012.

© 2009, 2012 MVP Books

Photograph copyrights as indicated with captions.

MVP Books titles are also available at discounts in bulk quantity for industrial or sales-promotional use. For details write to Special Sales Manager at Quayside Publishing Group, 400 First Avenue North, Suite 300, Minneapolis, MN 55401 USA.

To find out more about our books, visit us online at www.mvpbooks.com.

Library of Congress Cataloging-in-Publication Data

Freedman, Lew.
 New York Giants : the complete illustrated history
/ Lew Freedman ; foreword by Pat Summerall. -- Rev. ed.
    p. cm.
 ISBN 978-0-7603-4395-1 (hardback)
 1. New York Giants (Football team)--History. 2.
Football--New York (State)--New York--History. I. Title.
 GV956.N4F74 2012
 796.332'64097471--dc23

2012012637

ISBN-13: 978-0-7603-4395-1

Printed in China

CONTENTS

FOREWORD
BY PAT SUMMERALL

Pat Summerall played in the National Football League between 1952 and 1961 and then became a nationally renowned television sports commentator.

When I joined the New York Giants in 1958, coming over from the Chicago Cardinals, the Giants had just moved into Yankee Stadium and that move had a big effect on fans. The aura of Yankee Stadium, all of the championships the Yankees won and the sheer "glow" of the Yankees changed the entire outlook of New York towards the Giants. The championship and the move was the beginning of the increase in the Giants' popularity.

The Cardinals had told me that I was going to be a

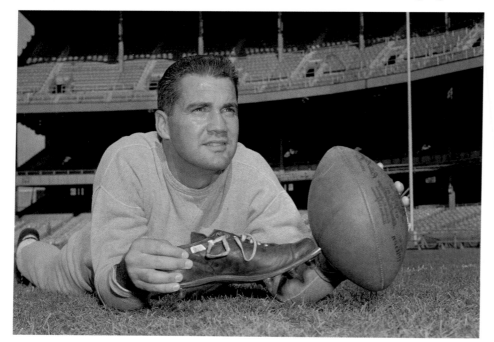

Pat Summerall as a young place kicker with the New York Giants in the late 1950s. *Bettmann/Corbis*

key member of the team and two weeks later they traded me. I had just about decided I wasn't going to play any more football, but I knew Jim Lee Howell, the Giants' coach. He had been at the University of Arkansas when I was there and he had a great assistant coaching staff with Vince Lombardi and Tom Landry. Jim had been a marine lieutenant during World War II and he was a tough disciplinarian. You had better be on time and you had better be where you were supposed to be.

Lombardi and Landry both became Hall of Fame coaches, and they were our assistants. When I first went to the Giants we were in training camp in Oregon and a bunch of us went out drinking beer and renewing old acquaintances. The next day the meeting room was raucous and one of the other assistant coaches tried to quiet the room, but was making no progress.

All of a sudden, this guy walked in, cleared his throat, and the whole room went silent. I said to the player sitting next to me, "Who the hell is that?" He said, "That's Lombardi. You'll know soon enough." And he was right about that.

The whole atmosphere of being with the New York Giants was entirely different from being with the Cardinals. It was a much classier operation. The owners, the Mara family, had that reputation and they lived up to it. The players on the Giants may not have been physically much better, but mentally they were. There were a lot of smart players on the Giants in the late 1950s and early 1960s.

The 1958 season was a great year to join the Giants. I was always listed as an end and a kicker on rosters, but I was mostly the kicker. As the season wound down we were in a tough battle to win the Eastern Conference against the Cleveland Browns. We had to beat them to force a playoff and I was sent onto the field in a blizzard to attempt a long field goal. Jim Lee Howell called the play for the kick. The wind was swirling and the snow covered the yard markers. The line of scrimmage was near mid-field and nobody thought we would try for a field goal. When I jogged into the huddle our quarterback, Charlie Conerly, said, "What the hell are you doing here?"

Officially, the kick was listed as being from 49 yards, but nobody really knows how far it was. Some guy wrote that it was 52 yards. Some people said it was 55 yards. I know it was a long way. I knew I had to hit it in the sweet spot to get it that far, especially in weather conditions like that. I knew as soon as I touched it that I had hit it where I wanted to hit it. So I knew it was going to get there for distance, but I didn't know if it was going to be true enough. I could see the goal post and I could see the ball on its flight. It behaved like a knuckleball, breaking back and forth. I just hoped that it would break through the uprights. It did.

When I ran back to the sidelines, Lombardi grabbed me and hugged me and yelled, "You son of a bitch, you know you can't kick it that far." We won the game and that is still considered one of the most famous plays in Giants history. It comes up all of the time. It regularly gets discussed. We won that game and beat the Browns again and that put us into the championship game.

The NFL title game in 1958 between the Giants and the Baltimore Colts is the game that has been called "the greatest game ever played." It had such a strong influence on television, fans, and on the league. It was the first sudden-death overtime game. But I don't think any of us Giants who were in the game thought it was the best game we had played. We lost four fumbles and we lost the game, 23–17.

I think it was the most important game ever played. It was the first overtime game and it was a championship game and people had never seen anything like that. It carried a lot of aura with it. I can understand why it was called the best game.

That time period was a terrific stretch in Giants' history. We reached the championship game again in 1959—and lost to the Colts again—and the Giants won the Eastern Conference in 1961, 1962, and 1963, too. By then I had retired and begun my broadcasting career.

Only a few years later there was a revolution in place kicking. Like all those who had come before me, I was a straightaway kicker. By the middle of the 1960s, the Giants had this kicker named Pete Gogolak who came over from the Buffalo Bills in the American Football League and he kicked his field goals and extra points soccer style, approaching with a couple of steps from the side.

I saw him kick it and I tried to kick the same way a couple of times because it was a novelty. If I came back later in life as a kicker I would kick soccer style. It's so much easier on your leg. It's more like a golf swing. With straightaway kicking you just use the muscles in your thigh. Your leg gets very fatigued very quickly. Soccer style is more like a swing.

The Giants had been around New York for years under the ownership of the Mara family, but the teams I played with helped establish the popularity of the sport more firmly. We had a lot of good guys and great players who were very bright. Sam Huff, Dick Modelzewski, Andy Robustelli, Kyle Rote, and our backup quarterback Don Heinrich were some of them.

Everybody seems to remember me as a Giant and as one of those Giants. Nobody even remembers the Chicago Cardinals. When I say I played for the Chicago Cardinals, people say, "When were they in Chicago?" I was a sports broadcaster for so long that some fans don't even realize that I played.

The Giants were regarded as a classy organization when I joined the team and I think they are still regarded as the same classy organization now. I think the Giants are viewed as one of the fairest, most classy teams. Maybe I think that because I was a Giant, but I think a lot of that is attributable to the Mara family. Tim, the founder, and his sons Jack, and particularly Wellington, who was regarded as a pillar of the league and established the Giants' reputation. The Maras go back to 1925, to the early days of the NFL, and that's pretty special.

Working together, Pat Summerall and John Madden (seen in 1983) became the most respected and popular NFL television announcing duo.
Wally McNamee/Corbis

INTRODUCTION

The Giants' distinctive blue helmet with white NY lettering sits on the field before the NFC divisional playoff game against the Dallas Cowboys at Texas Stadium in January 2008.
Chris Graythen/Getty Images

The name was already taken by the National League baseball club, but how fitting to apply the moniker to the New York football team anyway when it began playing in the new National Football League in 1925: Giants.

It was the right match with the right city.

New York was America's most gigantic city, a teeming, energetic metropolis that seemed, to those who lived in the rural hinterlands (and other not-so-rural cities of the USA) larger than life in so many ways. The founders of the team could not foresee a day and age when almost all of the players on the roster would be behemoths, but Giants was an appropriate name, nonetheless.

In the "roaring twenties," America thought big on many fronts, and what the heck, there was probably some residual goodwill in appropriating the nickname from John McGraw's diamond twirlers and sluggers. It was the age of Babe Ruth, Jack Dempsey and Gene Tunney, Bobby Jones, Bill Tilden, and Red Grange, a time when being a giant was part of the landscape in popular sports.

At least they sounded big from the start. The New York "football" Giants, as famed team announcer Chris Schenkel often put it, to differentiate the pigskin carriers from the horsehide wallopers, struggled to establish an identity initially, at least partially because the Great Depression followed hard on the heels of the great prosperity of the 1920s. But gridiron success cemented the enduring popularity of the team in the minds of New Yorkers. The football players may have had a name in common with the Giants' baseball players, but one thing the football team had going for it during the first 35 years of its existence was almost no fractionalization of the fan base. One could root for the Yankees, Dodgers, or Giants in baseball, but in football, the Giants unified the local sports fans.

After some financially shaky beginnings, the Giants emerged as one of the most stable NFL franchises, partly because of secure ownership. Other teams might pass from hand to hand, but the Mara clan

tenaciously clung to the Giants. Football business was the family business. Father Tim Mara was the clear-eyed founder, but his sons, Wellington and John, were the wide-eyed, fuzzy-cheeked inheritors, who made the Giants their lives' work from the time they were boys. Wellington's Giants commitment spanned 80 years.

No team is going to have a run of success of 80-plus years, but the Giants were winners more often than not, and the Giants sprinkled their championships around, from decade to decade. The Giants were present and accounted for once the NFL organized conference against conference championships in the 1930s. They had their shots in the 1940s. They had their glory in the 1950s and 1960s. And the Giants have won four world titles in the Super Bowl era, while participating in the biggest single game on the American sports scene five times.

They have blessed their sports fans with stars in every generation, including Benny Friedman, one of the league's first great quarterbacks, Tuffy Leemans, Mel Hein, Emlen Tunnell, Charlie Conerly, Sam Huff, Frank Gifford, Roosevelt Brown, Andy Robustelli, Phil Simms, Lawrence Taylor, Michael Strahan, and Tiki Barber.

As an organization, despite their down moments, the Giants reeked of class. Their elegant dark blue jerseys and helmets with the "NY" on the hard shell headgear projected that simple statement. There was no mistaking a Giants' uniform, and the nation got to know the Giants well. As of the start of the 2009 season, the New Yorkers had appeared in 44 post-season games since 1933.

The Giants participated in 14 NFL championship games before the Super Bowl existed, winning three of them. In 2012 the Giants won their fourth Super Bowl.

The famed 1925 national tour that the Chicago Bears made with the legendary Red Grange (left) gave the New York Giants a tremendous financial boost by attracting 70,000 fans to the Polo Grounds during the Giants' first year of NFL play.
Bettmann/Corbis

There have been great moments and great players, as any franchise with longevity can claim, but the Giants have had more than their share. The teams of the late 1950s and early 1960s captured the attention of the entire country, and more than in any other Giants era, the names of the key players from that period seem to be revered and admired. Over time, some 29 players and coaches who either wore Giants' blue or coached those who did have been elected to the Pro Football Hall of Fame in Canton, Ohio. They were not all Giants for their entire careers, but they left at least some mark in New York.

Perhaps the most exciting time was the late 1950s, when the pro game was first outgrowing the shadow of college football. Drama followed the Giants. The Giants participated in the event called "the greatest game ever played" in 1958 against the Colts, the first overtime championship. The Giants were TV favorites at a time when TV exposure elevated the sport's popularity ahead of baseball for the first time. The Giants were the heroes of a second "sneaker" game over the Bears in 1956. Giants' assistant coaches outgrew their britches and became legends elsewhere, Tom Landry in Dallas and Vince Lombardi in Green Bay. The Giants gave the football universe "The Violent World of Sam Huff," a television documentary, and the Giants gave the football world the final, noble seasons of bald and bleeding Y.A. Tittle.

Pro football was a young sport when the Giants were founded. Pro football has matured and become more sophisticated in the intervening years, with the use of clever and creative offenses and defenses, improved and safer uniforms, and the introduction of substances summarized as "artificial turf."

Wellington Mara recalled that as a nine-year-old boy in 1925 he was sitting on the Giants' bench and overheard a command from first coach Bob Folwell. Folwell told a player entering the game to give the opponents hell. Mara decided that pro football must be some tough game. He was right. Football is a tough game, and it takes Giants to play it well.

There was no doubt who these fans were cheering at a celebratory gathering at Giants Stadium after their team defeated the New England Patriots for the Super Bowl title in 2008.
Tony Kurdzuk/Star Ledger/Corbis

An aerial view of a packed Giants Stadium during a September 2008 New York Giants–Cincinnati Bengals game.
David Drapkin/Getty Images

THE 1920s
PRO FOOTBALL COMES TO NEW YORK

Tim Mara was a New York sports promoter and bookmaker when he was approached about buying a franchise in the fledgling National Football League. He shelled out $500 and introduced the New York football Giants to his home city.
Bettmann/Corbis

Tim Mara was a bookmaker in New York at a time when the profession was legitimate, and so it was no surprise that he was a betting man. Mara wagered a chunk of his bank account on pro football making it big in the biggest city in the United States.

It doesn't sound like much—a pittance really—but even the $500 franchise fee that Mara paid (unless it was $2,500 as sometimes rumored) bought a name, not a license to print money, nor even anything close to a guarantee of success. The National Football League was only five years old in 1925 when Mara made his sporting proposition, but most of the teams that had joined the fray in an automobile showroom in 1920 had already gone belly up. This was despite the aura of optimism that coddled American life during the 1920s, when all things seemed possible, when sporting figures became as popular as stars of the silent screen and as famous as the president of the United States. In fact, when Babe Ruth, the "Sultan of Swat," who not only saved baseball after the seamy Black Sox Scandal, but was also a signature figure of the excess of the times, battled Yankee management for an $80,000 contract, one point of argument was that he had enjoyed a better year than the president. Mara had only to gaze at the skyline to acknowledge that the baseball palace recently constructed in the Bronx was indeed the "House That Ruth Built."

Following the peace concluding World War I, it might be said of the 1920s, that a good time was had by all, especially heavyweight champ Jack Dempsey, golfer Bobby Jones, and college football star Red Grange. Prohibition governed the land, but Americans everywhere seemed to ache for a good party of any kind. So why not pro football? Yes, it was true that the game was viewed as brutal in some quarters, and to a large extent the image was earned. Large men wearing leather helmets for protection, or none at all, collided with full force, cracking bones and teeth with equanimity. But in this era of peace, the stock market was churning out a millionaire a minute, or so it seemed. It was a time of great prosperity, and Tim Mara took a flyer.

Tim Mara was born in New York City in 1887, an Irishman by heritage and inclination. His father died when he was young and Mara's schooling ended by his teens when his jobs selling newspapers and working as an usher in a theater overwhelmed his time and need to support his mother. Mara staked out regular customers as a newsboy, and the astute lad picked up on the nature of his clientele. The men who seemed to be best off were bookmakers. Mara talked his way into a job as a runner, as the collector of losing bets.

Before he was 20, Mara had started his own bookmaking business, a business he was able to build because he was charming to the customers and above all, honest handling money. As business improved, he moved off the street to a more coveted location—the race track. A good reputation helped Mara move in some of New York's sporting circles. He was friendly with fight promoter Billy Gibson and that association proved to be life-changing for Mara and his family.

In 1925, the most reliable teams in the NFL were the Chicago Bears and the Green Bay Packers. Teams representing other cities came and went like ducks

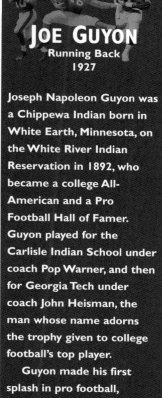

JOE GUYON
Running Back
1927

Joseph Napoleon Guyon was a Chippewa Indian born in White Earth, Minnesota, on the White River Indian Reservation in 1892, who became a college All-American and a Pro Football Hall of Famer. Guyon played for the Carlisle Indian School under coach Pop Warner, and then for Georgia Tech under coach John Heisman, the man whose name adorns the trophy given to college football's top player.

Guyon made his first splash in pro football, getting paid per game, before the National Football League took shape in 1920. He then teamed up with Jim Thorpe in the backfield for the Canton Bulldogs. Guyon also played minor league baseball under Joe McCarthy, who later won seven pennants with the New York Yankees.

Running, passing, tackling, punting, blocking—Guyon could do it all. He stood 6 feet 1 inch, weighed 180 pounds, and had tremendous speed. Guyon played just one season for the Giants in 1927, but the team won its first NFL title by compiling the league's best record of 11–1–1.

according to season. One minute the Duluth Eskimos were a member, the next they were out. And a league hoping to present itself as big-league needed to break into the New York market.

The first NFL commissioner was Jim Thorpe, acknowledged as the world's greatest athlete, who won Olympic gold medals in 1912 in the decathlon and pentathlon, starred as a running back with the Canton Bulldogs, and even played major league baseball. But Thorpe was a figurehead and lasted only a year on the job. By 1925, Thorpe, at 37, was in the backfield for the Giants making a brief comeback. His administrative replacement was a man named Joe Carr, better suited for the paperwork responsibilities. Carr had previously operated the Columbus Panhandles.

Carr sought an owner to run a football team in the nation's largest city. He first approached Gibson, who thought about the idea, but was about to scotch his involvement when Mara dropped by his office. He piped up that Mara might be interested in what Carr was selling. Mara admittedly knew less about pro football than he did about growing oranges in Florida, but that didn't scare him. When representatives of the first NFL teams gathered to found the league in Canton, Ohio, they were expected to pay a $100 franchise entry fee. There is no indication the teams paid those bills. But in Carr's pitch the price was $500.

Mara was just about 38 years old when he met

Five members of the pre-NFL Canton Bulldogs, one of pro football's first great teams, in 1919. From left to right: unidentified player, Pete Calac, Jim Thorpe, Joe Guyon, and Guy Chamberlin. Thorpe, the NFL's first commissioner, and Guyon, spent some time with the Giants early in franchise history.
Pro Football Hall of Fame/NFL/Getty Images

Carr. He was financially comfortable, married, and the father of two young boys. He was neither giddy about the idea of operating a professional sports franchise, nor put off by the suggestion. He thought he might be able to make a go of it, so he bought in with the famous understated words, "A New York franchise to operate anything ought to be worth $500," he said. Mara's son Wellington later said his father also noted that, "an empty store with chairs in it is worth more than $500 in New York."

Mara became proprietor of the New York football club, one that did not have a name and did not have a place to play. Partial to the New York Giants' baseball club, he adopted the same nickname, and soon enough started paying rent to the Giants for autumn usage of the Polo Grounds. Unlike many modern-day owners who immediately immerse themselves in areas of the football operation that they have no background for, Mara installed Gibson as team president and hired Harry March, who had promoted football in Canton, as team secretary.

Above: The New York Giants get instructions from head coach Bob Folwell and assistant coach Joe Alexander under the lights at the Polo Grounds, the team's first home field.
Bettmann/Corbis

Right: Wellington T. Mara (1916–2005), co-owner of the New York Giants, became involved with the family team as a child and stayed involved for 75 years. Like his father, Giants' founder Tim Mara, Wellington is also a Hall of Famer.
Bettmann/Corbis

Mara felt the times were right for a promoter with savvy. "The Giants were founded on a combination of brute strength and ignorance," he once said. "The players supplied the brute strength and I supplied the ignorance. But you have to remember that New York City in the 1920s was a virgin area for a smart promoter. There was money around and people would buy anything, or at least they could come around to see or hear it."

For his minimal investment, Mara thought it would be no trouble rousing enough New Yorkers to attend his games and help him turn a profit. The Giants hired Robert Folwell as their first coach, who came from the U.S. Naval Academy and had coached the University of Pennsylvania. Some prominent All-American players, from lineman Joe Alexander to tackle Century Milstead, signed. The Giants lost their first official game, 14–0, to Providence, but finished the season with an 8–4 record. The home opener against the Frankford Yellowjackets took place on October 18, and while attendance was about 25,000, only about half of the spectators paid. Not only did the Mara sons pass out free tickets to their school chums, but professional publicity men handed out free tickets all over town. Tim Mara walked the streets trying to sell tickets at half price, but often gave them away free.

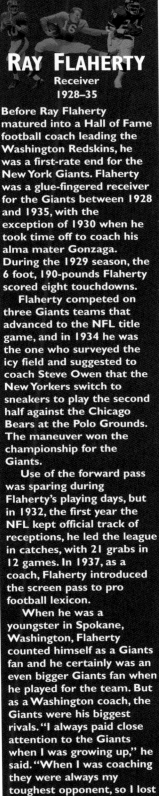

"My brother was in town from Wilkes-Barre, Pennsylvania, and a girl I was seeing from Parkersburg, West Virginia, also came up for the game."
—*Giants guard Al Bedner, on his motivation to play well in a 1926 New York showdown with the fledgling AFL Philadelphia Quakers.*

Winning was a nice perk, but the won-lost record didn't concern Mara as much as the lack of public interest. Attendance was abysmal and he lost money rapidly. A game against the Columbus Tigers might have drawn 1,000 fans. Mara's losses reached $45,000, making his purchase seem less like a bargain. But Mara's first reaction when someone urged him to sell was, "Where could I find anyone crazy enough to buy it?" Besides, Mara recognized he owned a family plaything. John and Wellington loved the team more than anything else in their lives. They mingled with the players and acted as ballboys. Mara said that if he sold the team his sons would kill him. "The boys would run me right out of the house if I did (sell)," Mara said.

The boys came on board as the first season started. The family was attending services at Our Lady of Esperanza Roman Catholic church on 156th Street and young Wellington distinctly heard his father tell a friend, "I'm gonna try to put football over on New York today." John Mara, who was 17, walked the sidelines at the first home game with his father. Wellington, nine, sat in the stands at the Polo Grounds with his mother Lizette. As is common at many games, the fans sat on the bench side of the team they favored. Only that side was in the shade and it was surprisingly chilly on a sunny day. That night, Wellington's mother complained to Tim Mara that she was worried Wellington would catch a cold and why didn't he locate the Giants' bench on the sunny side of the stadium? The move was made—permanently.

In the 1920s, pro football was a country cousin of college football. The college game was well-established and players such as Knute Rockne had made Notre Dame a household name. The service academies were powerhouses. Each school could claim a backlog of alumni sure to support the old university. Pro football teams had no ready-made fan bases, however. They were starting from scratch in the communities they purported to represent. They had a good product, and they knew the caliber of play was better than college ball, but there was still a "show-me" body of thought about the ability of pro teams to beat the best college teams.

Ray Flaherty, an early star end for the Giants, became coach of the Redskins in 1936. Here he is giving instructions to quarterbacks Frank Filchock (30) and Sammy Baugh (33) at a workout before leaving for New York to meet the Giants at the Polo Grounds.
Bettmann/Corbis

RAY FLAHERTY
Receiver
1928–35

Before Ray Flaherty matured into a Hall of Fame football coach leading the Washington Redskins, he was a first-rate end for the New York Giants. Flaherty was a glue-fingered receiver for the Giants between 1928 and 1935, with the exception of 1930 when he took time off to coach his alma mater Gonzaga. During the 1929 season, the 6 foot, 190-pounds Flaherty scored eight touchdowns.

Flaherty competed on three Giants teams that advanced to the NFL title game, and in 1934 he was the one who surveyed the icy field and suggested to coach Steve Owen that the New Yorkers switch to sneakers to play the second half against the Chicago Bears at the Polo Grounds. The maneuver won the championship for the Giants.

Use of the forward pass was sparing during Flaherty's playing days, but in 1932, the first year the NFL kept official track of receptions, he led the league in catches, with 21 grabs in 12 games. In 1937, as a coach, Flaherty introduced the screen pass to pro football lexicon.

When he was a youngster in Spokane, Washington, Flaherty counted himself as a Giants fan and he certainly was an even bigger Giants fan when he played for the team. But as a Washington coach, the Giants were his biggest rivals. "I always paid close attention to the Giants when I was growing up," he said. "When I was coaching they were always my toughest opponent, so I lost my love for them."

WILBUR "PETE" HENRY

Tackle
1927

Wilbur Henry was called "Pete" by some and "Fats" by others, and apparently only immediate members of his family called him Wilbur. A Hall of Famer who passed through New York briefly (in an era when there were no long-term contracts), he stopped by at the right time.

Henry stood 6 feet tall and weighed 250-pounds. He looked more like a beer salesman, or a beer keg, than a football player. His was not a weight-lifting, sculpted look, so he earned the "Fats" nickname. No one made fun of Henry when they ran up against him on the field, however. He looked like a round mound, but played 60 minutes of football, going both ways at tackle. When he signed with the Canton Bulldogs, it was front-page news in that Ohio town. When he came to New York in 1927, he solidified the Giants' stingy defense. Also belying his size, Henry was a prominent punter and kicker who recorded a 94-yard punt for Akron in 1923.

A winner of 11 letters at Washington and Lee University, Henry not only starred in football, but in baseball, basketball, and track and field. The football boss was Bob Folwell, the same coach who led the Giants in their first season. Henry later served as athletic director at his alma mater. One sportswriter said of Henry, "He was as mild and gentle as one of Sabu's pet elephants off the field, but he became a terror when unleashed on the gridiron."

The single-most important football figure in the 1920s, and perhaps in the history of the sport, was Harold "Red" Grange, the "Wheaton Ice Man." Grange was a charismatic star for the University of Illinois, a player who almost solely wrecked Michigan with his slashing running ability. Grange made headline news all over the country. He was the most famous player in the land. There was no one in the pro game remotely comparable in name recognition. Grange's exploits were well-publicized, but in the days before television, only those within easy driving distance of Champaign, Illinois, or other Big Ten venues saw him play.

As the end of Grange's college career approached, he was propositioned by a promoter named C.C. Pyle, who, because of his bold schemes, was nicknamed "Cash and Carry" Pyle. Pyle became Grange's agent. Through shrewd dealing he placed Grange with the Chicago Bears for an elaborate football tour. The tour was a wild success for Grange (it made him rich), for Pyle (it made him rich, too), for the Bears, for the NFL, and for many teams that scheduled the Grange-led squad. Sensing a score, Tim Mara signed up his Giants to face the Bears featuring Grange at the Polo Grounds.

The game was played December 6, 1925, and while the Bears were victorious, 19–7, Mara did not care. About 70,000 fans turned out and he walked

Above: Red Grange of the Chicago Bears during the 1925 game against the Giants at the Polo Grounds in New York City that helped establish the popularity of pro football in the Big Apple. *Bettmann/Corbis*

Below: The way the game looked in the 1920s: the Giants run a play against the Chicago Bears in the Polo Grounds. *Bettmann/Corbis*

"It was like bouncing off a rubber ball. I never budged him once."
—Pottsville Maroons' lineman Charlie Berry, on trying to block Giants Hall of Fame lineman "Fats" Henry.

away with $143,000 in receipts. That single day not only wiped out Mara's debt, it wiped out his doubt that the Giants could make it in New York. "This really established the sport of professional football in New York," Wellington Mara said years later.

After Grange's spectacular tour ended, Pyle wanted his own franchise in the NFL, featuring his running back, in New York. The league refused. So Pyle started his own league and went after the Giants and Tim Mara head-to-head with his newly formed New York Yankees gridiron team. Although Mara was entrenched in the established league, to some it felt as if he fielded the inferior product because the other guys had Grange, "the Galloping Ghost," who had earned his primary nickname by being so difficult to tackle. Things got worse when Folwell jumped leagues to coach the Philadelphia Quakers.

The Giants and Philadelphia actually met for a championship game of sorts in 1926, New York

representing the NFL and the Quakers Pyle's AFL. The program from that game on December 12 featured Giants' running back Jack McBride on the cover. Mara wanted to shut Pyle's mouth about just who had the best team and league.

"Everyone on the Giants wanted to win that one," said tackle Babe Parnell. "The first-place Quakers thought the seventh-place Giants were pushovers, but we kicked the bleep out of them." Parnell's description may not have been poetic, but it was accurate, with the Giants triumphing 31–0 at the Polo Grounds. It was a challenging day for a rough game. Some 15 inches of snow were scraped off the field and the physical play along the line was memorable. Al Bedner said the Quakers' linemen did not live up to their peaceful nickname. "They started holding me early in the game," Bedner said. "I was a boxer and wrestler, so I knew how to handle this."

While Tim Mara hired good football people, the Giants were successful in four of their first five years. Some players made as little as $100 a game. Some made $400 a game. Perhaps Mara's most unusual contract was his pact with Jim Thorpe in 1925. Not even Thorpe pretended he could play with the same verve as he had shown in his prime. Nor did he possess the same stamina at 37 he had at 27. So Mara inked Thorpe to a contract paying him $250 for each half he played.

The Giants unleash a punt. Note the good old days of 1920s football when helmets did not have face masks.
Bettmann/Corbis

Jack McBride was one of the Giants' first star backfield performers in the 1920s and 1930s. However, he didn't always land on his feet after a tackle. *Bettmann/Corbis*

"Cal Hubbard was the mountain that moved like a man. He played end or tackle and some awed foes persist in the belief that he played them at one and the same time."
—*Pro Football Hall of Fame press release.*

As young as the team was, as fresh on the scene as the Giants were, and as late in the decade as they began, the Giants still managed to field some of the greatest football players of all time under their banner before the 1930s. Many of them were one-year wonders, just starting out or just finishing careers, or wooed by the upstart American Football League. Thorpe was one such player. Joe Guyon, another future Hall of Famer, played just one season in 1927, but was a world champion with the Canton Bulldogs in 1919 and 1920. Like his running mate Thorpe, Guyon was an alumnus of the Carlisle Indian School and his nickname during his playing days was "Indian Joe." Guyon grew up on an Indian reservation in Minnesota and his formal schooling ended in the sixth grade—until he discovered his sports ability. His athletic skills provided additional educational opportunities at Carlisle and Georgia Tech. "It was hard trying to make anything out of yourself," Guyon said. "Sports were one of the few ways a youngster could pull himself up."

Guyon was a multi-talented back who could run, throw, and kick, and was a prolific scorer. Near the end of the 1927 season, in a close game with the Bears, Guyon threw the winning touchdown pass. That was also the game in which George Halas tried to level Guyon and put him out with an injury. Guyon turned the tables and delivered a swift, hard kick to Halas' mid-

Giants Season-Opening Games, 1925–29

1925	October 11	at Providence, R.I.	Loss 14–0
1926	September 26	at Hartford, Conn.	Win 21–0
1927	September 25	at Providence, R.I.	Win 8–0
1928	September 30	at Pottsville, Pa.	Win 12–6
1929	September 29	at Orange, N.J.	Tie 0–0

Feared Hall of Famer Cal Hubbard was the dominant lineman of his era, starting in the late 1920s when players went both ways on offense and defense.
Bettmann/Corbis

CAL HUBBARD
Tackle
1927–28, 1936

Cal Hubbard was the first king-sized Giant. When men who weighed less than 200 pounds still played on the offensive and defensive lines, the 6 feet 5 inches Hubbard, whose weight was variously listed at between 250- and 280-pounds during his career, could scare opponents half to death just by shouting "Boo!"

Hubbard was a tackle and an end; he was one of the most important reasons why the intimidating defense of the Giants in 1927 surrendered an absurdly low 20 points in 13 games. Hubbard, who was inducted into the Pro Football Hall of Fame when it opened in 1963, was also a major league baseball umpire and is in the Baseball Hall of Fame, as well. "The best I ever saw was Cal Hubbard," said Jimmy Conzelmen a fellow football Hall of Famer of the then-Chicago Cardinals.

Hubbard was remarkably fast for his size, something else that bothered running backs trying to zip past him, and he hit very hard. Hubbard was called a human bowling ball for the wreckage he wreaked, and he didn't leave many spares when he rolled along. Old football comrades must have gotten a chuckle out of the description "The Enforcer," which was applied to Hubbard when he laid down the law in baseball.

The big man played 1927 and 1928 for the Giants, and spent the bulk of his career with the Packers, returning to New York for one more season in 1936. Hubbard was voted the best tackle in the NFL's first 50 years of play.

Jim Thorpe (wearing a baseball uniform in this 1914 photo) was one of the greatest athletes of all time, playing major league baseball as well as football, and winning two gold medals at the 1912 Olympics.
Bettmann/Corbis

section, dropping him on the spot. Guyon shouted that Halas had clipped him and the referee fell for the scam. As Halas was carried off the field, the ref marched off a 15-yard penalty on Chicago. Giants' linemen admonished Halas, saying, "George, you should know better than to try to sneak up on an Indian."

That Bears game was a war. Steve Owen had joined the Giants in 1926 and remained with the team until 1953, including his long tenure as coach. He played in the 1927 game, all 60 minutes, and said it was the toughest game of his career. His opposite number was Bears' tackle Jim McMillen, who later became a prominent professional wrestler and through his largesse during the Depression helped bail out the Bears when George Halas was about to default on a payment.

"When the gun went off, both of us just sat on the ground in the middle of the field," Owen said. "He smiled in a tired way, reached over to me, and we shook hands. We didn't say a word. We couldn't. It was fully five minutes before we got up to go to the dressing room." Jack McBride scored two touchdowns. Although the game was only one of those listed on the regular schedule, it was apparent to each team that the game was championship in nature.

Some memorable players were briefly attired in Giants blue. Ray Flaherty was a star receiver with New York before becoming a Hall of Fame coach with the Redskins.

The Giants signed the first throwing quarterback, Benny Friedman, in 1929. It was a time when throwing the ball in the regular course of offensive play was nearly as unusual as spotting a UFO in the sky. Friedman was a small man, with a listed playing size of 5 feet 8 inches and 172-pounds, but with an abnormally powerful arm. Friedman was ahead of his time and was fortunate that Tim Mara was an innovative owner who recognized Friedman's attributes and drawing power and brought him to New York (even if it meant purchasing an entire team to do so).

In the 2000s, pro football teams are used to the sight of big men with big bellies manning the offensive and defensive lines. They don't cover much ground, but they look as if they could bench-press a car. Each club easily has 10 players on the roster that weigh at least 300 pounds. In the 1920s, it was rare for any team to have a 250-pounder. Many linemen were the size of defensive backs today, around 200 pounds. But the Giants came up with players who were among the best good, big players of all time, very early in their existence.

Wilbur Henry became famous with the Canton Bulldogs even before the NFL was founded. He weighed 250 pounds and appeared to have the build of a farmer who lifted bales of hay, but didn't work out in an organized way. His appearance was deceiving. Born in 1897 in Mansfield, Ohio, Henry's initial reputation was forged in his home state. In old pictures his body does not appear distinctively different from W.C. Fields', but if the two men had gone one-on-one at the line of scrimmage, Henry, who became a charter

"He taught us all plenty."
—Chicago Bears founder and coach George Halas, on Giants coach Steve Owen's defensive wizardry.

member of the Pro Football Hall of Fame in 1963, might have killed Fields with a block. One of Henry's most valuable attributes was tremendous strength in his hands. More than one opponent struggled futilely against that grip.

Football experts lined up to proclaim Henry one of the greatest tackles they ever saw. John Heisman, his Georgia Tech coach, added that Henry was "the greatest punt blocker the game has ever known." And Walter Camp, the coach known as "the Father of American Football," said Henry was so overwhelming on defense, that teams re-arranged their whole attacks to run away from him on the field.

Henry, who played both offense and defense, once booted a 50-yard drop-kick field goal. In 1922, in a game against the Buffalo All-Americans, the coach gave orders for his team to put Henry out of business. "Everyone rack him up at once," player-coach Tommy Hughitt said. "We'll show him who's boss." The All-Americans ran their offensive handoffs at Henry every single play. The strategy was jettisoned in about two minutes. Henry wiped out one entire side of the Buffalo line and threw the ball carrier for a loss.

What Henry demonstrated is a lesson that is still being learned by those who dismiss a man's capabilities because of size. It is possible to be both a huge man and possess quick feet. A sportswriter once wrote of Henry, "He walks on feathers." If anyone was going to call Henry "Fats," he had better be smiling at the time.

Cal Hubbard contributed to the Giants' great 1927 team, stuck around for 1928, then found a home in Green Bay until he returned to New York in 1936. Hubbard was even larger than Henry, a player who stood 6 feet 5 inches and weighed perhaps as much as 280 pounds, unheard of for the time. Hubbard possessed great strength. He could bulldoze his way to the ball and was a human Great Wall of China in fending off blockers hoping to enter his team's backfield. After retiring from football, Hubbard became a Major League umpire.

Pulitzer Prize–winning columnist Arthur Daley of the *New York Times* called Hubbard a "Bunyan of the gridiron." Hubbard was so admired that when the NFL selected an all-time team in 1969 to commemorate its first half-century of existence, he was picked as the best tackle ever. "I really was dumbfounded," Hubbard said. "There have been so many great players since I

played that I was surprised that they could remember."

There were no long-term contracts in the 1920s—an owner would have looked at a player as if he was completely nuts if he had been asked for one—and since pro football was not the most secure profession, some players took a year off here or there. One player who came and stayed and stayed . . . and stayed, was Steve Owen. Owen played for the Giants from 1926

Head coach Steve Owen, pictured at a training camp in August 1936, began his association with the Giants as a player in the 1920s, and he stayed with the organization for more than a quarter of a century. *NFL Photos/Getty Images*

to 1931 and again in 1933. But he remained with the organization as head coach for another 23 years. Praised as a defensive genius, Owen became as close to the Maras as any non-relative. Owen stood 5 feet 10 inches, but played at 240 pounds and was nicknamed "Stout Steve." Owen was a fierce competitor who was a recognized star on the line. He played college ball at tiny Phillips College in Oklahoma and turned pro in 1924 with the Kansas City Cowboys, a team that played all of its games on the road before

expiring. Owen won 150 games as coach before retiring under pressure in 1953.

Owen was part of the first four decades of the Giants' operation, as much a part of the fabric of the team as the blue jerseys and the Mara boys.

ny 1920s ny
NEW YORK GIANTS
YEAR BY YEAR

1925	8–4
1926	8–4–1
1927	11–1–1
1928	4–7–2
1929	13–1–1

When Mara made Owen the full-time street-clothes coach after a period as player-coach, he said, "I'm tired of buying uniforms for you. Steve, you're our new coach."

Mara, who gradually became a bigger public figure in New York through his ownership of the Giants and friendships with Mayor Jimmy Walker and Governor Al Smith, appreciated the stability Owen brought to the role at age 34. He had had trying times going head-to-head with Pyle, and he put the upstart league out of business with the crushing of the Quakers. From then on, New York was almost indisputably a Giants' football town.

Still, the Giants had bounced from coach to coach until Owen became the boss. After Folwell's one-year-and-out tenure, Joseph Alexander took over as player-coach in 1926 and the team finished 8–4–1, another solid job. Then, in 1927, the Giants, under Earl Potteiger reached new heights. The team finished 11–1–1 behind a surreal defense. The Giants gave up only 20 points in 13 games, while the offense scored 197 points. The defense recorded 11 shutouts. In the 1920s, before the NFL split its teams into Eastern and Western Divisions, the annual league champion was chosen based on the best record. The 1927 season marked the Giants' first title in team history. The Giants under Poetteiger were nowhere nearly as lethal the next season, falling to 4–7–2, before rebounding in 1929 to a 13–1–1 record under LeRoy Andrews. Andrews did not last another complete season, but soon enough the head coaching spot was a position that gave Tim Mara nothing but contentment. And by the end of the 1920s Mara realized he had made a worthwhile investment in acquiring the New York football club.

Jim Thorpe (20) was in his prime with the Canton Bulldogs. In addition to being able to out-run most foes, Thorpe was also a crisp tackler, as he showed bringing down a Buffalo player in a 1920 game.
Bettmann/Corbis

THE 1930s

2 NEW YORK CATCHES ON TO FOOTBALL

Until more thorough reviews of estate papers are commissioned to determine the inner workings of America's wealthiest families, it seems likely that never has a 14-year-old boy been a more active owner of a professional sports franchise than Wellington Mara.

Tim Mara was at best half-joking when he told peers that his sons would run him off if he sold the New York Giants. In 1930, Mara sanctioned his boys' devotion by officially making them owners of the club. John, who went by the name of Jack more often, was 22. Wellington was 14. Wellington was no giddy schoolboy. He was immersed in Giants' business and

Right: New York Mayor Jimmy Walker greeted the visiting Notre Dame All-Stars at city hall before they took the gridiron for a charity game against the professional New York Giants.
Bettmann/Corbis

Far right: Harry Newman was known for his elusiveness coming out of the backfield as one of the first prominent Giants quarterbacks. Here he shows why, twisting away from teammate Tod Goodwin during practice in October 1935 at the Polo Grounds.
Underwood & Underwood/Corbis

that season turned out a memorable scouting report on the Staten Island Stapletons, warning the Giants not to be overconfident. Given that the Giants won 9–7 in the first meeting and lost 7–6 the second time the teams played, Wellington's words were hardly reckless. For the rest of their lives together, Jack and Wellington maintained the same division of responsibility running the team. Jack represented the Giants in financial matters and Wellington scouted personnel.

The early 1930s were a challenging time across the United States. The stock market crash wiped out millions. The Oklahoma dust storms sent people West. Citizens driven from homes by bank foreclosures set up squatters' camps. There were few jobs and less hope. Tim Mara had to watch his pennies, as well. Salaries were cut, players left, but the game rolled on. By 1933, when the National Football League broke its teams up into Eastern and Western Conferences to create two sets of standings leading to a championship game, the Giants had their foothold in New York.

Carefully nurturing the team, always on the lookout for useful players and ideas that would boost the gate and draw larger crowds, Tim Mara built a football team

> "Tim (Mara) was a fine fellow. Tim Mara was easier to deal with as far as a contract was concerned (than son Jack). Jack, being a lawyer, was a bit tougher to get anything out of."
> —Hall of Fame center-linebacker Mel Hein.

his city could support with pride. Mara was always on the prowl for players who could make a splash. The P.T. Barnum in him sometimes led down some unusual paths and alleys. It was one thing to shell out for proven All-American talent like Benny Friedman from Michigan and center Mel Hein from Washington State, but Mara might have been better served if the habit of the day wasn't to take someone's word at face value on a player's pedigree.

The wacky "roaring twenties" produced a variety of characters criss-crossing the front pages of America's newspapers. One of the flakiest individuals of the times was a gentleman known as "Shipwreck" Kelly, who

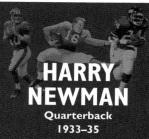

HARRY NEWMAN
**Quarterback
1933–35**

It might be said that Harry Newman chose the wrong profession. He was a pro football player, but given his canny business acumen, he probably should have hung out with people named Rockefeller.

In the early days of pro football, when players were lucky to wring much more than $150 per game out of an owner, especially in the Depression of the 1930s, Newman's skills gave him solid bargaining power. Perhaps inspired by the financial success of Big Ten compatriot Red Grange, when Newman came out of Michigan and signed with the Giants in 1933, his deal called for receiving 10 percent of gate receipts above $11,000. The next year he argued for 20 percent. In one of the great showdowns of the 1934 season, Newman said he collected a career high $7,200 playing against the Bears in a game that attracted 54,000 people. The Giants really couldn't afford him after that and Newman played only three years professionally.

He had been a star already at Michigan, where the Wolverines only lost one game in three years; one of Newman's teammates was a lineman named Gerald Ford later 38th president of the United States. Newman's finest season with the Giants was 1933, when he threw for 11 touchdowns and ran for three more. After 1935, Newman tried to help jump-start an alternative league to the NFL, but it fizzled out within two seasons.

"Heck, I can't kick getting $25,000 a year playing ball when millionaires were selling apples."
—Quarterback Harry Newman, on his pay in 1934 during the Great Depression.

Heavyweight fighter Primo Carnera (left) and Ken Strong, the Giants' all-around star, stopped in for a 1935 hospital visit to cheer up West Coast heavyweight contender Art Lasky, whose bout with the flu replaced his scheduled bout with champ Jimmy Braddock. *Bettmann/Corbis*

made it a habit to sit atop flagpoles as adoring crowds looked on. Originally a Hollywood stunt man, Alvin Kelly sat on a flagpole for 49 days as 20,000 people studied him in Atlantic City, New Jersey.

When a young man walked into Tim Mara's office in 1932 and introduced himself as Shipwreck Kelly, the Giants' owner could be forgiven if his thoughts immediately linked the body in the flesh to flagpoles. But no, the man protested, he was another Shipwreck Kelly altogether, the Shipwreck who had played

halfback for the University of Kentucky. Supporting the scouting thoroughness of young Wellington, then 16, Mara whipped out a file bulging with newspaper clippings of Kelly the football player, and as he flourished them, Tim Mara said, "I've heard of you, my boy." In a thick southern accent, Shipwreck Kelly replied, "I'd like to play football this fall with your Giants. I hear it's a right smart team."

Kelly wanted a percentage of the gate to sign and Mara said that while he would love to have his talents, he could not abide the Kentuckian's terms. Yet Kelly showed up unannounced at Giants training camp a bit later. Coach Steve Owen greeted him with the comment, "Glad to have you, but we really weren't expecting you." Kelly answered enigmatically. "That's why I came," he said. "I do the most astonishing things."

Shipwreck briefly lived up to his press clippings. For

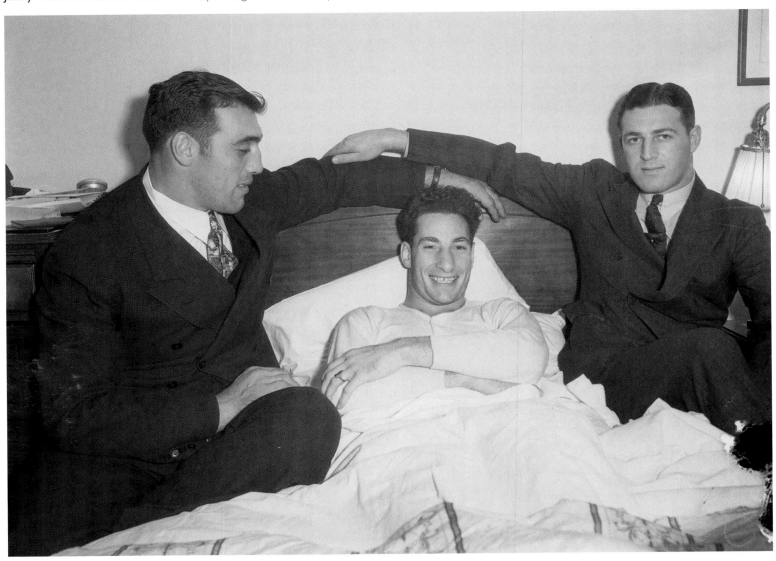

half a season he was an impressive runner and he could punt, but he was a no-show for the Giants' sixth game. When players asked of Kelly's whereabouts, one sarcastically said, "Maybe he's sitting on a flagpole." Owen suspended Kelly, ending his Giants' career. Future sightings of Kelly in New York night-spots suggested that his disappearance was related to drinking. "Shipwreck" was more than a nickname—it was a state of being.

The Giants had better luck when they hired Mel Hein on reputation. From the moment Hein was inserted into the starting lineup as the center and a linebacker, he was immovable. Not only did he repel all challenges for his job, for 15 years it often seemed as if he repelled all rushers and running backs. Opposing teams just could not penetrate behind Hein when he rose up to protect the quarterback. He was a brick wall with feet. Wellington Mara said that Hein was the greatest Giants' player in the team's first 50 years. When Hein died, Al Davis, owner of the Oakland Raiders, who had worked with Hein at USC, called him, "truly a football legend and a giant among men."

When Hein named his all-time opponent team it was sprinkled with such famous names as quarterback Sammy Baugh and tackle Bronko Nagurski. Nagurski, Hein said, was the toughest player he ever saw in a very rugged sport. "Those were tough years in pro football," Hein said of his days. Hein was an iron man on both sides of the ball, 60 minutes a game for 15 years, and later in life he wondered if he played more than anyone. "I can't prove this with any statistics," Hein said, "but I may have played more minutes than anybody in pro football history."

One aspect of their style that made the Giants more effective than most teams in the pro game's early years was an acknowledgement that the passing game could add a dangerous dimension. Most football was similar to the hand-to-hand combat of war. But just as early airplanes were showing the world that distances could be shrunk by air, football coaches were starting to see the parallel. Having the machinery in place would not do the trick by itself, and good pilots were needed. When it came to leading aerial attack offenses, they were very much at a premium. That's where Benny Friedman came in. There was still a body of opinion prevalent in the United States that college football was purer because the boys were amateurs, being true to their schools instead of dirtying their hands by taking money. The naivety of such viewpoints dissipated with time. A more difficult opinion to dislodge was the thought that college teams played a higher caliber of football than the pros. Pro athletes who knew better laughed at the notion. "I like the pro game best," Friedman said. "We play surer football

because we know more."

The slender Friedman had a ripe build for injury, but he never got hurt. He said his old Michigan coach, the legendary Fielding Yost, taught him the proper way to carry the ball when running in the open field so he wasn't dismembered. "About all you see of the good ball carrier is his feet and head," Friedman said. "He isn't at all exposed." Later in life, Friedman watched NFL quarterbacks scrambling and grimaced when they got creamed by a muscular, swift linebacker. "The poor guys," he said of those in the quarterback brotherhood. "They don't know what they don't know."

Another major Giants acquisition in 1933 was Ken Strong. At 6 feet and 206 pounds, Strong lived up to his name on all fronts. Strong was from Connecticut and attended New York University. The Giants had their eye on Strong from a young age, but when Strong finished school they lost him to the Staten Island Stapletons. The only thing the New York Giants and Staten Island Stapletons have in common to writers of NFL history is that they both received their mail in the state of New York. Yet Strong spent four seasons with Staten Island before the Giants wrested him away.

Elmer Kenneth Strong Jr. could pass the ball a little, run the ball well, and kick the ball very well. Once he finally joined the Giants' roster he stayed until 1947, with time out for World War II, and is considered one of the most important and best Giants players of all, earning Hall of Fame induction in 1967. Strong had dark, wavy hair, a streamlined body, and large hands. He set a wide range of Giants' team records, particularly in kicking after World War II. Much confusion attended the Giants' initial attempts to sign Strong after college, who after all was starring right under the Maras' noses. Jack Mara was a student at Fordham at the time and he saw Strong in games with NYU. Wellington the teenager scouted him. "We wanted him for the Giants very badly," Wellington said. "My father had this employee who was instructed to make every effort to sign Ken Strong. But he failed and we were very upset when Ken signed with the Staten Island Stapletons."

Four years later, when the Staten Island team folded, Tim Mara went after Strong by himself, without trusting a secondary functionary to do the work. It was only then, in conversation with Strong, that Mara learned why the employee let him down. Mara had told the worker to go as high as $10,000 for Strong. The man apparently offered Strong $5,000, which underbid Staten Island and undermined Mara's plans. The courtship of Strong this time resulted in a wedding.

In its first decade, the NFL had gone through a shakedown phase, shedding financially weak teams in small markets. Rules were approved to open up the

Colorful Brooklyn Dodgers' halfback John Simms "Shipwreck" Kelly and ahead-of-his-time throwing quarterback Benny Friedman pose for an early 1930s photo in Brooklyn, New York. *Pro Football Hall of Fame/NFL/Getty Images*

MEL HEIN
CENTER, 1931–1945

The story of how Mel Hein became a member of the New York Giants humorously stalked him throughout his pro football career. It demonstrated that Hein may have had a better relationship with the U.S. Postal Service than anyone besides Santa Claus.

Hein, who was born in 1909 in Redding, California, was a remarkable two-way player as a center and linebacker who played all 60 minutes of a game, but even more notably showed up ready to play in every game for 15 seasons starting in 1931. Lou Gehrig, the Yankees' first baseman who set the major league baseball mark for consecutive games played, was not the only Iron Man in New York. Hein played in 170 straight Giants' games.

However, Hein might not have played any games in a New York uniform if his original intentions were carried out. The 6 feet 3 inches, 230-pounds Hein graduated from Washington State University and wrote to a few pro teams offering his services. Despite All-American recognition in his final year with the Cougars, Hein still had to clamor to be noticed. Pro scouting was very much an inexact science in the early 1930s and Pullman, Washington, was out of the mainstream.

Hein heard through the grapevine that the Giants were intrigued by his abilities, but officially he heard nothing. Meanwhile, the Providence Steamrollers put a contract where their mouth was with a deal calling for $125 a game. Hein signed the contract and put it in the mail, then went out on the road with his

basketball team. Ray Flaherty, the Giants end, sought Hein out to ask if he had received his New York contract yet. Hein said he had not, but it didn't matter anymore because he had mailed a contract to Providence the day before.

"What are they paying you?" Flaherty asked. Hein told him and Flaherty said that was too bad because the Giants were offering $150 a game. Then Flaherty dreamed up a half-baked scheme. He urged Hein to get his home postmaster to send a telegram to the postmaster in Providence asking him to hold up the envelope at the other end.

Hein approached his local postmaster, who refused to take the action, but said Hein might try himself, while warning that the chances were slim. Hein sent a telegram and amazingly intercepted his letter and got the Providence postmaster to return it. Hein ripped up the Providence contract and signed the newly arrived Giants' contract. Hein believed his $150-a-game pact made him the best paid lineman in the league and he was quite satisfied. "You could buy a loaf of bread for a nickel and get a full meal for 35 cents in the Automat back then," Hein said. "And you had no income tax."

Hein's physical prowess and smart blocking—especially his pass-blocking ability—led to his being named All-Pro eight years in a row between 1933 and 1941. His No. 7 jersey was retired by the Giants, and when the Pro Football Hall of Fame opened in 1963, Hein was a member of the first class inducted. In 1938, Hein attained the unique distinction of being named the National Football League's Most Valuable Player—as a lineman. The chances of such a thing as a center being singled out in that manner in the modern game are roughly akin to Brett Favre playing an entire season without wearing a helmet.

During Hein's career it was expected that most players would go both ways on offense and defense, but he took his participation a step further, almost never missing a snap. According to biographical material written by the Pro Football Hall of Fame, Hein only once called a timeout during his career. The dramatic event occurred a decade into his career in 1941 when Hein signaled for a break in the action while his broken nose was fixed. The timeout ended, Hein stayed in the game, and the action resumed. The longer Hein played, the more numerous were those fans who applied his nickname, "Old Indestructible."

It wasn't as if the Giants didn't appreciate Hein's excellence and reliability, but during the Depression, wages were suppressed and the Mara family did not throw around dollar bills as if they were confetti falling at a Canyon of Heroes parade. Two years into his career, Hein's salary was upped to $175 a game and in 1938 he was practically a magnate, making $225 per game.

Hein entered the pro game fully developed, as savvy as any veteran, and opponents realized it immediately. George Halas, the coach and chief executive officer of the Chicago Bears, the Giants' top rival, said he game-planned to try to pick on Hein as a newcomer, but it didn't work. "Even as a rookie in 1931 there was no one like him," Halas said. "Usually, you look for rookies on another team and try to take advantage of them. We tried working on Hein, but from the start he was too smart."

Hein's talent was immediately recognized by Giants' coach Steve Owen. But Owen spent more time admiring Hein's style than offering pointers, even though as a former offensive lineman he might have. Over the years, Owen never took credit for Hein's outstanding performance. "I don't think I ever taught him anything," Owen said. "He always had excellent judgment."

The superiority of that judgment was noted by many others who observed football, and when Hein retired he was in demand as an off-field leader. In 1946, Hein became head coach at Union College in Schenectady, New York. In 1947 and 1948, Hein coached linemen for the Los Angeles Dons of the All-America Football Conference. Staying in the same neighborhood, Hein also coached linemen for the Los Angeles Rams in 1949 and 1950 and from 1951 to 1966 for the University of Southern California Trojans. Then Hein moved into the front office of the American Football League, working to help the upstart league survive.

Far left: Mel Hein in 1938: one of the early iron men of the game.
NFL/Getty Images

Left: The inaugural Hall of Fame class of 1963 pose with their statues. Top row (L–R) Sammy Baugh, Robert Hubbard, Bronko Nagurski, George Halas, Red Grange; bottom row (L–R) Ernie Nevers, Dutch Clark, Curly Lambeau, Mel Hein, Blood McNally, and Don Hutson.
Pro Football Hall of Fame/Getty Images

game and encourage more passing, and owners counted on the new title game to increase end-of-season excitement with a champ chosen on the field, not by acclamation.

The Giants completed the 1933 regular season with an 11–3 mark. At 10–2–1, the Chicago Bears had the best record in the West. The championship contest was set for December 17 and not even the game's magnates could have imagined a game so rich in drama. If a genie had granted them three wishes the patrons of the sport would not have been so bold as to ask for the type of action they witnessed in the normal flow of play. More than 75 years later, the contest remains one of the greatest championship games in NFL history.

Approximately 30,000 fans attended the title game at Wrigley Field in Chicago. The Bears, relying on the older style of power football, dominated the Giants 33–13 in first downs. But the Giants gained 201 yards through the air on 12-of-17 throwing by Harry Newman to stay in contention. It was a seesaw game with plot twists, surprises, and lead changes that kept the fans warm on a cold day that began in the mist and fog, which accounted for slippery footing on the field. Newman had been recruited as a fresh quarterback and Wellington Mara described just what the Giants

wanted from Newman when he called the newcomer "a clone of Friedman."

In another sneak preview of an offensive weapon that would grow both in importance and popularity as the NFL aged, the Bears' early scoring came on field goals by Jack Manders for a 6–0 Chicago lead. Newman, who was chosen All-Pro that season, brought the Giants back with a second-quarter, 29-yard touchdown pass to Hall of Fame end Morris "Red" Badgro. Ken Strong kicked the extra point for the Giants and New York had a 7–6 lead. Badgro's catch was the first touchdown pass grabbed in an NFL playoff game. Years later he recalled the play as an easy one. He ran across the middle, was open, caught the ball, and when defenders failed to close in he ran all the way. "The safety man wasn't there, so I ran downfield for a touchdown," Badgro said.

One of the most fascinating plays in the history of the NFL was attempted by the Giants during this game. It was the sort of play that the Marx Brothers would use in the movie *Horse Feathers,* or that in years to come would register more as a comic play in parodies of football games. Early in the game, the Giants lined up for an offensive play as usual, with center Mel Hein's hands on the leather. Before the snap, the left end dropped back into the backfield as a

The Chicago Bears' Bronko Nagurski was an unstoppable force as a ball carrier and tackler. The Giants discovered just how difficult it could be to bring him down on this 8-yard gain in the 1934 championship game at the Polo Grounds.
Bettmann/Corbis

wingback and the wingback on the right side moved up to the line of scrimmage. That shift made Hein an eligible receiver.

Hein hiked the ball to Harry Newman, who quickly handed it back in the swirling mix of players. Newman faded back as if to pass and Hein slipped the ball into his jersey. While the Bears rush focused on Newman, Hein began walking slowly downfield, apparently minding his own business. Impatient to make the trick play work, Hein started to run. Bear defender Keith Molesworth got suspicious and chased Hein down. Hein made a significant gain, but the Giants did not score. (The only other time in his career Hein attempted this play, he was smothered and later pronounced it essentially a one-trick pony, a play that would be a surprise only once.)

The teams traded points throughout the game, with Manders kicking three field goals. However, in the fourth period, Newman threw an 8-yard strike to Strong in the end zone and it appeared as if the Giants would prevail, 21–16. But the Bears had one more drive in them after a disappointing Strong punt gave Chicago field possession at the New York 47-yard-line.

Two plays later, Bronko Nagurski, taking the snap, faded back and threw a jump pass to end Bill Hewitt, the last NFL player to compete without wearing a helmet. Hewitt gathered in the pass, but as Giants' tacklers circled him like a school of sharks, Hewitt stunned onlookers by flipping a lateral to end Bill Karr. Karr finished off the 33-yard touchdown play and the Bears had the winning score.

The Giants made one more run at the Bears as the clock ticked down. A pass play was designed to reach Badgro, but the redhead could not shake off the coverage of Red Grange, who was playing in the defensive backfield for Chicago. Badgro said he was always haunted by his inability to break free for an opportunity to win the game. "If I had gotten by Red Grange, I would have scored," Badgro said in an interview 61 years after the game. "Grange had me around the middle. His arms were around the ball and I couldn't get rid of it (in order to attempt a lateral). If I get by him, we win the game."

Although there have been few more suspenseful NFL title games or Super Bowls, the rematch between the Giants and Bears, a year later in 1934, eclipsed the debut game for legendary status. Not because of the final score, but because of the unusual events.

The Giants were not nearly as strong in 1934 as they had been in 1933, finishing 8–5. The Bears, meanwhile, breezed through the regular season 13–0, appearing to be the top team of all time. So even as the same teams lined up on December 9, 1934, this time at the Polo Grounds, they seemed to be the same

Starting Lineups for the First Official NFL Championship Game
December 17, 1933
at Wrigley Field, Chicago

Chicago Bears 23, New York Giants 21

GIANTS

Left end	Red Badgro
Left tackle	Len Grant
Left Guard	Butch Gibson
Center	Mel Hein
Right Guard	Potsy Jones
Right tackle	Bill Owen
Right end	Ray Flaherty
Quarterback	Harry Newman
Left halfback	Ken Strong
Right halfback	Dale Burnett
Fullback	Bo Molenda

BEARS

Left end	Bill Hewitt
Left tackle	Link Lyman
Left guard	Zuck Carlson
Center	Ookie Miller
Right guard	Joe Kopcha
Right tackle	George Musso
Right end	Bill Karr
Quarterback	Carl Brumbaugh
Left halfback	Keith Molesworth
Right halfback	Gene Ronzani
Fullback	Bronko Nagurski

Score

	1	2	3	4	F
Giants	0	7	7	7	21
Bears	3	3	10	7	23

The New York Giants got their fill of Chicago star Bronko Nagurski (3) in several big games in the early days of their rivalry, including the December 1934 title game that the Giants won, 30–13. Here Mel Hein (7) caught up to the Bronk for the tackle.
Pro Football Hall of Fame/Getty Images

Opposite: The switch from cleats to rubber-soled shoes was the decisive factor in the Giants' defeat of the Chicago Bears on December 9, 1934, in the famous "Sneaker Game."
Pro Football Hall of Fame/Getty Images

teams in name only.

Not only were the Bears favored because of their sterling record and by virtue of defeating New York twice during the regular season, but the weather was unfavorable for the Giants. When they awoke they were confronted by bitterly cold temperatures. It was a day to lounge around indoors. Even worse for the Giants, quarterback Harry Newman and end Red Badgro were sidelined with injuries. No single pre-game angle provided the Giants with any optimism.

Giants' president Jack Mara was the first to inspect the field and see the frozen mess that the weather had produced. How would his backs retain their footing on the slick field? Coach Steve Owen received the news with consternation. But almost immediately, Ray Flaherty, the star end and team captain, came up with a potential remedy. Flaherty recalled that when he was in college, playing for Gonzaga, the team encountered similar conditions. "Coach, why not wear basketball shoes?" Flaherty suggested.

On the surface, Flaherty's idea was as welcome as the invention of the light bulb. But the game was being played on a Sunday and all of New York's sporting goods stores were closed. Where could the Giants find a few dozen pairs of sneakers on short notice when

most of the metropolis was busy at church? The solution to the ice problem was in mind, but not in hand. When Owen spied Abe Cohen in the locker room, he was struck by inspiration. Cohen, a tailor by trade, was a hardcore Giants fan who helped out as a clubhouse attendant, but also worked part-time for Manhattan College's athletic program. He had a key to the school's locker room and equipment room, so the Giants instructed him to zoom across town and borrow as many pairs of sneakers as he could.

Game time was rapidly approaching when Cohen hailed a taxi. Over time the story has been muddled as to whether Cohen obtained the sneakers by hook (simply using a key for access) or crook (breaking into lockers after obtaining access to the right room), but action began at the Polo Grounds without him.

On a brutal day for maintaining balance before a chilled 37,000 fans, the Bears several times made plays that might have put the game out of reach. The bruising back Bronko Nagurski scored two touchdowns that were called back because of penalties. Kicker Jack Manders missed two field goals, probably because of poor footing. The Bears could have built an insurmountable lead, but settled for a 10–3 margin at halftime.

"We didn't exactly get rich, did we?"
—Hall of Fame end Morris "Red"
Badgro, on playing for $150 a game in
the 1930s.

Half the game had been played before Cohen re-appeared bearing nine pairs of sneakers, all he could come up with. Center Mel Hein and guard Potsy Jones, two of the more stationary Giants players, went without rubber soles. The Giants caused a stir when they ran onto the field for the second half, but the payoff was not immediate. An enraged George Halas, coaching the Bears, ordered his players to step on the Giants' feet with their cleats. At the end of the third quarter, the Bears led 13–3. The Giants had made up nothing on the scoreboard, but Flaherty said the comparatively solid footing created "a runner's paradise."

The basketball shoes did not offer as much protection to Ken Strong's toe when he booted, and he broke a nail on one kick. However, in the fourth quarter, when backup quarterback Ed Danowski fired a 28-yard TD pass to Ike Frankian and Strong ran 42 yards for another touchdown, the Giants were true believers in their sneakers. "They were slipping and sliding," said Newman of the Bears' attempts to make tackles. "They couldn't touch anybody."

Strong scored on an 11-yard run and Danowski added another touchdown on a 6-yard run. The Giants scored 27 points in the fourth quarter (17 in the game for Strong), and defeated the Bears, 30–13. "They just out-smarted us," said Nagurski.

Afterwards, Strong praised Cohen's efforts. "Abe, you were the real hero of this game," the player said. "We never could have won without you." Or at least without the footwear he supplied. The game forevermore came to be called "The Sneaker Game," but certainly no more than one in 10 Giants fans at best can recall Abe Cohen, the man who delivered the sneakers to the locker room.

The memorable encounter was the first championship claimed with Owen at the helm. The one-time player was an unlikely figure to be named head coach of a professional football team representing the largest city in the country. Owen was born in Cleo Springs, Oklahoma, a speck on the map. His high school was located in Aline, a larger speck. He attended college at Phillips, which didn't even feature on most collegiate maps.

Even as a young man, Owen was a sizable specimen, tipping the scales at about 240 pounds, and the legend surrounding his introduction to football is half cornpone and the other half folklore, with perhaps a tiny kernel of truth mixed in. Supposedly, the young

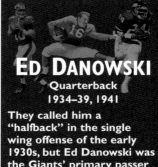

ED DANOWSKI
Quarterback
1934–39, 1941

They called him a "halfback" in the single wing offense of the early 1930s, but Ed Danowski was the Giants' primary passer at the time.

Danowski was a New Yorker all of the way. He grew up on Long Island, attended Fordham University, where he played on the football team, and then joined the Giants. After serving in the Navy during World War II, he returned to Fordham and coached football from 1946 to 1964.

A key player during the Giants' shocking disposal of the Chicago Bears during the 1934 National Football League championship game, Danowski frequently talked of how the team switched into sneakers to out-fox George Halas and the Bears to earn the title.

The most touchdown passes Danowski threw in his seven Giants seasons was 10 in 1935. He also kept the ball to rush on many occasions with a season-high of 335 yards in 1935.

In an art that died a few years after Danowski retired in 1941, the 6 feet 1 inch, 198-pound back specialized in quick kicks, booting punts at unexpected moments before teams were ready, thus pinning foes in their own territory where the Giants' defense gained advantageous field position. An Associated Press cartoon extolling Danowski's variety of talents during his playing days pictured a baffled enemy returner as the ball sailed into the distance, accompanied by the words, "He (Danowski) is forever embarrassing opposing safety men with long kicks over their heads."

BENNY FRIEDMANN
QUARTERBACK, 1929–1931

The first great National Football League quarterback was the strong-armed, improvisationally gifted, Benny Friedman. In 1929 the one-time Michigan All-American threw for 20 touchdown passes with the New York Giants, at a time when the words "touchdown pass" practically required a foreign language translator.

Friedman, 5 feet 8 inches and 172 pounds, grew up in Cleveland, and was one of the first pro football players to realize that the shortest distance between two end zones was through the air. Friedman played for the legendary Fielding Yost in Ann Arbor and although he might have been overshadowed in the Big Ten by Illinois' Red Grange, Friedman was not shy about tooting his own horn. Although that rubbed some the wrong way, it was not so easy to gain attention as a throwing quarterback, even as a two-time All-American. Yost called Friedman "one of the greatest passers and smartest quarterbacks in history."

The pint-sized thrower spent three of his eight NFL seasons with the Giants, from 1929 through 1931. In Jewish publications battling against anti-semitism, Friedman was a hero. Friedman made his biggest impression on the biggest stage. He shined on Broadway. "We are not a people apart," Friedman said. "Physically, and in general mental attitudes, there is nothing that distinguishes the Jewish athlete from any other. You're either a man, or you're not."

Paul Gallico, the New York newspaper sportswriter and author of *The Poseiden Adventure*, once joined Giants' coach LeRoy Andrews on the sideline during a game as Friedman made play after play to overcome the Providence Steamrollers. Gallico's story in *Liberty Magazine* was headlined "The Greatest Football Player in the World."

In the article, Gallico listens to Andrews predict an upcoming play and then watches as Friedman executes it for a touchdown. "Didn't I tell you? Didn't I tell you that play was coming!" Andrews exulted to Gallico after the done deal. "I'll bet there have been more than 50 times since I've been with Friedman as a pro that I've mentally called for a play like that and Benny has seen the same thing and called it himself."

How Friedman became a Giant was an adventure story in itself. When Friedman emerged from college he signed with the Cleveland Bulldogs, the club representing his home town, where he was born in 1905. Friedman threw 11 touchdown passes during his rookie year. The next year, Friedman signed on with the Detroit Wolverines, a team trying to capitalize on the popularity of the Michigan Wolverines, Friedman's old college.

With Detroit, Friedman was a one-man army, leading the league in passing touchdowns, rushing touchdowns and scoring at a time when the NFL did not yet keep close track of yardage gained. He was the most explosive, spectacular player in the league, and Giants' owner Tim Mara felt Friedman was just the elixir his team needed to make a big public relations splash and erase the red ink of debt. Mara initiated trade talks with Detroit, but Detroit did not want to part with Friedman at any price.

After being rebuffed, Mara approached the owners of the pro Wolverines again. This time he made an offer they couldn't refuse—he bought the whole team. As soon as the deal was consummated, Mara folded Detroit and signed Friedman (and some of his teammates) for the Giants.

The deck was stacked against successful passing at the time when

(Left to right) Giants' quarterback Benny Friedman, Bo Molenda, and Red Grange. *Bettmann/Corbis*

Friedman broke into the NFL. The ball was not nearly as aerodynamic as it is today; it was much rounder, making it difficult to grasp. There were no sophisticated passing attacks. Under the rules, throwers had to retreat at least five yards behind the line of scrimmage before making a pass. If a quarterback threw an incomplete pass into the end zone, the opposing team received the ball at its own 20-yard-line. That is more like the punt rule of today. Also, if a quarterback threw two incompletions in a row, his team was penalized. Passing had definitely not caught on yet around the league, but Friedman still turned it into a weapon.

George Halas, founder of the Chicago Bears, their long-time coach, and one of the founders of the NFL, was involved in some of the rule changes that opened up the passing game, but said before that Friedman was still able to sting unsuspecting defenses. He called Friedman "a pioneer" of the passing game.

"Benny Friedman was the first pro quarterback to exploit the strategic possibilities of the pass," Halas said. "Benny starred for the New York Giants in 1929. He couldn't flip our 'cantaloupe' (23 inches around) with the accuracy of a modern-day Johnny Unitas, but he jolted our defenses with surprise passes on first and second down."

Football has always been a rough game, and in the days when players wore comparatively sub-standard equipment, with few checks on the types of hitting allowed, they took a beating.

Friedman got clobbered fairly often and once as he limped to the sideline he commented on it to Dr. Joe Alexander who had been the Giants' coach in 1926. Alexander told Friedman:

"I used to be as stupid as you until I learned something. Take a copy of Liberty Magazine, rip it in half, and you have the perfect shin guard. It worked wonders for me."

That same night, Friedman attended a dinner party where a woman approached him for an opinion. She said she would never let her son play such a violent game as football, but his legs were taking a serious bruising playing soccer, and did Friedman have any advice? He did. A few moments later the woman said, "We don't subscribe to *Liberty*. Will the *New Yorker* do?"

Friedman later coached small school Brandeis, but was mostly out of the public eye and despite active lobbying by him and early NFL stars, was overlooked for the Hall of Fame until long after his death in 1982. In 2005, Friedman was at last voted into the Hall.

David Friedman (far right), nephew of Benny Friedman, appears on behalf of his uncle at Friedman's induction to the Pro Football Hall of Fame. Also present are Steven Towns, representing enshrinee Fritz Pollard; Steve Young; and Dan Marino.
David Maxwell/epa/Corbis

The Giants sent a team representative to round up sneakers for as many players as possible, and the switch of footwear gave the Giants a second-half advantage on an icy field and helped them to the 1934 title game victory.
Pro Football Hall of Fame/Getty Images

cowhand was riding his pony along a road in rural Oklahoma and came upon a school field. Holding the reins in one hand and resting his other arm on the saddle, Owen gazed at the activity for a while.

Owen did not have the slightest idea what the students were doing for exercise. When a coach approached him, Owen asked, "What are they playing?" The man replied, "Football. Would you like to try it?" Owen dismounted and asked what he was supposed to do. The coach instructed him to grab a kickoff and try to run to the other end of the field, past the goal posts, without being tackled by the guys on the field. Skipping around tacklers, faking this way and that, Owen ran the length of the field, and then said, "What do I do now?" The coach said, "Try it again, this

"The first time I saw New York, I was on horseback."
—Long-time player and coach Steve Owen, on riding the Kansas City Cowboys' mascot for a photo opportunity a year before he joined the Giants.

time without your spurs."

A good story, and perfect for a New York audience told with the proper drawl, but Owen apparently didn't begin playing football until he was in college. He discovered he was pretty good at it and became a

RED BADGRO
End
1930–35

One of his college teammates at the University of Southern California certainly became more famous, but it was not because Marion Morrison outdid Morris "Red" Badgro on the gridiron. Badgro was a four-time All-Pro with the Giants. That other guy, nicknamed "Duke," made a few cowboy flicks and became better known as John Wayne.

At 6 feet and 190-pounds, Badgro played offensive and defensive end for the Giants. He was an elusive pass catcher and a hard hitter for New York's 1930s title teams. A three-sport athlete for the Trojans, Badgro continued to show his versatility by playing major league baseball with the St. Louis Browns in 1929 and 1930.

Red Grange, a contemporary and rival, called Badgro "one of the best half-dozen ends I ever saw." When the NFL split the league into two conferences for a formal method of settling its annual championship in 1933, Badgro caught the first title-game TD pass.

Badgro had been retired for nearly 50 years when he was finally chosen for the Hall of Fame in 1981. He was frequently asked if he belonged there. "I think anybody who plays pro football dreams of being in the Hall of Fame," he said. "I look at the people in the Hall of Fame and I think I accomplished just as much or more than a lot of them."

New York Giants back Eddie Miller demonstrates his holding style for Ward Cuff's kicks. Note the flashy, two-tone ball.
Gjon Mili/Time Life Pictures/Getty Images

professional with the Giants in 1926. He discovered he was pretty smart at it, too, and became their coach for more than a generation.

Owen played for the long-forgotten Kansas City Cowboys first. He was fond of the team nickname, but neither he nor any of the other players were fond of the fact that the Cowboys played no home games. That spelled doom for the franchise, but before the

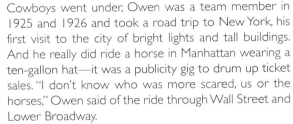

"I made her quit smoking and she makes me keep training, eat salads every day, watch my weight, practice every day except Monday and (stop) the gambling."
—Ward Cuff, on the influence of his wife Doris.

Cowboys went under, Owen was a team member in 1925 and 1926 and took a road trip to New York, his first visit to the city of bright lights and tall buildings. And he really did ride a horse in Manhattan wearing a ten-gallon hat—it was a publicity gig to drum up ticket sales. "I don't know who was more scared, us or the horses," Owen said of the ride through Wall Street and Lower Broadway.

The funny part of the Giants' 1933 and 1934 championship games against the Bears was how many points were scored. Owen was a defensive coach all the way. He abhorred teams running up and down the field imitating a track meet. "I would rather win by 3–0 than lose by 38–36."

Playing for the big trophy at the end of the season meant more than anything. Year after year the Giants positioned themselves for a chance to take home the title. In 1935, the Giants won the East again, finishing 9–3, and earning the opportunity for the crown for a third straight season. This time they met the Detroit Lions, who not long before had moved to the motor city after dumping their old identity as the Portsmouth Spartans.

The third time was not the charm for the Giants. They were manhandled by the Lions, 26–7, in the championship game played on December 15 in Detroit. The winners scored two touchdowns in the first quarter and two in the fourth. Only 15,000 fans showed up at the University of Detroit Stadium in snowy, muddy, sleeting weather. The Giants still had Ken Strong and Ed Danowski working for them, but the Dutch Clark-led Lions offense was superior and Detroit broke the game open in the fourth quarter. A 35-yard run by Strong provided New York's only touchdown. The poor attendance was a factor in the low payoffs to the participants. Winning a world championship meant only $240 per man to the Lions, and the runners-up collected just $160 apiece.

The terrible weather was predicted and it was felt that the high winds and wetness would ground the Giants' passing game. That proved true, but the Lions managed fairly well through the air, prompting *New York Times* sportswriter John Drebinger to note, "what took the experts most by surprise was the fact that under these very trying conditions the Lions actually outplayed the Giants at their own game."

While the Giants could not be expected to finish in first place every season, the team returned to the championship game representing the East once again in 1938, this time facing the Green Bay Packers. The Packers were one of the old-guard teams, led by Curly Lambeau, and the last survivor of the small-market, Midwestern clubs that had been the cornerstone of the NFL when it began. The Packers had dominated the league between 1929 and 1931 when the team with the best record was declared champion, but had not reached a playoff showdown before.

More than 48,000 people paid their way into the Polo Grounds to see a 23–17 New York win that once again turned out to be as good a show as the circus or anything playing on Broadway. The scoring bounced back and forth. The Giants led 9–0 and 9–7, then 16–7. Green Bay, behind quarterback Cecil Isbell, went ahead

17–16. The winning score culminated with a 62-yard drive in the third quarter when Giants' quarterback Ed Danowski passed for six points to Hank Soar.

New York Times reporter Arthur Daley was quite flowery in his description of the events of the day, "The Giants and the Packers delved into the realm of fiction for a storybook football game," Daley wrote. "At the end the spectators were too emotionally exhausted even to try to rip down the goal posts." Given the casualty list, with Hein suffering a concussion complete with memory loss from a kick to the cheekbone, Johnny Dell Isola being hospitalized with a spinal concussion, and Ward Cuff enduring a possible fracture of the sternum, the Giants paid with pain for their victory.

They did recover sufficiently to sweep through the regular season 9–1–1 in 1939 to set up a rematch with the Packers in Green Bay. This time—their fifth appearance in the title game in the decade—the

Chuck Gelatka (left), coach Steve Owen (center), and Gerry Donnerlein of the Giants in 1937. *Bettmann/Corbis*

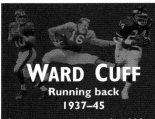

WARD CUFF
**Running back
1937–45**

It was no surprise that Ward Cuff was an all-around threat when he played nine of his 11 NFL seasons for the Giants between 1937 and 1947. He rushed the ball, ran back punts, and was a place kicker extraordinaire. But that routinely followed the pattern of his earlier life.

Cuff grew up in Redwood Falls, Minnesota and he attended Marquette. At 6 feet 1inch and 195-pounds (a weight he maintained for decades), he was wooed for his ability to throw the javelin, play hockey, and oh yeah, a little bit of football. Giants' coach Steve Owen had his eye on Cuff as a prospect from his freshman year on in Milwaukee.

Cuff was such a big track star that he qualified for the U.S. Olympic team, traveling to Berlin in 1936, but opted to stay home because he didn't want to miss out on any of the football season.

Although Cuff did many things well for the Giants, his field-goal kicking paid the most dividends. Few teams counted on going for a three-pointer during Cuff's era, and he scored 411 points in his career, about 350 of them with his foot. Cuff had a phobia about hospitals and played hurt instead of taking treatment.

"I loved every wonderful minute of it," Cuff said later of his pro career years, while working as a recreation administrator for Boeing the airline manufacturer after his retirement from the game.

Giants were crushed, losing to the Pack 27–0. The Packers, with Arnie Herber, a future Hall of Famer at the controls, were starting to pick up the nuances of the passing game and make it work for them. The Giants still featured several of their most reliable weapons of the past, from Danowski at quarterback, to Ward Cuff and Tuffy Leemans, but December 10, 1939 in Wisconsin was not their day.

Certain elements of the New York Giants' world were effectively established by the end of the 1930s. The team, it was obvious, was going to be a factor in the disbursement of titles just about every year. And the team was also in good hands with the Maras presiding over its operation. Tim Mara once said that his son Jack was a good fit to oversee the books because he didn't like to spend money any more than his old man. Wellington, on the other hand, was passionate about the men and the game they played. "Well was so obsessed with the Giants that Jack knew the team was in capable hands," wrote Dave Klein, a sportswriter for the *Newark Star-Ledger.* Wellington Mara said he and his brother took on the roles for which they were best suited. Jack,

he said, was great for the financial end of the business because he "was the worrywart of the family." Wellington made it his mission to find the best football players available.

New York Giants' lineup in 1937. Backfield, left to right: Kink Richards, Ed Danowski, Dale Burnett, and Les Corzine. Line: Len Grant, Del Isosa, Art White, Mel Hein, John Haden, and Jim Poole.
Bettmann/Corbis

1930s
NEW YORK GIANTS
YEAR BY YEAR

1930	13–4
1931	7–6–1
1932	4–6–2
1933	11–3
1934	8–5
1935	9–3
1936	5–6–1
1937	6–3–2
1938	8–2–1
1939	9–1–1

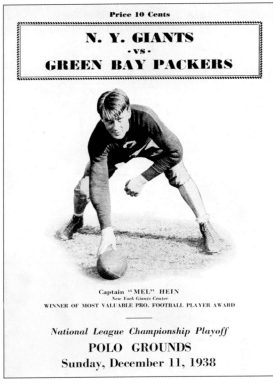

Price 10 Cents

N. Y. GIANTS
- vs -
GREEN BAY PACKERS

Captain "MEL" HEIN
New York Giants Center
WINNER OF MOST VALUABLE PRO. FOOTBALL PLAYER AWARD

National League Championship Playoff
POLO GROUNDS
Sunday, December 11, 1938

Left: The 1938 NFL championship game program cover featured Giants' Hall of Fame center Mel Hein. The Giants defeated the Green Bay Packers 23–17 on December 11, 1938, at the Polo Grounds.
Pro Football Hall of Fame/Getty Images

THE 1940s
GOOD TIMES AND TROUBLED TIMES

George Kracum (10) of the Brooklyn Dodgers peels off yardage at the Polo Grounds as the Dodgers defeat the New York Giants, 21–7.
Bettmann/Corbis

The violent march of Nazi Germany and Imperial Japan defined the decade of the 1940s by spreading death and destruction all over the world. The futures of nations were at stake and by comparison the professional sports teams that had helped develop civic pride in cities around the country faded into insignificance.

When Pearl Harbor was bombed by the Japanese air force on December 7, 1941, coincidentally the day the Giants were honoring Tuffy Leemans with a special day, the fantasy world of sports took a back seat to the all-too-harsh reality of the outside world. When asked for his opinion, President Franklin D. Roosevelt decreed that major league baseball should play on as a diversion for workers and residents on the home front. Pro football and other sports took their cues from baseball, the widely recognized "national pastime." With the country preoccupied by much

"If I am remembered for nothing else, I'd like to be remembered for discovering Tuffy Leemans."
—Wellington Mara, on signing the fullback out of George Washington University.

more important matters, the war years were not kind to pro football. Players one minute became soldiers the next, gone for two or more years, or gone for good, killed, wounded, or simply because their skills eroded.

The show went on, but precariously. Some teams could not make it financially. Some teams merged temporarily to survive. The Giants, unlike the Pittsburgh Steelers and Philadelphia Eagles, which briefly became one club, the Steagles, stood on their own, and the Maras remained in charge, holding things together.

The Giants approached 1940 with optimism. They were coming off two straight championship game

Attendees at a 1942 Banshees' Club Gridiron luncheon at the Waldorf Astoria Hotel included (left to right) Giants' coach Steve Owen, sports columnist Dan Parker, Lt. Col. Lawrence "Biff" Jones, sports editor and writer Edward Cochrane, and humorist Arthur "Bugs" Baer.
Bettmann/Corbis

appearances, one victory, one defeat, and with Stout Steve Owen still in command of the on-field activity, believed they would be contenders again. However, Tuffy Leemans was sidelined with a back injury midway through the year and the team finished 6–4–1.

Alphonse Leemans, nicknamed "Tuffy," was famous for being as tough a player as his nickname implied during his time with the New York Giants.
Pro Football Hall Of Fame/Getty Images

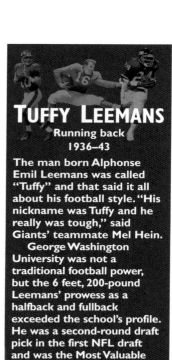

TUFFY LEEMANS
Running back
1936–43

The man born Alphonse Emil Leemans was called "Tuffy" and that said it all about his football style. "His nickname was Tuffy and he really was tough," said Giants' teammate Mel Hein.

George Washington University was not a traditional football power, but the 6 feet, 200-pound Leemans' prowess as a halfback and fullback exceeded the school's profile. He was a second-round draft pick in the first NFL draft and was the Most Valuable Player in the 1936 College All-Star game before starting an eight-season, injury-plagued career that landed him in the Pro Football Hall of Fame.

Leemans ran for 830 yards as a Giant rookie, to lead the league in rushing in 1936. Leemans was an all-around star running, passing, and catching the ball, and became respected as a hard tackler on defense. After he became an indispensable player, the team honored Leemans with a special "Tuffy Leemans Day." The Giants met the Brooklyn Dodgers at the Polo Grounds, but the happy occasion turned somber on December 7, 1941.

The ex-Giant was not selected for the Hall of Fame until 1978, just six months before his sudden death from a heart attack at 66, but he exulted in his enshrinement. "It's like all of a sudden, I'm a celebrity again," he said.

Leemans said he always appreciated his nickname. It complimented the manner in which he played the game and made others forget his real name. "When your first name is Alphonse, any nickname will do," Leemans said.

Above: Using the old, straight-ahead style of kicking, Ward Cuff of the Giants misses a 38-yard field goal in a November 1941 game against the Washington Redskins. Ed Danowski holds.
Bettmann/Corbis

Right: Giants' back Tuffy Leemans records a short gain in a game in the Polo Grounds against the Washington Redskins, as Washington's Wayne Millner (40) leapt through the air in an attempt to tackle him.
Bettmann/Corbis

In 1937, Owen introduced an offense called the "A" formation and gradually implemented it into the team's repertoire. A chief innovation was an unbalanced offensive line, with four linemen to the right of the center and only two to the left. He also shifted backfield members around in different ways so that they were not aligned three across behind the quarterback. The key one featured an unbalanced backfield with more runners to the left, or the weak side. Owen termed the variations his plans B, C, and D. He leaned towards more regular use of A, however.

All of this tinkering was a surprise to Giant players because Owen was admittedly first and foremost a defensive coach and he was not someone who relied much on trick plays offensively. Run, run, and run some more, the conservative approach, appealed to Owen.

Leemans was the ideal performer for Owen. He was a player acknowledged as giving 100 percent effort 100 percent of the time. He grew up in Superior, Wisconsin and as a teenager during vacation breaks from high school worked on iron ore boats as a fireman shoveling coal. He built muscle the hard way, and described himself as being "of hardy Belgian stock." Leemans showed contempt for any player who didn't give his all. Once, when a Giants rookie lineman missed a block, Leeman dressed him down. The young player made the situation worse by suggesting it didn't make any difference because they were getting paid anyway. A furious Leemans retorted, "Son, I'm going to give you a break. On the next play I want you to fake an injury. Then go to the sidelines and get off this squad as fast as you can. We don't want men like you on this team, or in pro ball."

The Giants returned to the championship game in 1941 for the third time in four seasons. The regular season had ended on Pearl Harbor day and two weeks later New York met the Bears at Wrigley Field. The country was distracted and only 13,341 fans watched Chicago crush the Giants, 37–9. The Giants led 6–3 after the first quarter on a 31-yard pass from Leemans to George Franck. The Bears led 9–6 at halftime, but a Ward Cuff 16-yard field-goal for the Giants tied the score 9–9 in the third quarter. But the Bears erupted after that and dominated the Giants the rest of the afternoon.

This was the last season resembling normalcy in the NFL until 1946. The United States was at war for real and any comparisons to football as war were now in poor taste. During the war years 52 members of the New York Giants served in the military. End Jack Lummus, who earned the Congressional Medal of Honor, died on Iwo Jima. Al Blozis, a powerful, 250-pound tackle from Georgetown, who suited up for the Giants between 1942 and 1944, was killed near the end of the war in France.

Merle Hapes was a reliable newcomer as a running back, but Leemans was the primary thrower, although

Washington's Sammy Baugh (33), perhaps the greatest all-around NFL player ever, was a superb quarterback, but also a star safety. He is shown here in a 1943 game chasing down Giants' back Bill Paschal after a 35-yard gain.
Bettmann/Corbis

this was not his best talent. The Giants of 1942 barely resembled the multiple-division-winning Giants of preceding seasons, and finished 5–5–1. It was exactly what Leemans had expected. "I took one look at the squad and I felt like crying," Leemans said. "It hurt to see the Giants I loved having as miserable a group as we had there."

One by one, NFL players signed up to join the Army, the Navy, the Marines or the Air Force. One by one, players on the Giants roster shipped out to Europe or Asia. The ranks of able-bodied, high-quality players thinned. The Giants made a useful addition when they latched onto running back Bill Paschal out of Georgia Tech in 1943, but such finds were rare.

In January of 1942, Wellington Mara joined the Navy and was commissioned as a lieutenant. He served in the Pacific for three years, only rarely hearing details about the fortunes of his favorite football team. He had never before missed the team's training camp. Tim Mara and son Jack continued to run the Giants and it was later revealed that there had been discussions among some owners that the NFL should shut down for the war's duration. The Maras argued against the drastic move. Wellington later said his family

ny

Giants' early Pre-season Training Camps

1933	Pompton Lakes, New Jersey
1934–38	Pearl River, New York
1939	Superior, Wisconsin
1940	Pearl River, New York
1941–42	Superior, Wisconsin
1943–45	Bear Mountain, New York
1946	Superior, Wisconsin
1947–49	Pearl River, New York

committed to keeping the Giants in business, "even if we had to play 4Fs and high school players." The 4Fs abounded on rosters, as well as some recently retired players who were recalled.

Mel Hein had retired and was teaching and coaching at Union College in Schenectady, New York. When his team's schedule was suspended in 1944, Owen talked him into suiting up just for the games. Hein took the train back and forth to the city and without benefit of any contact in a year, was pressed into 60-minute service again on a brutally hot day. "What a toll it took," Hein said of his body-wide aches.

The 1943 Giants finished 6–3–1. They could beat the mediocre teams, but were overpowered by the good teams. The stinging 56–7 defeat hung on the Giants by the Bears was the worst loss in franchise history.

Players with talent were dear. Leemans retired after the 1944 season, but Pascal, who led the NFL in rushing in 1943 and 1944, played with distinction and Ward Cuff was still around as a versatile contributor. Hein was commuting. Ken Strong re-upped to help out. And Hank Soar obtained Army leave to play in a Giants game. Owen supposedly asked him, "Hank, how's your pass defense these days?" The reply from

"The Giants were in trouble because of a heavy draft call. So for three years I worked under those circumstances."
—Mel Hein, explaining why he coached Union College and still played Sundays for New York during World War II without practicing.

Soar? "Wonderful, Steve. Here it is," he said, pulling out his three-day pass signed by a colonel. "No MP can stop me." Owen would have preferred if no Redskin could stop Soar.

The 1940s were definitely not the good-old days of the Giants franchise, and it is regarded as a decade of struggle—at least the first six years. Yet the Giants did record some successes against the backdrop of national gloom. Whether it was finding the necessary number of capable players, of convincing aging veterans to hang on for just another season, or taking to the streets to drum up spectators, the management team of Tim and Jack Mara, plus coach Steve Owen pieced together a 1944 club that went 8–4–1 and advanced to the NFL championship game against the Green Bay Packers.

The Packers were experiencing a renaissance of sorts. Still under the tutelage of Curly Lambeau, the icon of northern Wisconsin, Green Bay had an explosive passing offense still built around legendary receiver Don Hutson. Hutson was a pass catcher ahead of his time, who developed routes that flummoxed defenses, and he retired with every receiving record. Ironically, in 1944, the Giants quarterback was Arnie Herber, a future Hall of Famer, who had spent much of his career throwing to Hutson. The title encounter was a hard-fought game, with Green Bay winning, 14–7.

For once, the Packers adopted a counterintuitive strategy. The Giants, who were limping along with a multitude of injuries, were determined not to let Hutson defeat them. They shadowed him tightly and double-teamed him, but the Packers rarely pushed the issue through the air. They out-foxed the Giants by sticking to the run game. As 46,016 spectators watched at the Polo Grounds, Green Bay handed off repeatedly to fullback Ted Fritsch, who scored two touchdowns while Hutson occupied the defense. The Giants' offense was limited. Paschal's previously sprained ankle confined him mostly to the bench. Herber was active throwing, but he could not connect with receivers for big plays. As for Hutson, he kicked two extra points, was exemplary in the defensive

The Giants opened their 1944 Bear Mountain pre-season training camp with 45 hopeful roster candidates on hand for a workout, as coach Steve Owen looked on.
Bettmann/Corbis

backfield, and was mostly a decoy on pass routes.

World War II ended in 1945 and things began to revert to normality in American society. That included pro football. The Giants were a patchwork club, still clinging to several aging players as younger and fitter soldiers returned to civilian life. The Giants did not make the transition rapidly enough, however, and recorded a horrible 3–6–1 season. The 1945 team was neither a war-years squad nor a back-to-business bunch. So helpful when key players were fighting in the real trenches overseas, Herber and Hein couldn't keep the Giants rolling for one more year. Old reliable Steve Owen remained at the controls and it was up to him, with the approval and cooperation of the Maras, to start over with fresh faces for the 1946 season and build the new Giants.

The work began behind center. Frank Filchock was a veteran quarterback out of Indiana University who had played for Pittsburgh and the Redskins. In Washington he was Sammy Baugh's understudy, possibly the best all-around football player of all time. In 1946, Filchock escaped to the Giants, where for one important season he was the key man running the offense. Filchock was 5 feet 11 inches and 193 pounds with a strong, but erratic arm and some running ability. He set Giants records throwing for 12 touchdowns and 1,262 yards, and rushed for 371 yards, too. The

Above: Giants' receiver John Weiss, who grabbed a pass from Marion Pugh, eludes a Washington tackler en route for a touchdown in an October 1945 game at the Polo Grounds. *Bettmann/Corbis*

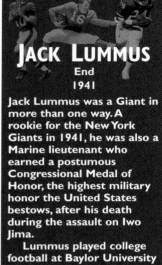

JACK LUMMUS
End
1941

Jack Lummus was a Giant in more than one way. A rookie for the New York Giants in 1941, he was also a Marine lieutenant who earned a postumous Congressional Medal of Honor, the highest military honor the United States bestows, after his death during the assault on Iwo Jima.

Lummus played college football at Baylor University and broke into the Giants' lineup as a 6 feet, 3 inches, 200-pound, two-way end. Soon after Pearl Harbor was bombed and the football season concluded, Lummus enlisted in the Marines.

His No. 29 Giants uniform and his football cleats were put aside and Lummus became the leader of a rifle platoon as U.S. troops sought to take control of the Pacific Island from the Japanese. According to accounts of the battle, Lummus made a single-handed charge on an enemy gun setup. He was knocked down by the blast of a hand grenade, but destroyed the Japanese obstacle.

Another hand grenade wounded Lummus in the shoulder, but he shot out a second, dug-in Japanese vantage point. As Lummus held his spot he yelled for his men to follow, but before they reached him a massive explosion battered the officer. Lummus had stepped on a land mine that tore off his legs. Still conscious, he ordered the men ahead, and then was taken to a field hospital. Before he died on March 8, 1945, it was reported that Lummus said to a doctor, "I guess the New York Giants have lost the services of a damned good end."

(Left to right) John Mara, president of the New York Giants; Dan Reeves, owner of the Cleveland Rams; George Preston Marshall, owner of the Washington Redskins; and Earl "Curly" Lambeau, Green Bay Packers coach, at a 1946 National Football League meeting discussing strategy on how to hold off a challenge from the new All-America Football Conference. *Bettmann/Corbis*

Below: Frank Filchock (center) escaped his role as backup to Washington great Sammy Baugh and signed with the Giants in 1946. Looking on are Wellington Mara (left), vice president and secretary of the club, and John Mara (right), president and treasurer. *Bettmann/Corbis*

KEN STRONG

**Running back, kicker
1933–35, 1939, 1944–47**

He certainly had the name for the game. Ken Strong was that—and much more. Strong was an All-American for the New York University Violets before playing for the Staten Island Stapletons and the Giants. Passing was not the Hall of Famer's strongest suit, but he dabbled at it when needed. He specialized in busting out of the backfield for key runs, returning punts spectacularly, and providing a useful weapon kicking in tight games.

Strong broke into professional football in 1929, joined the Giants in 1933 and lit out for a rival league between 1936 and 1938. He rejoined the Giants in 1939, retired, but came back to the Giants again during World War II and stuck with the club from 1944 to 1947. By then he was 41.

A key contributor in the famous Sneaker Game victory, Strong also turned in a memorable performance in a 3–0 win over the Bears in 1933. Strong kicked the game-winning field goal three times, because twice the Giants were whistled offside. Strong was a kicker-only when he played in the mid-1940s, and did not even wear shoulder pads in games.

However, in the last game of the 1944 season, with the Giants leading the Washington Redskins, 31–0, Strong asked coach Steve Owen for one last rushing attempt. Strong's son, Ken Jr., had mentioned never seeing his dad do anything on a football field except kick. Owen assented. Later, Strong discovered that Ken Jr. had a cold and had not attended the game.

Do-it-all Giants' star Ken Strong had two stays with the club, first in the 1930s and again at the end of World War II.
Pro Football Hall of Fame/NFL/Getty Images

"With the possible exception of Jim Thorpe, Ken Strong can do more things better than any back I ever saw."
—*Sportswriter Grantland Rice.*

good numbers earned him All-Pro recognition, but he also heaved 25 interceptions.

Young linemen Tex Coulter and Jim White, who was also an all-star, bolstered Filchock's protection, and running back Merle Hapes returned from military service. The rejuvenated Giants won the Eastern Division with a 7–3–1 mark after blasting Washington 31–0 in the final regular-season game, a result that no doubt made Filchock happy. Once again, the Giants were in the NFL title game against the Bears.

Primed to return to the winner's circle, the Giants were shocked on the eve of the December 14, 1946 championship game and later on that day when word spread that two key members of the offense were embroiled in a scandal. The night before the game Tim Mara was informed by Commissioner Bert Bell that police authorities were investigating Filchock and Hapes for allegedly taking bribes to throw the game. Police had detained both players and interrogated them.

The next day, as kickoff approached and a short-notice investigation was led by Bell, the Giants' preparation was distracted. Bell handed down a decision based on what was known at the time. He was told that Hapes (who admitted the fact) had been offered a $3,500 bribe from a noted gambler, but turned it down. However, he had not reported it to any football authority. Filchock knew the gambler and associated with him over dinner many times, but said he was not offered the same $3,500 bribe. Bell banned Hapes from the game, but allowed Filchock to play.

The 58,346 fans at the Polo Grounds were unaware of the burgeoning scandal, though it was breaking on the radio. The bribery allegations cast a pall over the Giants players. The game itself was tight, but not viewed as a classic. "The Giants-Bears football game was smothered under such a thick blanket of honesty that it looked as if it was fixed both ways," wrote the esteemed *New York Herald Tribune* sportswriter Stanley Woodward. "What with Frank Filchock and Sid Luckman consistently firing passes into the hands of the enemy and their associates fumbling and stumbling all over the field, it was no thing of beauty. Everyone was nervous and the District Attorney had the field."

Luckman, a Hall of Famer-to-be, was a throwing quarterback, the dream leader of Bears' owner George Halas, who loved him like a son. Unlike many of the top

Looking on unhappily during a 1946 game as the Chicago Bears advance the ball are a trio of New York players all named Frank: Filchock, Reagan, and Liebel. One of their staunch rooters, President Franklin D. Roosevelt's postmaster general, Jim Farley is behind Liebel. *Bettmann/Corbis*

Perhaps the biggest shock was that the Bears even had a play in their playbook that called for Luckman to run. Who knew? It was called "Bingo, keep it." Luckman asked Halas for permission to go for it and the coach assented. The fake handoff was to George McAfee, a marvelously talented running back, who under ordinary circumstances would have been trusted with the ball. Certainly the Giants thought so, given that the entire defense followed McAfee and allowed Luckman to tip-toe into the end zone unmolested.

Once the result was in, Filchock was finished with the Giants. It was determined that he had lied about the bribe offer (and he later confessed). Bell expelled him from the league. He played in the Canadian Football League for four seasons, splitting his time between Hamilton and Montreal, but was then allowed to return to the Colts in 1950 for whom he played one game. In April of 1947 Hapes was banned by Bell and although his suspension was lifted in 1954, he never played in the NFL again. The loss of Hapes and Filchock wounded the Giants' offense. An awful start to the 1947 season prompted a trade of Bill Paschal to the Boston Yankees for quarterback Paul Governali. As an All-American graduate of nearby Columbia, with the catchy nickname of "Pitchin' Paul," Governali's skills were well-known to Wellington Mara. He was installed as the Giants' starter immediately and in just eight games set team records for touchdown passes with 14 and yards gained with 1,461. The Giants finished the season 2–8–2, but they were feeling better about themselves. With just three

Above: NFL commissioner Bert Bell is shown at a 1947 press conference in Philadelphia announcing his decision to suspend Merle Hapes and Frank Filchock, the two New York Giants players involved in an attempted bribe scandal. *Bettmann/Corbis*

quarterbacks of the 1930s and 1940s, Luckman was not a runner. Only he made an exception against the Giants. With the game deadlocked, 14–14, Luckman surprised the defense with a fake handoff followed by a bootleg around end. He scampered 19 yards for the winning touchdown in a 24–14 triumph.

Giants' runner George Cherverko takes off around right end in a 1947 game against the Chicago Cardinals, with Ray Apolskis (75) and Mal Rutner (80) in pursuit. *Bettmann/Corbis*

"During the years I quarterbacked the Giants, we never had any real speedsters as receivers."
—*Charlie Conerly.*

pro seasons on his resume following World War II service, Governali was young and promising and seemed to have a lock on the Giants' quarterback position for the foreseeable future.

That perception did not last long. In 1948, Charlie Conerly, a war hero who had been taken in the NFL draft by the Washington Redskins previously, completed his college career at the University of Mississippi. He was an All-American and considered the best rookie prospect at his position. But Washington was no longer in need of a quarterback. The Redskins still had Sammy Baugh manning the job and Harry Gilmer on deck. So the Giants traded for Conerly. Poor Governali was benched and after the 1948 season retired and turned to earning a master's degree and college coaching. Conerly became a legend in New York.

The arrival of Conerly coincided with the signing of All-American end Bill Swiacki, out of Columbia, and defensive back Emlen Tunnell, from Iowa. Conerly and Tunnell became all-stars and became the cornerstones of the re-emerging Giants. But so much change all at once contributed to a soft 4–8 record. The season was more of warm-up for the future.

As much as they coveted the polished and rugged Conerly as their quarterback of the future, the Maras blanched at the price. The All-America Football Conference had come into existence as a competitor league and flashed big dollars at selected players. The Brooklyn Dodgers reportedly offered Conerly a $110,000 deal. The Giants were forced to ante up or lose their man. While Tunnell was signed for $5,000 plus some incidental bonuses, it took $62,500 over five seasons, plus a $10,000 signing bonus to wrap up Conerly. He was worth it.

Conerly stepped in immediately and was a hit. He completed 54.2 percent of his passes for 2,175 yards and 22 touchdowns. In one game against the Pittsburgh Steelers, Conerly completed a league record 36 passes that was not eclipsed for 16 years. The Giants had a major-league passing game, the best they had ever fielded. Swiacki caught 39 passes with 10 touchdowns. Tunnell, the Giants' first African-American player and later the first African-American assistant coach in the National Football League, intercepted seven passes as a rookie, en route to his lifetime total of 79, the second-most in history. The Giants struggled

Charlie Conerly, the All-American quarterback from the University of Mississippi, as a 1948 rookie. He became one of the team's most popular figures. *Bettmann/Corbis*

for wins in 1948, but they had the look of a team on the upswing and they did provide excitement.

Owen had always been proud of his defenses and thought defense-first when tailoring a game plan. He knew that the Giants of the late 1940s were going to endure some growing pains, but he did not envision a wholesale collapse of his beloved defensive eleven. For once in his life, the defense gave Owen heartburn. The 1948 club allowed 388 points in 12 games, or a painful average of 32.3 points a game. Sprinkled into the mix were games when the Giants permitted 41, 45, 63, and 52 points. Despite being 50 years old that season, Owen might have been tempted to put himself in uniform for the first time in a decade-and-a-half.

Improvement came incrementally to the Giants. In 1949, through careful drafting, trading and seeking out unsigned players, they kept beefing up and acquiring

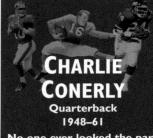

CHARLIE CONERLY
Quarterback
1948–61

No one ever looked the part of the craggy-faced, savvy pro football leader more than Charlie Conerly, the beloved Giants' quarterback who broke into the lineup in 1948 and stayed until 1961.

A World War II Marine who became an All-American at the University of Mississippi, Conerly was portrayed as a 24-year-old rookie-of-the-year. Later he said that he was 27 when he took his first NFL snap. Before he took his last one, Conerly was portraying the Marlboro Man astride a horse on billboards around the nation.

Conerly was the epitome of "The Old Pro," the man looked up to in the huddle and revered as a go-to quarterback when the clock was ticking down. He threw 173 touchdown passes for nearly 20,000 yards and led the NFL in passing in 1959 at age 38, a year after being the signal-caller in the first sudden death overtime game against the Baltimore Colts. Conerly played in three Pro Bowls and four NFL championship games for the Giants.

Also a cotton farmer in Mississippi, Conerly spoke more with his actions, acquiring a reputation for being taciturn. "He's the toughest quarterback in the league and I guess tough guys don't have to talk much," said Giants' coach Allie Sherman.

No one pushed Conerly into retirement and at a Toots Shor luncheon honoring his career, Jack Mara encouraged him to play one more season. "If you change your mind and decide to return, Charlie, you can still keep the watch."

Famed quarterback Charlie Conerly calls the signals in a 1962 game near the end of his 15-season career.
Bettmann/Corbis

fresh talent. One discovery was right on the roster all of the time. Gene "Choo-Choo" Roberts, formerly of the University of Tennessee-Chattanooga, joined the Giants in 1947. He hardly played that season. In 1948, he gained 491 yards rushing. However, in 1949 he became a star, running for 634 yards, catching 35

passes and scoring 17 touchdowns for 102 points, a total that led the league.

By the end of the decade, Owen had ditched his "A" formation offense in favor of the traditional "T" formation which provided the best opportunity to excel for throwing quarterbacks. Conerly may have

been fleet afoot earlier in life, but he was never a jackrabbit in the pros and he only got slower as he absorbed more hits from defenders who penetrated his porous offensive line.

The Giants and the Bears were used to playing one another when the stakes were high, with championships on the line, but neither team was in the title hunt in 1949. However, they did produce a thrill-a-minute game, which was won 35–28 by the Giants during the regular season. Just 30,587 fans attended the October game in the Polo Grounds, evidence that the teams were not up to their usual standards. The game was knotted at 28–28

EMLEN TUNNELL
DEFENSIVE BACK, 1948–1958

Nearly 50 years after his retirement, Emlen Tunnell is still considered the best defensive back in NFL history, a supreme talent who awed his teammates and the fans who watched him as he batted passes to himself in the air and wiggled in and out of tacklers' grasps.

The first African-American player in New York Giants history was a walk-on. Although that is a college term applied to players who are not on scholarship and show up to try out for the squad, the description fits. Tunnell, who was born in 1925, was a star athlete in the Philadelphia suburbs, growing up in the shadow of Villanova University in a neighborhood called Garrett Hill. He enrolled at the University of Toledo, where he broke his neck playing football, but served in the Coast Guard during World War II, surviving a torpedoed boat.

After the war, Tunnell transferred to the University of Iowa, where he enrolled on the G.I. Bill. As a youth, Tunnell said he adopted the advice of his mother Catherine and sought to defuse any type of potentially tense racial matter with humor. His joking, story-telling persona became a trademark.

While at Iowa, Tunnell was approached by a scout from the fledgling All-America Football Conference, who counted out $5,000 in cash as an inducement to turn pro. Then, unexpectedly, he received a questionnaire from the New York Giants. Although Tunnell had another season of eligibility at Iowa, he decided in 1948 that it was time to make some money. Inspired by the routine Giants paperwork he hitchhiked to New York intent on convincing the Giants to give him a job. When he arrived in the big city knowing no one, he found a low-class hotel room for 75 cents a night.

The next day he walked over to

the old Giants offices on 42nd Street and talked his way first into a meeting with general manager Ray Walsh and then owner Tim Mara. In varying accounts of Tunnell's unannounced visit to the Giants, most indicate the team had no idea who he was. Coach Steve Owen is quoted as saying, "Never heard of you." But Tunnell had been a star in the Big Ten. He said the Giants knew who he was, but that walking in off the street the way he had they just didn't know if he was who he said he was.

Tim Mara had appraised Tunnell quietly, liking both his style and approach on his unannounced call at the Giants' offices. Wellington Mara, the personnel chief, said, "If you have enough guts to walk in here and ask for a job, I'm going to give you a chance." Tunnell signed a $5,000 contract that included two $500 bonuses and the relationship forged that autumn lasted the rest of his life (with only a short break of a few years with the Green Bay Packers), first on the field, then as the first black assistant coach in the NFL and also as a scout.

Exhibiting a down-to-earth personality, Tunnell was friendly with Giants' players on both sides of the ball, fans, organization officials, and people from all walks of life. He grew up poor, with his mother working as a domestic in a white area, and always was comfortable with integrated circumstances. If Tunnell was All-Pro as a defensive back and punt returner, perhaps his best skill was making conversation. "I'll bet you I have more bartender friends than anyone," he said once. "And I don't drink much. I just like to go in somewhere and talk."

Tunnell broke in with the Giants in 1948 and was a fixture at safety for 11 seasons. He intercepted a team record 74 passes before moving on to Green Bay for the final couple of years of

Emlen Tunnell, the Giants' first black player shakes hands with Vince Lombardi (who got his NFL start as a New York assistant coach) after joining him in Green Bay in 1961. *Bettmann/Corbis*

his Hall of Fame career. Tunnell's lifetime total of 79 interceptions is the second highest in league history. He intercepted ten alone in the 1949 season, and at one point intercepted a pass five games in a row. His team interception yardage return total of 1,240 remains a Giants' record by more than 500, even though it is a half-century old.

"Emlen Tunnell was one of the greatest football players of all time," said Harland Svare, a Tunnell contemporary as a linebacker with the Giants.

In addition, Tunnell's total of 261 punt returns remains the team mark, and his yardage total of 2,214 is second on the Giants' list. Long-time teammate Frank Gifford said that it was fun just to observe the way Tunnell gathered in a punt and took off downfield. "I used to love to watch him catch a punt," Gifford said. "He caught it like Willie Mays. He had the softest hands I've ever seen."

Tunnell was a critical player as the Giants matured during the 1950s. He played for the 1956 champs, and at one point competed in 150 straight games. He ended his playing career with Green Bay in 1962, again a champion. Although Tunnell once said he could make tackles until he was 50 years old, his legs were slowing down when he made the move to scout, then assistant coach. During one stretch, Tunnell embarked on a three-month, 51-college campus scouting mission for the Giants that was the

"Never heard of you."
—Coach Steve Owen upon first meeting future Hall of Fame defensive back Emlen Tunnell.

Jules Verne around-the-nation journey of talent searches. In May of 1963 he was hired as the first African-American NFL assistant coach.

As an assistant, Tunnell said he could relate to younger players, especially African-American players who came out of comparatively sequestered traditionally all-black schools. He also said race had never been a factor in his pro football career. When he was with the Packers, he said, he probably ate dinner at former Alabama quarterback Bart Starr's home 20 times and discussed race with southern lineman Dave Hanner regularly.

Tunnell was elected to the Hall of Fame in 1967 and was caught off-guard by the timing. "A lot of people who know me kept telling me I'd make it," he said, "but I figured it would be a long time coming." It was just as well that the honor was not so terribly long in coming because the Giants and the football world were shocked in 1975 when Tunnell, only 50, died of a heart attack.

Emlen Tunnell (45) had a tremendous knack for big plays, making interceptions and returning punts and kicks for the Giants. Alex Sandusky (68) of the Baltimore Colts helps run Tunnell out of bounds, while Stan West (62) of the Giants and Dick Young (24) of the Colts follow in a 1955 contest. *Bettmann/Corbis*

Bill Austin (75) is about to wrap up Detroit's Bob Smith (40) in a tackle after Smith caught a pass from quarterback Frank Tripucka in a 1949 game. New York defensive back Emlen Tunnell takes a tumble after missing out on an interception.
Bettmann/Corbis

in the fourth quarter when Conerly unleashed a sideline bullet to Choo-Choo Roberts. Roberts tucked the ball under his arm and completed an 85-yard TD romp.

In 1949, the Giants moved in a fresh direction offensively that was still pretty much unheard of around the league. Since the creation of the NFL, teams had relied on regular players who handled other full-time jobs to take care of their place-kicking duties. Lou Groza was an exceptional kicker, but also a full-time tackle for the Browns. Lou Michaels was a defensive end and kicker. George Blanda was a quarterback and kicker.

That season the Giants departed from the norm and hired Ben Agajanian to kick extra points and field goals. Agajanian, was first paid to kick by a minor league outfit called the Hollywood Bears. Agajanian, who was born in 1919 in Santa Ana, California, played for 13 different pro teams, including the Giants twice.

"I won a lot of games for them. The 50-yard kick was kind of a mental barrier. I used to compute the maximum range by the atmospheric conditions."
—Ben Agajanian, the NFL's first full-time place kicker.

He was the first kicking specialist in the game and he was regarded with the same skepticism that audiences brought to the viewing of dancing bears. He was a student at the University of New Mexico in 1939 when he sliced off the toes on his right foot in an accident on a freight elevator. He immediately asked the surgeon if he would be able to kick again. The doctor's answer was, "What will you do

with the cane?"

Agajanian, who stood 6 feet tall and weighed 215 pounds, had a square-toed shoe made and resumed kicking the football. His biggest obstacle was not his amputation, but the closed-mindedness of coaches who with limited rosters sought all-around players. One coach called him "excess baggage" and said, "We can't afford to pay a guy to just sit around and kick a field goal once in a while." Obviously, that coach did not have a crystal ball that would allow him to see into the future.

It was difficult for Agajanian to convince pro teams that he was valuable enough to keep around. There were no kicking coaches and there were no organized workouts for kickers in the framework of head coaches' practices. Still, Agajanian sold Wellington Mara on the notion that hiring him would be worthwhile. Agajanian's home remained in California where he started some businesses. Mara actually signed Agajanian to a deal where he only had to fly in for the games. He could operate his other businesses and practice on his own.

"I won a lot of games for them," Agajanian said. That was in his second incarnation with the Giants, between 1954 and 1957 when Jim Lee Howell had succeeded Owen as head coach. The purist in Howell did not like Agajanian at all. Agajanian used to methodically examine the weather and the wind and Howell sarcastically asked, "What's your range today?" Later that day, Agajanian booted a 50-yard-field goal to best the Redskins, a kick that 60 years ago was of nearly unthinkable length. "It's 50 today," Agajanian retorted to Howell.

Agajanian kicked for pay until he was 45 years old and then became a kicking coach, bringing his expertise to pro teams in training camps and sometimes during the season as a consultant. In 1964, he was traveling with the San Diego Chargers as an aide and was ordered to suit up and kick. The guru played in three games that autumn more or less against his will. "I hate to get hit," he said, "because at my age it hurts. So I kicked the ball and ran as fast as I could to the sidelines." His last NFL kicking job with the Chargers ended abruptly. He pulled a groin muscle and fled to his home as quickly as possible, retiring with 525 points. Many years had passed since his body was in the kind of prime shape it had been with the 1949 Giants. But Agajanian had begun a revolution.

1940s NEW YORK GIANTS YEAR BY YEAR

Year	Record
1940	6–4–1
1941	8–3
1942	5–5–1
1943	6–3–1
1944	8–1–1
1945	3–6–1
1946	7–3–1
1947	2–8–2
1948	4–8
1949	6–6

Ben Agajanian was the first full-time kicker in the NFL, despite losing a portion of his foot in an accident as a young man. Agajanian played a year for the Giants in the 1940s and again in the 1950s, but is shown here wearing a Los Angeles Dons uniform in 1947. *Bettmann/Corbis*

CHAPTER 4

THE 1950s
PEACE AND PROSPERITY

Careers and lives were altered for the survivors of World War II, but American euphoria reigned as the nation's soldiers came home in the late 1940s and ushered in a new outlook, a new enthusiasm, and a new level of prosperity. Young American families bought automobiles and took to the open road with a vigor never before seen. And those who stayed home made sure to invest in the most popular new appliance —the television set.

New energy seemed to infuse American sports franchises, as well, and pro football embraced the new optimism on several fronts. The old standby teams of the NFL were reinvigorated. Potential new owners appeared and fielded new teams in the All-America Football Conference. By 1950, it was apparent that the established NFL would once again fend off the challenge of an upstart league, this time absorbing some of the most potent teams into the league as full members. The teams that folded, however, flooded the market with established players, giving teams like the Giants a chance to strengthen their rosters.

The opportunity arose at a time when coach Steve

Right: Pete Pihos (left) of the Eagles leaps high, but can't catch a pass from Bobby Thomason during a 1954 game against the Giants in the Polo Grounds. At right is New York defensive back Tom Landry, the future legendary coach with the Dallas Cowboys. *Bettmann/Corbis*

Dan Reeves of the Los Angeles Rams, James D. Clark of the Philadelphia Eagles, and John Mara of the New York Giants gather for a 1950 NFL owners meeting. *Bettmann/Corbis*

Owen and the Maras were beginning to see the fruits of their rebuilding efforts behind quarterback Charlie Conerly, and the additions served the Giants well. New York added tackle Arnie Weinmeister, a future Hall of Fame lineman, and defensive back Tom Landry. Landry, who after retiring stayed on as an assistant coach, invented the 4-3 defense at the end of the decade, and then departed for his own Hall of Fame coaching career leading the Dallas Cowboys.

Opportunity was the watchword in a post-World War II economy, both in society and professional sport. Weinmeister had two years of experience in the AAFC before the Giants scooped him up. He had no learning curve. As many players still did, Weinmeister, who had excelled at the University of Washington, went both ways, but preferred the role of defensive tackle over offensive protector. "Blocking for the passer is as formidable a job as the tackle can have," Weinmeister said. "He must hold up the wall, or pocket, for his quarterback for an appreciable time while the defensive player or players against him can use their hands. It is a tough assignment to recover from that pushing around to maintain the pocket." Conerly was not the most mobile of quarterbacks, even in his mid-20s, but he also slowed as the years passed.

Landry's playing career is virtually forgotten outside New York because of his 29-year tenure with the Cowboys, and his image as a suited man on the sidelines, wearing a hat, with arms folded and an emotionless expression on his face. Landry was born in 1924 in Mission, Texas and played for the University of Texas. He flew 30 missions as a bomber pilot during World War II. After one season in the All-America Conference, he played six seasons for the Giants and intercepted 31 passes.

His last couple of seasons he was the de facto defensive coach, and allowed a free hand in designing defensive formations. He said:

One must remember that in those days football was a fairly simple game. We had maybe a couple of offensive formations, a couple of defensive changes. That's all we had. So we didn't spend a lot of time like the staffs do today. We would come in and practice in the morning, and then the coaches would meet right after lunch. Then most would go home.

The new decade brought new success. After a few years of hardscrabble hustle, when the Giants eked out whatever wins they could, the 1950 team exploded with a 10–2 mark. Ordinarily that would be good enough to put the Giants into the championship game, but the Cleveland Browns, accepted into the league from the All-America Conference, were a little better. This marked the beginning of a fresh rivalry that would help define New York's decade.

Meanwhile, the Maras exhibited a magic touch on the personnel front, the hallmark of a great organization. In 1951, the Giants drafted Southern Methodist University star Kyle Rote, a receiver who became so respected and revered among teammates,

Arnie Weinmeister was the cornerstone of the offensive line in the early 1950s as the team rebuilt from a disappointing stretch in the 1940s. *NFL Photos/Getty Images*

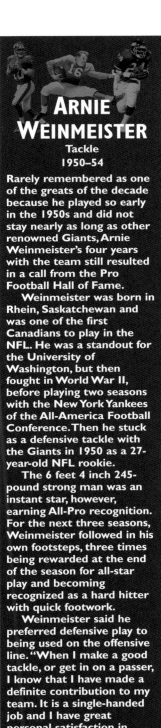

ARNIE WEINMEISTER
Tackle
1950–54

Rarely remembered as one of the greats of the decade because he played so early in the 1950s and did not stay nearly as long as other renowned Giants, Arnie Weinmeister's four years with the team still resulted in a call from the Pro Football Hall of Fame.

Weinmeister was born in Rhein, Saskatchewan and was one of the first Canadians to play in the NFL. He was a standout for the University of Washington, but then fought in World War II, before playing two seasons with the New York Yankees of the All-America Football Conference. Then he stuck as a defensive tackle with the Giants in 1950 as a 27-year-old NFL rookie.

The 6 feet 4 inch 245-pound strong man was an instant star, however, earning All-Pro recognition. For the next three seasons, Weinmeister followed in his own footsteps, three times being rewarded at the end of the season for all-star play and becoming recognized as a hard hitter with quick footwork.

Weinmeister said he preferred defensive play to being used on the offensive line. "When I make a good tackle, or get in on a passer, I know that I have made a definite contribution to my team. It is a single-handed job and I have great personal satisfaction in knowing I am holding the other team down."

The combined six years Weinmeister played professionally in the two leagues, before becoming a high-ranking Teamsters union official in Seattle, was one of the shortest careers of any Hall of Famer.

A family orchestra: Giants' receiver Kyle Rote plays the "bull fiddle tub" as his wife Betty and their sons accompany him on the piano in 1958.
Bettmann/Corbis

that at least a half-dozen named sons of their own Kyle. That did not include Kyle Rote Jr., who became a major soccer star. Frank Gifford was drafted from the University of Southern California in 1952. Hall of Fame tackle Roosevelt Brown was added in 1953. Piece by piece throughout the mid-1950s, the Giants added key components. These were players who embarked on long careers with the club, extending into the mid-1960s: from defensive end Andy Robustelli and middle linebacker Sam Huff, to center Ray Wietecha and guard Jack Stroud, from fullbacks Mel Triplett and Alex Webster to defenders Jim Katcavage and Harland Svare. And the Giants still featured Conerly and sticky-fingered safety Emlen Tunnell. Tunnell intercepted 79 passes and earned the nickname "Mr. Offense on Defense" for his explosive running back punts and kicks. In one game against the Chicago Cardinals in 1951, Tunnell recorded 178 yards in return yards, including an 82-yard punt return for a touchdown.

Even the linemen became household names as the franchise boomed in popularity, made headlines with divisional and league championships, and in 1958 competed in the contest against the Baltimore that came to be known as the greatest game ever played.

"I wouldn't be in the Hall of Fame if it weren't for him."
—Halfback Frank Gifford on Hall of Fame tackle Roosevelt Brown.

The 1950s were one of the most momentous decades in Giant history.

Kyle Rote was born in 1928 and by the time he was a 6 foot 190-pound rookie for the Giants in 1951, he had become a Texas football hero, which on the Texas ranking scale may rank ahead even of oil man or cattle rancher. The All-American's special moment came in the Cotton Bowl in 1949, when Southern Methodist University faced a highly favored Notre Dame team. It turned into Irish against Rote, Notre Dame finally prevailing 27–20. But Rote earned a new reputation for tenacity and fearlessness.

Rote was a run, pass and catch all-around star for Southern Methodist, but early in his pro career he suffered a severe knee injury. That setback moved him to wide receiver for the Giants. Because the Giants had so many weapons, Rote was often overshadowed, but

Frank Gifford was a star at the University of Southern California and was a versatile offensive and defensive performer for the Giants throughout the 1950s.
Bettmann/Corbis

had a knack for making clutch plays. He caught his 20-or-so passes a season for years and then in the early 1960s Rote had years when he grabbed 42 and 53. Talk about patience.

Rote discussed how he made himself into a better receiver. "Playing basketball helps," he said. "As a pro you also have more opportunity to study films. You can improve on your ability to catch the ball, but there are some people who can never catch it. It's easier for a back to become an end than vice-versa."

Frank Gifford was the golden boy. He was a star for Southern California who acted in movies as a part-time job. Gifford was a triple-threat player and was willing to do it all in the same game (as well as play defensive back). Gifford and Conerly, who were roommates on the road, became as close as brothers and that didn't hurt their ability to connect on pass plays.

Gifford, who once tutored Tony Curtis on how to play quarterback for his role in the movie The All-American and babysat Jamie Lee Curtis (later telling her that she had wet his clothes as he held her), felt Hollywood glory had it all over pro football. Gifford was surprised how unglamorous the pro world was at the time. "It was the ugly duckling of sports," Gifford said. "It ranked just a notch above wrestling."

New York newspapers reserved most of their coverage for the three contending major league baseball teams. Gifford's friends back in California didn't even know what he was doing when he went east for a few months each year. Giant players thought he was "suspect" because he was from California, and he was sure that Owen cared only about defense. Gifford recoiled at the snuff juice that dribbled down Owen's chin onto his clothing and once said that the old-fashioned boss had such a strong aversion to flying that the team was bound to crisscross the country by train in slow motion feeling like "Lewis and Clark." Gifford was discouraged on some fronts, but was determined to succeed—and he did, not only becoming an eight-time Pro Bowl player, but having his No. 16 Giants jersey retired. But all of that came after Gifford's most miserable year in football.

The Giants had continued to play at a high level, finishing 9-2-1 in 1951 and 7-5 in 1952, Gifford's rookie year. But things were starting to fray around the edges, and in 1953 the Giants' anemic offense and faltering defense produced a 3-9 record. This was a turning point in franchise history.

Stout Steve Owen had been a fixture on the New York Giants' team masthead for more than a quarter of a century, first as a player, then as coach. He had presided over tremendous triumphs and some disappointing defeats. Always he had rebounded. In the late 1940s he had introduced an "A" formation offense

"I broke in playing defensive end at 197 pounds (in 1954). Imagine that today!"
—Linebacker Cliff Livingston in 1965.

that for a few years gave the Giants an advantage scoring points. In 1950, Owen invented the "umbrella defense" that was aimed at crushing teams' increasing use of the pass. In the umbrella scheme, Owen lined up his men in a 6-1-4 formation. When the ball was snapped, the outside defender on the right and the outside defender on the left dropped back into pass coverage or to read swiftly developing runs instead of putting more pressure on the quarterback. The innovative defensive scheme made a splash around the NFL and ultimately led to modification into the enduring 4-3-4 defense introduced by Tom Landry a few years later.

In the immediate aftermath of its creation, the umbrella worked well against the Cleveland Browns and their juggernaut led by quarterback Otto Graham. The Giants contained the Browns better than any other team in the league, but the Browns, under the savvy play-calling of coach Paul Brown, still often got the best of the Giants in the final standings.

The slump to 3–9 in 1953 had fatal consequences for Owen's future. With heavy hearts, the Mara brains' trust decided that despite his long-time allegiance to the team and their extraordinary fondness for the man, Owen the coach had to step down. It was a shocking moment. Owen did not see the change coming and reacted bitterly. The Maras, already torn by what they felt was a requirement to oust a coach who had given them nothing but loyalty, expressed regret.

Owen had been a four-time all-star tackle for the

The Umbrella Defense

In 1950 coach Steve Owen introduced the so-called "umbrella defense" to the National Football League. The 11-man defense formed at the line of scrimmage in a 6-1-4 alignment. Then when the ball was snapped, the left end and the right end dropped back into linebacker roles for pass coverage. This maneuver essentially created the 4-3-4 alignment that revolutionized defensive football.

"The only way I can explain it is like I was starry-eyed, taking in something I'd never seen the likes of before."
—Southerner Roosevelt Brown on seeing New York for the first time.

Giants before he became head coach in 1931. He led the team through the Great Depression when resources were scarce, and through the war years when manpower was scarce. Owen's record was 153–100–17 and his clubs won eight division titles and two NFL titles. He was elected to the Hall of Fame in 1966. But in 1954 he was unemployed. Officially, Owen resigned, but he would never have done so if not pressured. He didn't give up—they gave up on him. The Giants tried to provide Owen a soft landing with a scouting job, but he eventually coached Edmonton and Calgary in the Canadian Football League. "He was hurt and wanted no part of that," Wellington Mara said of Owen's departure and the scouting offer.

The Maras coaching search did not go any farther than the neighborhood. They asked Jim Lee Howell, a former New York player and long-time assistant coach, to take over. Howell was initially reluctant. He asked the Giants to provide an assistant coach who was an expert on defense and an assistant coach who was an expert on offense. Most head coaches with ambition want to be the sole voice of authority. Howell sought the opposite. He wanted to be the overseer. It was an egoless position to take. Landry took full control of the

defense, first as a player-coach, and the organization brought in a fresh face to operate the offense. The newcomer had been a prominent assistant coach at Army (the U.S. Military Academy) under the legendary Red Blaik. His name was Vince Lombardi and the Giants offered the platform for Lombardi to establish his NFL bona fides.

Jim Howell had a respectable resume, playing on 1937 and 1938 NFL title-game teams, and was a familiar assistant. Although he offered a free hand to his top assistants he was not an easy-going mark for players to push around.

New York's first season under Howell demonstrated improvement. The 1954 Giants finished 7–5, and the following year, the 1955 Giants finished 6–5–1. The Giants continued to draft well and trade intelligently, and the talent showed up at all positions. Hall of Fame tackle Rosey Brown was grabbed in the 27th round in 1953, perhaps the greatest draft choice for value of all time. Defensive back Dick Nolan was the team's fourth pick in the 1954 draft. Rosey Grier, the 300-pound defensive tackle who later became a guitar player and made waves as a man who enjoyed needlepoint, was the Giants' second pick in 1955. Safety Jim Patton, who intercepted 52 passes in his New York career, was the eighth choice that year. In 1956, the Giants grabbed future Hall of Fame linebacker Sam Huff with their third pick, defensive end Jim Katcavage with the fourth pick, and kicker Don Chandler with the fifth pick. What a defense the Giants were building! Owen had an influence on that at first, but the team never slowed, adding critical pieces to a

The New York Giants of 1954. Among those shown are Charlie Conerly (42), Frank Gifford (16), and Roosevelt Brown (second from right in three-point stance), all of them stars of the decade. *Bettmann/Corbis*

powerhouse unit, even after he was gone.

Linebacker Cliff Livingston was a hard-living, fun-loving player who joined the team in 1954 after starring at the University of California and serving in the Army. His older brother Howie had been a Giants' player, as well. Livingston's escapades off the field were almost as common. After attending a pool party in California, Livingston was in a frenzy to find his missing clothes and be on time for the team plane home. He never found the clothes, jumped in a taxi wearing just a bathing suit, and made the plane, only to be fined $200 anyway for his improper attire.

In many ways, Livingston was an unusual member of the team. He weighed 208 pounds in his prime, light even in the 1950s for an outside linebacker. He rode his bicycle avidly for long distances as a conditioning measure—up to 1,000 miles before summer training camp—at a time when such conditioning was extremely rare. He also modeled for TV commercials in Hollywood during the off-season. And despite being small for his position, Livingston was forced to admit he was slower than the average turtle, too. "Let's say I'm quick," Livingston told a sports writer once. "I'd rather be quick than fast." Livingston lasted eight seasons with the Giants regardless of how his speed was classified, and 12 in the NFL.

Harland Svare, whose nickname was "Swede," was one of Livingston's linebacker partners. Svare, who was not much bigger than Livingston at 6 feet and 214-pounds, came out of Washington State and was drafted by the Los Angeles Rams in 1953. He joined the Giants in 1955 and had a long career as a player, coach and front office administrator. He credited Landry's expertise for making him a better player, and for molding the unit of 11 defensive players that was the most popular in team history. "Our defensive team was not the most talented in the league," Svare said, "but what set us apart was that we had a lot of intelligent guys on that team and operated a defense like nobody else had before." Svare learned well, and when he took over the Rams at 31, he became the youngest NFL head coach ever. "I spent a lot of time studying," said Svare, who said he had not planned to coach. "I committed all positions to memory. I was the only guy who knew everything by heart. I was like one of those smart kids in school that nobody liked."

Landry's genius was forging a squad that not only

Linebacker Sam Huff came out of the University of West Virginia and brought new prestige and fame to defensive players by receiving national media attention.
NFL/Getty Images

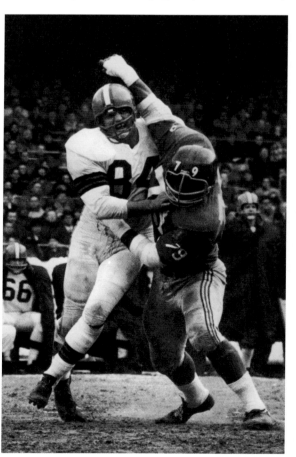

Tackle Roosevelt Brown (79) fighting off a Cleveland Browns defensive end in a game at Yankee Stadium in a typical late 1950s battle between the rivals.
Robert Riger/Getty Images

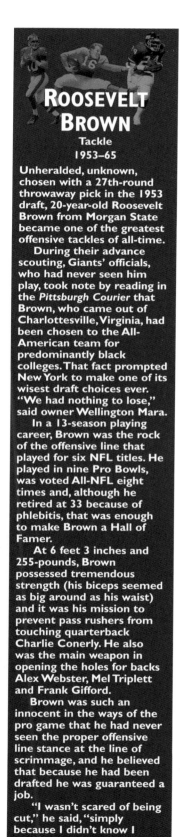

ROOSEVELT BROWN

Tackle
1953–65

Unheralded, unknown, chosen with a 27th-round throwaway pick in the 1953 draft, 20-year-old Roosevelt Brown from Morgan State became one of the greatest offensive tackles of all-time.

During their advance scouting, Giants' officials, who had never seen him play, took note by reading in the *Pittsburgh Courier* that Brown, who came out of Charlottesville, Virginia, had been chosen to the All-American team for predominantly black colleges. That fact prompted New York to make one of its wisest draft choices ever. "We had nothing to lose," said owner Wellington Mara.

In a 13-season playing career, Brown was the rock of the offensive line that played for six NFL titles. He played in nine Pro Bowls, was voted All-NFL eight times and, although he retired at 33 because of phlebitis, that was enough to make Brown a Hall of Famer.

At 6 feet 3 inches and 255-pounds, Brown possessed tremendous strength (his biceps seemed as big around as his waist) and it was his mission to prevent pass rushers from touching quarterback Charlie Conerly. He also was the main weapon in opening the holes for backs Alex Webster, Mel Triplett and Frank Gifford.

Brown was such an innocent in the ways of the pro game that he had never seen the proper offensive line stance at the line of scrimmage, and he believed that because he had been drafted he was guaranteed a job.

"I wasn't scared of being cut," he said, "simply because I didn't know I could get cut."

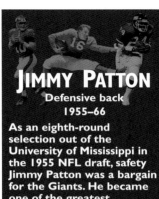

JIMMY PATTON

Defensive back
1955–66

As an eighth-round selection out of the University of Mississippi in the 1955 NFL draft, safety Jimmy Patton was a bargain for the Giants. He became one of the greatest defensive backs in team history, with 52 interceptions in a 12-year career.

Patton stood just 5 feet 10 inches and was a lithe 175-pounds, but when he tackled a ball carrier the reverberations registered in Greenwich Village. As a rookie, Patton returned both a kickoff (98 yards) and a punt (69 yards) for touchdowns in the same game against the Washington Redskins. In 1958, when the Giants reached the NFL title game, Patton's 11 interceptions led the league. Patton was a five-time all-star and was part of six conference title Giant clubs and one world championship team.

A fearless player, Patton would thrust his body into harm's way with each tackle when he positioned himself for head-on collisions. Sometimes that was like a Volkswagen steeling itself for a full-speed meeting with a Mack truck.

"Patton certainly didn't lack courage," said Giants coach Jim Lee Howell, "but he just didn't have the size to bang those big guys without getting hurt." Howell said the coaches ultimately showed Patton how to tackle by using angles in order to preserve his bones.

Patton's hobbies were hunting and fishing, and after his retirement he worked as an assistant coach and a scout for the Giants until his untimely death in a car crash in Georgia when he was 39 years old.

Baltimore Colts' fullback Alan Ameche (35) fighting for yardage as Giants' defensive back Jimmy Patton (20) makes the tackle in the NFL championship game of 1958. The dramatic 23–17 Colts' win at Yankee Stadium was the league's first overtime game and has been called the greatest game ever played. *NFL/Getty Images*

played a new style with the 4-3-4 alignment, but that featured the right players with the proper skills in the right positions. That's why the one-by-one additions were so important.

Tunnell had been around in the defensive backfield and he may have been the most purely talented safety ever. Then Jim Patton, out of Mississippi, came along and complemented Tunnell perfectly. Patton was quick, with great anticipation and superb hands. "Jimmy Patton was the toughest little SOB I ever knew," said Allie Sherman, a Giants' assistant coach, then head coach during Patton's 12-season New York career. "The man was a magnificent football player. He had the perfect attitude. On the field, he hated everyone."

Dick Nolan, who became a distinguished head coach, helped man the rear guard in the secondary and was another player who learned the Giants' way from Landry, a man he greatly respected. "Landry was a real good teacher," Nolan said. "He was a very detailed guy. He dissected opponents clinically. You didn't question what he told you to do because you knew it was going to work."

Dick Lynch became the fourth member of the secondary who excelled with skill and longevity, starting in 1958. In fact, Lynch, a former Notre Dame star, stayed on as a Giant broadcaster for four decades.

The third member of the linebacker corps, the man who filled the middle in the 4-3-4, was Sam Huff. Huff

was a star at West Virginia, an almost demonic tackler who didn't mind trash talking, and backed it up. Huff stood 6 feet 1 inch, weighed 230-pounds and was the perfect all-over-the-field tackler for the scheme. Huff intercepted 30 passes in his career, a high total for a linebacker. Despite the twang in his voice, Huff took to New York like a native, and New Yorkers loved his spirit. His No. 70 jersey was instantly recognizable. In 1960, at a time when pro football was not as widely viewed across the country, Huff became the subject of a one-man documentary on a CBS TV special. Huff was wired for sound in a Giants' practice and in an exhibition game for a film called *The Violent World of Sam Huff*, which was narrated by Walter Cronkite. Fans and TV viewers learned that sometimes players threatened to break each other's noses with punches during the heat of battle. Huff also appeared on the cover of *Time* magazine, a rarity for an athlete.

By 1958, when the Giants met the Colts in the memorable championship game, Huff was ready to boast of the defense's greatness. "Our defensive unit was truly something special," he said. "We'd been together for a few years and we were all close friends." Decades after the Giants of the 1950s did extraordinary things, true fans can name all members of the defense with little prompting. The front four consisted of Grier, Katcavage (who was drafted the same year as Huff, one position lower), defensive tackle Dick Modzelewski, and defensive end Andy Robustelli.

Modzelewski stood 6 feet 1 inch and weighed 255-pounds, but Huff called him "one of the strongest people I've ever seen." *New York Times* columnist Arthur Daley reported a public sighting of Modzelewski in street clothes in a hotel lobby, writing that an elderly man, considerably smaller than the player, asked, "Pardon me, sir, don't you ever take off your shoulder pads?" It only looked that way.

Dick's older brother Ed was a fullback with the Browns and was called "Big Mo." Younger Dick was "Little Mo." Both siblings had been stars at Maryland. Little Mo was drafted by the Redskins, but by 1956 was a fixture on the Giants' defensive line, just when the rivalry with Cleveland was at its hottest. Big Mo was still around, but in 1957 he was supplanted in the starting lineup by the magnificent Jim Brown, thought by many to be the best football player of all time.

Modzelewski was an immovable object on the line, but had a gentle side. He loved to cook and often invited teammates for dinner to eat pirogis and stuffed cabbage with meat and rice that he prepared. He eventually opened a restaurant. The Giants of that era were a special team in his mind. "It's a close-knit, family-type team," Little Mo said. "There's no bickering or squabbling. The players have tremendous pride and

"There is only one way to play this game and that is as hard and tough as you can."
—Hall of Fame defensive end Andy Robustelli.

spirit. Experience has done the most to make the Giants great. We always felt we could win the big game."

That family was made complete when Andy Robustelli came to the Giants from the Rams. He had spent five years on the West Coast, starting in 1951, but was a Connecticut guy and considered retiring. Even in the beginning, after graduation from tiny Arnold College, Robustelli was doubtful about playing pro ball. He had an offer to teach school for $2,400 and that looked better than traipsing to Los Angeles. He asked a friend for advice and the pal urged him to take the teaching money. "You won't get that kind of money or security from pro football," Robustelli said his friend said. "After all, you owe something to your wife and kids. I thought about it and discussed it with my wife. I never could have forgiven myself if I didn't give it a try."

Robustelli was good in California, better in New York. Going to the Giants rejuvenated his career. He was a terror as a pass rusher, became a Hall of Fame player, and ultimately returned to the Giants as general manager. "Andy makes the big play in the clutch," Lynch said.

Katcavage, who grew up in Pennsylvania and settled

The famous front four of the 1950s–60s Giants' defensive line: (left to right) Andy Robustelli, Rosey Grier, Dick Modzelewski, and Jim Katcavage. *Robert Riger/Getty Images*

Andy Robustelli was a Hall of Fame defensive end for the Giants in the 1950s and 1960s, and later returned to the team as a general manager. He modeled his old uniform at a special 2006 ceremony at Giants Stadium for the 50th anniversary of New York's world title team. *Michael P. Malarkey/NFL/Getty Images*

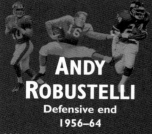

ANDY ROBUSTELLI
Defensive end
1956–64

When the great Giants teams of the 1950s are recalled, thoughts turn to the umbrella defense, and one of the cornerstones of that memorable 11 was Hall of Fame defensive end Andy Robustelli.

A graduate of Arnold College in Connecticut, Robustelli was an unlikely pro football star. He broke into the NFL with the Los Angeles Rams as a 19th-round draft choice in 1951 with a bonus payment consisting solely of the air fare to California. Robustelli nearly passed up pro ball to teach high school and it wasn't until the 6 feet, 230-pound player shifted from offense to defense that he found his niche.

Robustelli was a member of the Rams' 1951 title team, but after five seasons was prepared to quit because he wearied of playing so far from his Stamford, Connecticut home. The Rams obligingly traded him to New York. Neither the teams, nor the player, foresaw the glory ahead. Robustelli played 14 seasons and was a seven-time all-star. In a rarity, the Maxwell Club of Philadelphia named Robustelli, a defensive player, the best pro player in the game in 1962.

Robustelli's skills as a devastating pass rusher who stoked fear in quarterbacks were greatly admired by coach Allie Sherman. "Watch Andy on the field and you'll be studying a real master," Sherman said. "Terrific speed of mind, hands, and foot make him the best."

Several years after his 1964 retirement, the Mara family brought Robustelli back as "director of operations," essentially general manager.

there after he retired, played 14 seasons for the Giants. For most of that time he commuted to practice in New York by train from the City of Brotherly Love and didn't collect frequent rider miles. Sometimes, Katcavage took teasing heat from his teammates about this habit. Once, kicker Don Chandler shouted, "Everybody hustle today! Kat's gotta catch a train!"

Katcavage played in the shadow of Robustelli at the other defensive end, but when Robustelli retired, Katcavage got all-star mention. It was a better-late-than-never scenario, but gave football fans a fresh appreciation of Katcavage's prowess. Katcavage felt his best all-around season came in 1958, long before all-star voters noticed him, but he believed his best game occurred in 1961 against the Cardinals when he sacked the quarterback five times. He compared that achievement for a defensive lineman to "Mickey Mantle hitting four home runs in four times up." The moment Katcavage was cut in 1969, then-coach Alex Webster hired him to join the coaching staff.

Besides changing coaches and acquiring a multitude of prominent players, the Giants made one additional significant change in the 1950s. They moved to a new home stadium. The Giants became tenants at Yankee Stadium, primarily because it held more fans. Yankee Stadium had been the site of numerous memorable baseball games and the Yankee team, with its classic

"There is so much emotion involved in football. After a game, I've seen kids, grown men, all kinds of people, with tears in their eyes."
—All-Pro defensive back Emlen Tunnell.

pinstripe uniforms, was the epitome of class for many. From Babe Ruth to Joe DiMaggio to Mickey Mantle, Whitey Ford and Yogi Berra, the Yankees were synonymous with winning. There was a tinge of sadness departing from the Polo Grounds, but a sense of anticipation moving to the big house in the Bronx. "We felt like we were leaving a lot of tradition behind us," Wellington Mara said. "I know our players felt it was a little added incentive, 'We can't go out and louse up this place the way the Yankees have established it.' I think that definitely was an aura that overhung everybody."

The breakthrough for the new Giants under Howell, brimming with talent and aching to show it, came in 1956. During the regular season New York went 8–3–1. That was good enough to win the Eastern Conference. The victory advanced the Giants to their first title game since 1946, and once again the Chicago Bears were the foes. It was like a throwback game, rekindling days of the older NFL. George Halas still

Fullback Alex Webster runs with the ball after taking a handoff from quarterback Charlie Conerly (42, right) during a 1956 game against the Chicago Bears. The Giants won the NFL championship over the Bears by reprising their 1934 maneuver of switching game shoes to sneakers on an icy field.
Robert Riger/Getty Images

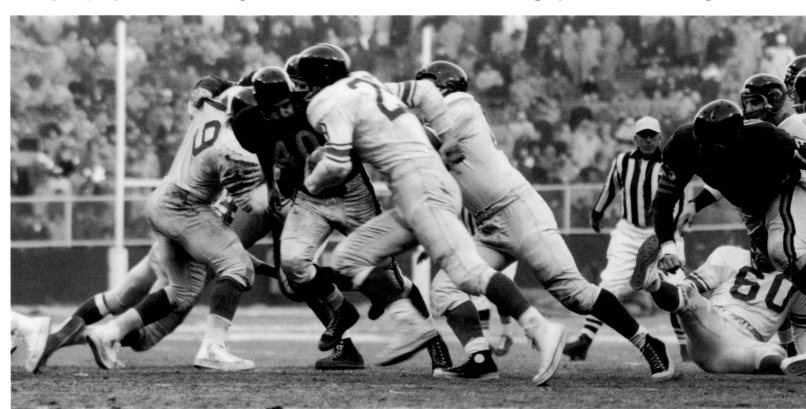

owned the Bears and the Maras still ran the Giants. Memory would play an important role in the December 30 game at Yankee Stadium.

The game attracted 56,836 fans on a wintry day with a frozen field. During the regular season, the teams played to a 17–17 tie, so the game figured to be close. Instead, the game turned into a romp. The Giants crushed Chicago 47–7, and it was a reprise of the 1934 "Sneakers Game." After the Giants changed into sneakers to take advantage of the Bears on an icy field in 1934, Halas vowed never to be out-smarted again.

Yet history repeated itself, and for a second time the Giants used sneakers. This time, Robustelli, who owned a sporting goods store in Stamford, Connecticut, took note of the plunging temperatures in advance of the title game and called his sneaker distributor. "I've been thinking that if the weather stays this cold we'll be playing Sunday's game on cement," Robustelli said. He ordered four dozen pairs of high-quality sneakers ranging in size from nine to 13. Before the game Howell asked players to test the turf. Gene Filipski wore sneakers, Ed Hughes wore regular cleats. Filipski's traction was fine. Hughes slipped when he ran. "Everyone wears sneakers," Howell announced in the locker room. The Giants wore the shoes on the icy field and trumped the Bears.

The game was never close. Filipski ran the opening

kickoff back 53 yards. The first Giant touchdown was scored on a 17-yard run by fullback Mel Triplett. Like Tunnell, Triplett, a 215-pound bruiser born in Mississippi, had attended Toledo University. He made a strong first impression as a rookie in 1955 and 1956. A headline on one newspaper story called him a "human bomb" and asked whether he was the best fullback since Bronko Nagurski. Jim Lee Howell called Triplett "one of pro football's future greats. He's got it all."

In a solid, eight-year career, Triplett scored 43 rushing touchdowns, but never quite lived up to the hype. What he did do well, a skill that always goes underappreciated, was block superbly in the backfield, helping to protect Conerly. "Blocking in this league is no picnic," Triplett said. "Most of the time I have to handle ends and linebackers who outweigh me by 40 pounds. And they seem to be getting bigger all the time."

Ben Agajanian, the toeless wonder, who had severed most of the digits on his kicking foot in an accident while in college, kicked the extra point, then added field goals of 17 yards and 43 all in the first quarter. Agajanian had spent more than a decade trying to convince coaches that it was valuable having a player on the roster that was a kicker only rather than a multi-tasker. This performance certainly helped the argument.

The Giants added 21 points in the second period, with Alex Webster scoring on runs of 3 yards and 1

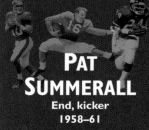

PAT SUMMERALL
End, kicker
1958–61

His football career ended so many years ago, and his broadcasting career, handling NFL games, tennis, golf and other events, lasted so long and was so popular, that many people Pat Summerall meets don't realize he was a prized kicker for the Giants.

The pride of Lake City, Florida, the 6 feet 4 inches 228-pound Summerall played some at end, but was best known for how he controlled a football with his toe. Summerall played college ball at the University of Arkansas and broke into the NFL in 1952 with the Detroit Lions. He spent four seasons with the old Chicago Cardinals and joined the Giants in 1957.

In 1958, Summerall made the most significant kick in Giants' history, when he booted a 49-yard field goal in a raging, blinding blizzard to boost New York over Cleveland in a game that led his team to the playoffs. No one truly knows how far the miraculous kick traveled because yard markers at Yankee Stadium were buried in snow. Summerall often says quarterback Charlie Conerly did a double take when the kicker entered the huddle and asked, "What the hell are you doing here?"

Summerall's right foot was a major weapon for the Giants. In 1959, he made a league-leading 20 of 29 field-goal attempts, and hit all 30 extra points for 90 points.

Long after he became established as a nationally famous sports broadcaster, Summerall contended with a highly publicized and successful battle against alcoholism that he said saved his life.

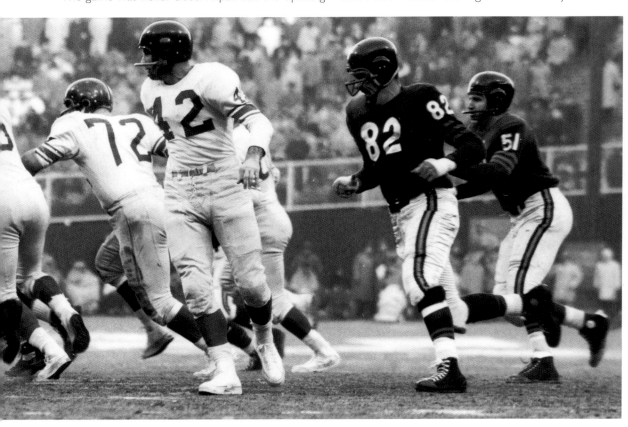

THE GREATEST GAME EVER PLAYED

The iconic photograph of Baltimore Colts' fullback Alan Ameche bursting through the Giants' defensive line, via a gaping hole created by his blockers, represents the moment of victory in the December 28, 1958 National Football League championship game.

Over time, Ameche's head-first, head-down touchdown run crossing the goal line has come to symbolize the league crossing a Rubicon as well, into the modern era of pro football. The Colts won a championship, 23–17, that day at Yankee Stadium, disappointing the Giants and their 64,185 fans, but that was the narrow view. The battle between the Giants and Colts became enshrined in lore as the "greatest game ever played."

Football historians have seized upon that long day as a turning point for the league, the singular event before a television audience of 45 million that arguably catapulted football into position as the most popular sport in the United States. The combination of intense drama, the New York site, and the first-ever sudden death overtime game sent pro football on its way to surpassing baseball as the nation's primary sport.

The hard-fought game was immediately viewed as a classic. For artistry and crisp play alone, except in the fourth quarter, the game did not qualify by any definition as the greatest ever played. But it was undeniably the most important game ever played. "It was a tremendous theatrical moment," said New York sportswriter Dave Anderson, a Pulitzer-Prize winner for commentary.

The Giants brought a 9–3 record into the championship game, but also had to win an extra Eastern Division playoff game because they had been tied with the Cleveland Browns. The Colts, led by quarterback Johnny Unitas, halfback Lenny Moore, end Raymond Berry, and such colorful defensive stars as Art "Fatso" Donovan, Gino Marchetti, and Gene "Big Daddy" Lipscomb, posted the same 9-3 regular-season mark.

The Giants took a 3–0 first-quarter lead on a Pat Summerall 36-yard field goal, but Baltimore led 14–3 at the half on touchdowns by Ameche and Berry. Fullback Mel Triplett scored a touchdown for the Giants in the third quarter, and Frank Gifford caught a touchdown pass from Charlie Conerly in the fourth period. The Giants led 17–14. Late in the fourth quarter, Unitas, who many consider the greatest quarterback of all time, led the Colts into field-goal range and Steve Myhra booted a 20-yarder with seven seconds left to forge the 17–17 end-of-regulation tie.

Gifford did not think the game was the greatest ever. "Baltimore was probably a better football team," he said years later, "but they don't win if I don't fumble three times."

The most pivotal moment occurred when it was 17–14 New York. Less than three minutes remained in regulation when the Giants handed off to Gifford seeking a short gain that would provide a first down. Gifford plunged off tackle. Marchetti grabbed his legs. Gifford went down, but was sure he made a first down and the Giants could run out the clock.

The Giants' Charlie Conerly releases a pass over Baltimore's charging defensive end Gino Marchetti in the classic 1958 title game. *Bettmann/Corbis*

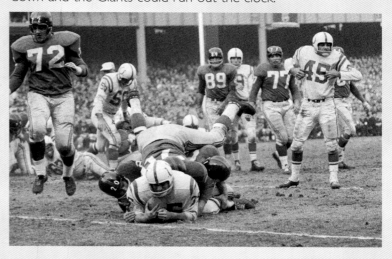

Colts' fullback Alan Ameche hugs the ball as he is buried beneath an avalanche of New York tacklers in the 1958 title game. The man on top of the pile, with his feet in the air, is Giants' Sam Huff (70). Also in on the tackle are Jim Patton (20) and Carl Karilivacz. *Bettmann/Corbis*

As Marchetti made the tackle, teammate Lipscomb, who weighed 290-pounds, fell on him. Marchetti started screaming because the big man had broken his leg. Gifford yelled at Marchetti to get up because the play was over, but Marchetti said, "Frank, I can't." In the confusion, officials held the ball. When they placed it, the ball was shy of the first down. The fuming Giants had to punt. Kicker Don Chandler pinned the Colts at their own 15-yard-line with 2:20 to go.

In an impressive showing of bravado and cool, Unitas repeatedly fired first-down passes to Berry to burn the Giants. Myhra made that tying field goal and the game went into overtime.

Overtime was an unheard-of-concept at the time. The provision in the rule book had never been used. Many of the players thought the game ended after the usual 60 minutes and that the teams were co-champions. In an oft-repeated exchange, Pat Summerall looked at teammate Kyle Rote and asked, "What happens now?" Rote said, "I think we play some more."

They did.

As fans buzzed and league and team officials made clear that the game would continue, a contest that began in midafternoon in New York continued into the early evening under the lights. The temperature had dropped and parts of the field turned from mud to ice. The title game was a fabulous showcase for the sport, taut with drama, and commissioner Bert Bell, who had worked so hard to sell a product that he knew would resonate with sports fans, reveled in the moment. It was Bell who over the years had argued with owners for the implementation of the sudden death rule so no championship game would ever end in a tie.

Marchetti, considered one of the toughest men to play the game, was carried off the field, but refused to leave the stadium for medical attention. He ordered his bearers to deposit him on the Colts sideline so he could watch. He was not the only spectator riveted to the action.

A second coin toss took place and the Giants won it. They chose to receive, a huge advantage in sudden-death play, where the first team to score wins. The Giants had their chance, but New York couldn't go anywhere and Chandler punted. Once again the Colts were stuck deep in their own territory, but once again, with the masterful Unitas calling the signals, the Colts inexorably ate up ground and drove the pigskin down the field. In the end, Ameche's spirit-crushing run covered just one yard.

When the Giants were ahead 17–14, a vote for the Most Valuable Player award took place and Charlie Conerly won it and apparently a new automobile. After the Colts' comeback, a second poll was taken, favoring Perian over Conerly, and Charlie's wife was heard to say later, "Mrs. Unitas is driving my car."

Whether the Giants-Colts encounter was the greatest game ever played or not, it put the NFL into the driver's seat on the American sports scene.

In one of the most famous pro football photographs of all time, Colt fullback Alan Ameche puts his head down and spurts through a huge hole to score the winning touchdown in overtime against the New York Giants during the 1958 NFL championship game on December 28, 1958, at Yankee Stadium.
Pro Football Hall of Fame/Getty Images

New York defenders Dick Modzelewski (77), Emlen Tunnell (45), and Sam Huff (70) smother Colts' runner Alan Ameche in overtime of the 1958 championship game, the first sudden-death game in NFL history.
Kidwiler Collection/Diamond Images/Getty Images

yard. Bears' fullback Rick Casares scored on a 9-yard run, Chicago's only touchdown of the day. The Giants scored three more touchdowns. "The Monsters of the Midway were supposed to be the roughest team in football," said Gifford, who scored the last touchdown on a 14-yard pass from Conerly. "As we quickly discovered, however, they had no idea what we were up to."

Winning the 1956 title seemed like the natural culmination of the building plan set into motion at the beginning of the decade. While most of the players on the squad were seasoned, most were still young. The Giants felt they could win for years. They were right—and wrong.

After a setback in 1957, when New York finished just 7–5, the Giants resumed their onslaught on the title game. Between 1956 and 1963, the Giants won six Eastern Conference crowns in eight seasons, spanning two decades. They missed out on a title game appearance only in 1957 and 1960. The instincts of the Maras and Howell were correct. They had assembled a special group.

Recovering from the 1957 disappointment, the Giants posted a 9–3 record in the regular season, equal-best in the conference along with the Cleveland Browns. The Browns and Paul Brown introduced yet another Brown that season: rookie Jim Brown, the 6 foot 2 inch, 232-pound force from Syracuse. He was just warming up in 1957, rushing for 942 yards. The total led the league. Over the next eight seasons, Brown led the NFL in rushing seven more times. He averaged an all-time best 5.2 yards per carry, scored 126 touchdowns, and totaled 12,312 yards, a record that stood for years.

It was like adding Captain America to an already very good lineup. And alas for the Giants, they had to play the Browns twice a season. The team rivalry heightened, but the Giants geared their defense toward stopping Brown. Usually, the point man was Sam Huff. He dogged Brown all over the field and compared to the rest of the league had measurable success against him periodically. No one stopped Jim Brown all of the time. The men developed a serious respect for one another's talents. "They built their whole offense around Jim Brown, but we shut him down," Huff said. "Landry had analyzed them perfectly."

By 1958, fans in Yankee Stadium were rooting for the defense with previously unknown gusto. Once merely an anonymous group, the personable, long-serving, high-achieving Giant defenders became celebrities. When Huff, Robustelli, Patton and Grier took the field the chant began. "Dee-fense! Dee-fense!" Defense became a two-syllable word that gave the unit identity. The chant also spread and has endured in other football cities. The roars greeting the defense were deafening. "It almost was a distraction," Svare said. "You couldn't hear anything."

To reach the title game against the Baltimore Colts in 1958, the road led through the Browns and Jim Brown. In a November game in Cleveland, the Giants triumphed, 21–17. Still, the Giants needed to win the last regular-season game in New York on December 14 to advance. In the most momentous kick in team history and one of the most important plays, Pat Summerall kicked a 49-yard field goal through blowing snow as the cornerstone of a 13–10 win. Although announced at that distance, no one was ever quite sure of the actual distance because the yard markers were invisible in the snow. Summerall thought it might have been 55 yards. When Summerall returned to the sideline, assistant coach Vince Lombardi hugged him and yelled, "You know you can't kick that far!"

The next week, the Giants eclipsed the Browns again, 10–0, winning a playoff. The only touchdown came on a spectacular razzle-dazzle play. Conerly handed off to Alex Webster. Gifford circled around on a reverse and took the ball from Webster. Downfield, as the Cleveland defense closed in, Gifford flipped a lateral to a trailing Conerly.

Those games belonged on the Giants' lifetime highlight reel, but the contest against the Colts eclipsed it for sheer drama. Baltimore won 23–17, in overtime. It was the first sudden-death game in NFL history, a classic game that has evermore been called "the greatest game ever played." The TV audience numbered roughly 45 million and fans talked about the game for weeks. Commissioner Bert Bell believed it was the game that put his league on the map for good

Jim Brown, the powerful Cleveland Browns' fullback, whom many consider the greatest football player of all time, and Giants' linebacker Sam Huff (at left, on ground) developed a highly publicized rivalry in the 1950s and 1960s. Jimmy Patton (20) is rushing up to try to help with the tackle.
Robert Riger/Getty Images

and elevated its value in the eyes of the TV networks. Historians looking back agree that whether or not the game was the best ever in quality or not, it was a milestone that "made the NFL."

Giant players would have been more thrilled about being a part of that history if they had actually won the game, which they felt they should have. Colts Hall-of-Fame quarterback Johnny Unitas and his seemingly telepathic ability to find receiver Raymond Berry accounted for the Baltimore win.

Exciting aftermath or not for the sport, the Giants felt let down. "I don't think any of us felt that was the greatest game ever played," Summerall said. "And I think all of us had the idea that this was not the greatest game we played. Certainly, we didn't play our best. And we didn't realize the magnitude of what it was."

The Giants regrouped and played well again in 1959, going 10–2, and limiting opponents to just 170 points in 12 games. This time the Giants didn't need a playoff to reach the title game, where once again the Baltimore Colts awaited. If the championship game of 1958 was an epic, this time around it was a Giants' letdown. The Colts trounced New York this time, 31–16. No overtime. Not even close. Still, the future looked bright. The NFL, riding the coat-tails of the monumental 1958 championship game, was more popular than ever. The Giants were still sufficiently well-stocked to keep on making solid runs at the title. And, as it so happened, harkening back to Tim Mara's words before the Giants' first game in 1925, when he had "put over pro football on New York." Giant players were as well-known as baseball players. Yankee Stadium sold out for football. The players drank and schmoozed with actors and ballplayers at Toot's Shor's saloon, hanging out with Mickey Mantle and TV star Jackie Gleason. Frank Gifford said he knew the Giants were major players in New York after they won the 1956 championship game. After that, he said, he didn't have to wait for a table at P.J. Clarke's, the venerable drinking establishment. It was now, "Right this way, Mr. Gifford."

Tim Mara, the bookmaker who had gambling in his blood, lived long enough to see his paltry $500 investment become a valuable property, as well known in the Big Apple as the Empire State Building. He had had the wisdom long before to turn the main operations of the club over to his enthusiastic sons. This advance preparation meant that when the team's founder died in 1959, the franchise did not flounder. Wellington and Jack had been in charge of the family business for years and they were still in charge. The man who bought the Giants on a lark and trusted his young sons to run the team properly, however, was gone. The patriarch lived on in family portraits and memories, but was no longer part of the discussions

about what the Giants were up to.

Tim Mara would never be forgotten by the family members he appointed to succeed him, but nor would he be forgotten by the league he helped build. In 1963, when the Pro Football Hall of Fame was established in Canton, Ohio, Tim Mara was one of the charter inductees.

1950s NEW YORK GIANTS YEAR BY YEAR

Year	Record
1950	10–2
1951	9–2–1
1952	7–5
1953	3–9
1954	7–5
1955	6–5–1
1956	8–3–1
1957	7–5
1958	9–3
1959	10–2

The Giants' defense, including Andy Rosbustelli (81, middle), waits for the start of the next play in a 1958 game against the Chicago Cardinals.
Robert Riger/Getty Images

THE 1960s

THE ALLIE SHERMAN REIGN

5

With an imposing cast of characters like Rosey Grier (76), Sam Huff (70), "Rosey" Brown (79), Dick Modzelewski (77), and Jim Katcavage (75) stopping opponents, Giants fans created the chant, "Dee-fense!"
Robert Riger/Getty Images

It was almost the best of times. The Giants put on a crowd-pleasing show and posted terrific results early in the 1960s, ruling the Eastern Division in three out of four years. They were giddy times in the Big Apple, with the profile of the team rising higher than ever. The continuity in the lineup nearly matched the Yankees, even if the Giants could not quite finish off the foes from the other conference with the regularity

of the baseball players in the World Series.

The Giants were blessed with a large group of outstanding players who held onto their jobs and prominence from the mid-1950s through the early 1960s. Charlie Conerly was a fixture at quarterback. Alex Webster was the fullback. Frank Gifford and Kyle Rote starred in the backfield. The defense was familiar, with long-term incumbents Andy Robustelli, Jimmy

> "If we had a smart-mouthed kid on the squad, Andy would take him alone in a corner and when they came back the kid would be shaking and he'd call everybody 'Sir' for the next year or so."
> —Alex Webster, on Andy Robustelli's toughness and stature on the Giants.

Patton, Jim Katcavage, Sam Huff, and Rosey Grier as popular as offensive stars in other cities.

Certainly there were changes. Harland Svare was gone, off to begin a coaching career. Emlen Tunnell retired, but stayed on as a coach. Jim Lee Howell led the Giants' resurgence in the late 1950s by allowing defensive coordinator Tom Landry and offensive coordinator Vince Lombardi a free hand. But the assistants became sought-after head coaching candidates elsewhere.

Although it is likely that both men imagined themselves one day taking over the Giants, Howell was entrenched. Lombardi was born in Brooklyn in 1913 and played for Fordham. He was one of the "seven blocks of granite" that comprised the school's famed line. He was a New York guy, but his destiny lay in Green Bay, Wisconsin. Lombardi went north and established his legend as perhaps the greatest pro football coach of all. In Green Bay, variations on the phrase, "Winning isn't everything, it's the only thing" stuck to him. Lombardi was gruff, sometimes harsh, set

Jim Lee Howell (center) Giants' director of personnel and former head coach, greets coach Allie Sherman; Tom Landry, head coach Dallas; Harland Svare, head coach L.A. Rams; and Vince Lombardi, head coach of the Green Bay Packers, during the National Football League draft meeting in 1962. All had previously been assistant coaches to Howell. *Bettmann/Corbis*

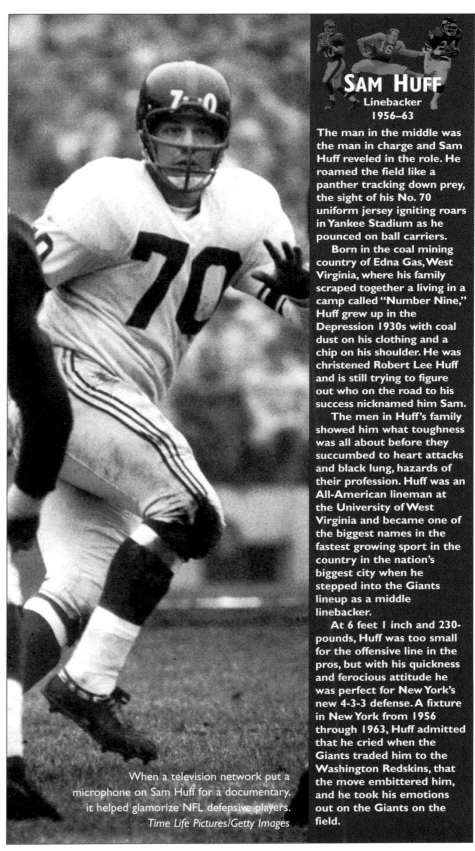

When a television network put a microphone on Sam Huff for a documentary, it helped glamorize NFL defensive players. *Time Life Pictures/Getty Images*

SAM HUFF
Linebacker
1956–63

The man in the middle was the man in charge and Sam Huff reveled in the role. He roamed the field like a panther tracking down prey, the sight of his No. 70 uniform jersey igniting roars in Yankee Stadium as he pounced on ball carriers.

Born in the coal mining country of Edna Gas, West Virginia, where his family scraped together a living in a camp called "Number Nine," Huff grew up in the Depression 1930s with coal dust on his clothing and a chip on his shoulder. He was christened Robert Lee Huff and is still trying to figure out who on the road to his success nicknamed him Sam.

The men in Huff's family showed him what toughness was all about before they succumbed to heart attacks and black lung, hazards of their profession. Huff was an All-American lineman at the University of West Virginia and became one of the biggest names in the fastest growing sport in the country in the nation's biggest city when he stepped into the Giants lineup as a middle linebacker.

At 6 feet 1 inch and 230-pounds, Huff was too small for the offensive line in the pros, but with his quickness and ferocious attitude he was perfect for New York's new 4-3-3 defense. A fixture in New York from 1956 through 1963, Huff admitted that he cried when the Giants traded him to the Washington Redskins, that the move embittered him, and he took his emotions out on the Giants on the field.

"A receiver has to have speed, hands, size, agility, quickness, and the intelligence to run patterns and recognize defenses."
—*Receiver Bob Schnelker.*

the new hero in town, lauded as the rejuvenator of a team that had stumbled.

Green Bay hosted the 1961 title game and 39,029 gleeful fans witnessed one of the most thorough wipeouts in the history of NFL championship games. The Packers crushed the Giants 37–0, and Paul Hornung, Jim Taylor, Bart Starr, Jim Ringo, Forrest Gregg, and Ray Nitschke began to etch their names into league legend. The Giants took a bruising. "It was a bad day," said Y. A. Tittle, the old pro who was a newcomer as the Giants' starting quarterback that season. "The dressing room was an awful scene. The Giants were a team of great pride and to have been crushed like this was a terrible blow. No one felt the loss more deeply than Allie Sherman. His eyes were moist and he was flushed with anger and humiliation."

Tittle had been the mainstay of the 49ers during the 1950s, but was pushed aside when San Francisco adopted a new offensive plan. "I was pretty sure I was going to retire," Tittle said. However, the Giants thought he could be valuable, maybe even the starter. They traded their 1960 No. 1 draft pick Lou Cordileone, a tackle, straight up for Tittle. In what became regarded as just about the best trade in New York history, even Cordileone said something like "Me and who else?" when he was swapped for Tittle.

Tittle remained reluctant to report, but Frank Gifford talked him into going to the Giants. "He told me that I was not just going to sit on the bench," Tittle said. "I probably wouldn't be in the Hall of Fame today if it hadn't been for that trade." Tittle was a terrific passer and wanted to prove that, despite a shoulder injury, he was not over the hill. Tittle said he was not warmly welcomed by some veteran Giants because Conerly was so revered, but he proved to be sharper and beat out Conerly for the first-string job during the season, although Conerly pitched some effective relief, too.

The Giants became Tittle's team in 1962. Conerly retired and Tittle's partnership with Del Shofner, which was forged in 1961 after the receiver came over from the Rams and caught 68 passes, truly blossomed. Tittle and Shofner became the most feared pass catching combination in the league during a three-year period. Shofner's yardage totaled more than 1,100 yards each season, and in 1962 when he grabbed 12 touchdown passes, he averaged 21.4 yards per catch.

Top: Y. A. Tittle and head coach Allie Sherman confer in 1961. *Vernon Biever/NFL/Getty Images*

Above: Del Shofner was Tittle's favorite receiver in the early 1960s, and the twosome dominated other teams en route to three straight Eastern Conference championships. *Vernon Biever/NFL/Getty Images*

Opposite: Tittle was a pocket passer, but he occasionally ran to escape rushing defenses. *Herbert Weitman/NFL/Getty Images*

the tone as a boss and yet was loved and respected by the players he led. He took over the dismal Packers in 1959 and put up a 7–5 record. Powerhouse years quickly followed.

Landry, a Texan by birth and upbringing, was tapped to become the head coach of the expansion Dallas Cowboys, starting with a 0–11–1 1960 season.

It is difficult to gauge if the Giants missed the services of their two top assistants so much that they tumbled to a 6–4–2 record, but after that season Howell abruptly announced his retirement. The Maras were caught off-guard. In Lombardi and Landry, they had possessed two head coaches in waiting. Now they were both gone. The Giants took a run at wooing Lombardi back home, but in good conscience he felt he could not walk away from Green Bay so soon.

Instead, the new coach was Allie Sherman. Sherman was a 5 foot 11 inch, 170-pound former Brooklyn College and Philadelphia Eagle quarterback, who had served as a Giants' assistant and a head coach in the Canadian Football League. He may not have been as hard-nosed as Lombardi, but he talked a tough game. "We don't simply prepare to play a game," Sherman said. "We prepare to WIN it." Win he did, right from the start.

The Giants of 1961 finished 10–3–1 and captured the Eastern Conference title. That earned them the chance to meet Lombardi's Packers. Lombardi had been weaving a spell in the cold country. The 1950s were as bleak as any in the history of the old line NFL franchise, but in 1960, at the end of his second season, their 8–4 record had the Packers in the title game. Although Green Bay lost to the Eagles, Lombardi was

Y.A. TITTLE
Quarterback
1961–64

Everyone knew someday Charlie Conerly would be replaced as the New York Giants' quarterback after holding the spot since 1948, but when it happened in 1961, 57,000 Yankee Stadium fans blinked in shock simultaneously. That was because the new quarterback, Y.A. Tittle, had also turned pro in 1948.

Hall of Famer Yelberton Abraham Tittle played collegiately at Louisiana State, and spent two years in the All-America Football Conference before joining the NFL in 1950 with Baltimore and spending 10 seasons with the San Francisco 49ers.

Tittle was a star in San Francisco, but became expendable when the 49ers committed to the shotgun formation and the younger John Brodie. The bald Tittle (hence his nickname, "the Bald Eagle") hardly represented a youth movement in New York. But he had a shotgun of an arm and during the first three seasons of the 1960s the player enjoyed the finest years of his career. And the Giants enjoyed the most explosive offensive period in their history.

Throwing to Frank Gifford, Kyle Rote and newly acquired Del Shofner, Tittle electrified Giants' fans. He threw a league-leading 33 touchdowns in 1962 and a then-record 36 touchdowns in 1963. That season he completed seven touchdown passes in one game, still the league mark. When Tittle led the Giants to the 1961 Eastern Division crown he felt he belonged. "I guess that was the best moment in my career," Tittle said, recalling how the fans counted down the final 30 seconds of the clinching game.

Above: Twice the Giants met the Green Bay Packers in the NFL championship game in the early 1960s, but the Packers had too many weapons, such as quarterback Bart Starr (15), and bested New York both times. *John Loengard/Time Life Pictures/Getty Images*

Right: Giants' end Del Shofner is tackled by Herb Adderley and Willie Wood of the Green Bay Packers, in a 16–7 loss in the 1962 NFL championship on December 30, 1962, at Yankee Stadium. *Vernon Biever/NFL/Getty Images*

Far right: Allie Sherman (left) with Frank Gifford (center) and Y.A. Tittle during a 1964 practice session. *Bettmann/Corbis*

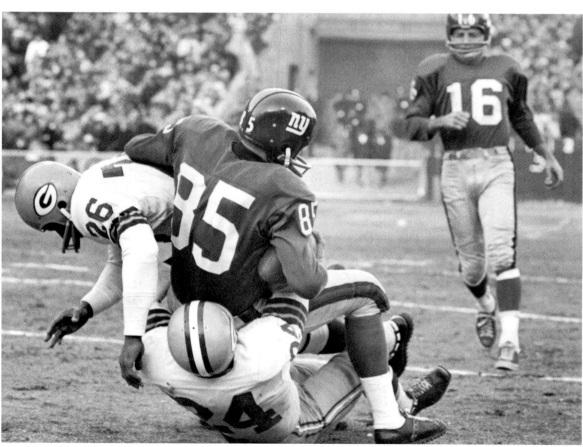

Shofner was a gazelle. At 6 feet 3 inches and weighing 186-pounds, whichever defensive backs he didn't out-run, he out-jumped. His long-legged running form was as fluid as water flowing from a faucet. While observers described Shofner as emotionless, he coped with an ulcer. "He's the best all-around receiver I've ever seen," said fellow receiver Frank Gifford.

Tittle's strong arm and Shofner's fleetness stretched the field and allowed the Giants to throw deep often. This suited Sherman well. He liked to go long. "I really couldn't tell you how I'd defend him if I had to," said Sherman of Shofner. When Shofner was asked about the ease of his running style, he said he adapted some techniques taught by a track expert. Shofner talked about "flowing" and added, "that's something I learned from my track coach at Baylor. You can get a lot more speed out of your body if you keep it loose. If you tighten it up, you're bound to lose some speed."

Although they did not possess Shofner's speed, two other Giant receivers bonded well with Tittle. Aaron Thomas was the tight end on the light side at 210-pounds who began to blossom with 22 catches in 1963. Thomas was more of a hybrid end, and for someone who was supposed to be more of a short-yardage guy, he recorded a phenomenal 17.4-yard per

catch average for his career. "A tight end can't go deep anymore," Thomas said as he switched to flanker. "That's what I do best—go deep."

Some people thought Thomas was stepping off a deep end when he retired after the 1970 season. He moved right into a seat on the New York Stock Exchange with the potential to increase his income nearly tenfold from his Giants' pay of $30,000. At the least he found a use for his degree from Oregon State.

One of the most overlooked players, who matured and endured in unexpected ways during his long stay with the Giants, was Joe Morrison. Morrison stood 6 feet 1 inch and weighed 210-pounds. He was a third-round draft pick out of Cincinnati in 1959, but if someone perused Morrison's position line in the Football Encyclopedia it would imply that the Giants didn't know what to do with him. Morrison is described as a halfback, flanker, wide receiver and fullback (special teams' play was forgotten). He was, in fact, all of those. In a career that ended in 1972, Morrison became one of the most valuable Giants. As time passed, Allie Sherman relied more and more on Morrison to perform a variety of tasks. One minute he was rushing the ball, the next minute he was catching it. The phrase "all-purpose player" was pretty much

RAY WIETECHA
Center
1953–62

After hiking the ball to the quarterback, most of the time the center disappears into a pile of big bodies at the line of scrimmage, throwing a semi-anonymous block and hoping no middle linebacker leaps over his head. The role of center is about as invisible as it gets, but Ray Wietecha was one regular who became an immovable rock in the middle of the Giants' offense, even though, at 6 feet 1 inch and 225-pounds, he was small for the position.

Wietecha was first noticed as a lineman at Michigan State, then Northwestern, both of the Big Ten, after he transferred, and he was one of the old reliables who fought their way into the Giants' lineup under Steve Owen and remained under the Allie Sherman regime, not retiring his cleats until 1962. By then he had been voted an all-star four times and served as the anchor for a powerful and cohesive front line.

Sherman loved Wietecha's knowledge and strength. "Wietecha is the best in the league," Sherman said. "Ray Wietecha is my quarterback up front. Ray calls out all the 'bastard' defenses. We face anything other than the standard 4-3, Ray spots it, calls it out, switches our blocking assignments on the line. And block? That man's a bear."

Unlike the early NFL players, Wietecha did not play both ways for the Giants, but he never missed a minute of time when the offense was on the field over a nine-season stretch.

Giants' cornerback Erich Barnes added speed and hard-hitting ability to the defensive secondary when he joined the team in the early 1960s. *NFL/NFL/Getty Images*

invented with Morrison in mind. At one point, Sherman said he would use Morrison at quarterback if injury called for it. "Joe's value to this team is his ability to come off the bench and give us a winning performance at almost any position," Sherman said. "Very few fellows can do this."

In a three-way deal that involved the Rams and Bears, the Giants complemented Shofner's arrival by picking up speed on the other side of the ball. Solid defensive back Linden Crow went West, quarterback Bill Wade arrived in Chicago, and the Giants acquired Erich Barnes for the secondary in 1961. Barnes intercepted seven passes for 195 return yards and two touchdowns on defense for the Giants. Barnes replaced the dimension lost when Emlen Tunnell retired.

Barnes was a play wrecker, the free-wheeling wild card in the defensive backfield. He was stealthy and sprang into the picture after the ball left the thrower's hands, making quarterbacks second-guess themselves. Barnes' most spectacular play was a team-record (still standing) 102-yard interception return on October 15, 1961 against the Dallas Cowboys. The pass was thrown by Eddie LeBaron, who probably still wishes he had a do-over. Barnes collected the ball in his own end zone and ran it all of the way to the Cowboys' end zone. There was some debate on the length of the return for a day or so, but 102 became official. "My only recollection is that I was so close to the sideline that my main thought was to stay inbounds and to avoid the little red flag in the ground where the goal-line and the sideline come together," Barnes said.

Pat Summerall's foot accounted for one of the greatest plays in Giants' history when he blasted that 49-yard field goal in the blizzard to beat Cleveland, but by 1962 the team's regular place-kicker was its full-time punter, Don Chandler. Chandler, who recorded a lifetime punting average of 43.5 yards a kick scored 104 points in 1962 and 106 in 1963 handling double duty. It's possible that Chandler was the last NFL booter to achieve as much in both disciplines.

Chandler, who played at 6 feet 2 inches and 205-pounds, had been an accomplished end at the University of Florida, but a severe shoulder injury discouraged him. He walked out of the Giants' camp as a rookie in 1956 and only returned when Vince Lombardi tracked him down at the airport. The permanently damaged shoulder did not prevent Chandler from kicking, however. "Sometimes I feel like the old, one-armed paper hanger," Chandler said. Even if his foot did all of the work, his first head coach, Jim Lee Howell, often credited Chandler for winning games with his punt placements. "There is no kicker in the game who is Don's equal under pressure," Howell said.

Although many of the stars of the 1950s persevered well into the 1960s, there were replacement models at selected spots. The 6 foot 243-pound Darrell Dess joined the Giants in 1959 and was a fixture at guard for a decade, playing on four Eastern championship teams. Dess' blocking style often meant leading with his head, as well as his shoulders, and he used to tell teammates that during the course of a game he shrunk an inch or so. In more somber moments after a long day of getting in his licks, Dess said his whole body ached. "I don't mind hitting people," Dess said. "I love the contact. It's getting hit in the head that bothers me. We're taught to block with our heads. If you block with a shoulder, the defensive man can slide off. If you hit him with your head and he slides off, then you've got him with your shoulder. But it's tough. I break helmets." Break helmets? That's dedication. Giants runners always understood that Dess was giving his all and Alex Webster unhesitatingly

Left: Don Chandler (34) barely got this punt off under pressure in a game against the Green Bay Packers. Chandler performed double duty for the Giants as a punter and place kicker.
John Loengard/Time Life Pictures/Getty Images

Right: Long-time teammates in the Giants' backfield, Alex Webster (29) and Frank Gifford in 1962, the year Gifford returned to the team after a year off following a concussion in a 1960 game.
Bettmann/Corbis

"It was the hardest thing I've had to do."
—Coach Alex Webster, on cutting former teammate Jim Katcavage in 1969.

said, "He's the best, the very best."

Ray Wietecha was a decade-long stalwart and when he retired, Greg Larson, a sixth-round draft pick out of the University of Minnesota in 1961, became the center and lodged himself in the lineup for 179 games, or through the 1973 season.

Wiectecha picked up the nickname "Iron Man," but the 6 feet 3 inch, 250-pound Larson actually played longer. Larson missed only three games in 13 seasons and was driven into retirement at age 34 because of a balky knee. He also had surgery for a double hernia, and operations on his elbow and nose, souvenirs of hand-to-hand combat on the line. Larson embraced being part of the three straight division winners in the early 1960s. "They were great days to be a Giant," Larson said. "New York went wild over us. Being on the team meant instant recognition. Just playing football and being part of a team with those guys was an

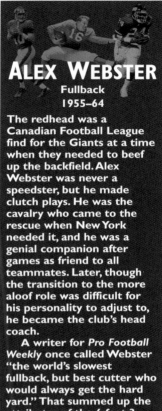

ALEX WEBSTER
Fullback
1955–64

The redhead was a Canadian Football League find for the Giants at a time when they needed to beef up the backfield. Alex Webster was never a speedster, but he made clutch plays. He was the cavalry who came to the rescue when New York needed it, and he was a genial companion after games as friend to all teammates. Later, though the transition to the more aloof role was difficult for his personality to adjust to, he became the club's head coach.

A writer for *Pro Football Weekly* once called Webster "the world's slowest fullback, but best cutter who would always get the hard yard." That summed up the attributes of the 6 feet 3 inch, 225-pound alumnus of North Carolina State who anchored a slot in the Giants' backfield from 1955 to 1964, and accumulated 4,638 yards on the ground and 56 touchdowns.

Some believed Webster would never recover from a severe left knee injury suffered during the 1960 season, but he fooled them. Loss of speed wasn't an issue and he was as tough as always. "I made my mind up I was going to make it," said Webster of his determination. "It was like starting all over again as a rookie. I had to win my job."

Webster will always be remembered by Giants' faithful as the man the team and quarterback Charlie Conerly turned to on handoffs when New York was in a third-down and two-yards-to-go scenario. The short yardage plays were not flashy, but they were critical.

incredible experience."

The 1961 Giants proved they could still win. But they wanted to show that they were the best team in football, not merely the best team in the East. The 1962 record of 12–2 was an improvement. The offense, under Tittle's guidance, rang up 398 points with seven games of at least 31 points. The defense gave a little bit more than those old chanters of "Dee-fense!" would have preferred, but the offense made up for most lapses.

Frank Gifford, who had been knocked unconscious by Chuck Bednarik's' crumbling hit in 1960, returned to the Giants in 1962 as a receiver after spending a year out of the game. He was a key component in that eye-catching offense. Gifford's departure had been announced as retirement, but once he was healthy he discovered he missed the sport too much. Gifford caught 39 passes and scored eight touchdowns and was named comeback player-of-the year in 1962. "I missed pro football," he said. "I don't know any kind of business you can get into where you can get as much excitement

once a week as you can playing pro football."

On the greatest single day of his long career, Tittle threw seven touchdown passes in a 49–34 win over Washington on October 28, 1962. The NFL record of seven had originally been set by the Bears' Sid Luckman in 1943 against the Giants, and Tittle tied it. The record still stands. Tittle also threw for 505 yards on 27 completions that day. "This was a day when everything fell into place," Tittle said. "Perhaps it was the kind of day that happens once in every quarterback's life. My receivers made flawless moves against the defenders. Our offensive line gave me great protection." The Giants and Sherman were confident that they were a year better for a rematch with Green Bay. The Packers and Lombardi did not believe they had slipped any. Yankee Stadium was the title game site on December 30 and it was a cold and blustery day. It was inhospitable weather for the passing game and the 64,892 fans.

The Frozen Tundra Packers felt at home and did everything but haul ice shanties onto the iced-over

Norm Snead (16) of the Washington Redskins (who later played for the Giants) attempts to pass but is thwarted by Giant Rosey Grier (76), who sacked him for a 5-yard loss in this 1961 game.
Bettmann/Corbis

Defensive tackle Rosey Grier in 1961. Besides playing pro football, Grier acted, played guitar and recorded music, and popularized needlepoint for men.
NFL/NFL/Getty Images

ROSEY GRIER
Defensive tackle
1955–56, 1958–62

Roosevelt Grier's nickname was "the Gentle Giant," but he was never called that by anyone who tried to tuck a pigskin into their chest and run past him. Grier, one of the first of the colossal defensive tackles at 6 feet 5 inches and about 300-pounds, wrapped up the optimistic ball carrier in a big hug and threw him to the ground. There was nothing gentle about that, except for the possibility that Grier might be kind enough to help the runner to his feet again.

Grier came out of Penn State and excelled in a 11-season career as one of the New York defenders who were treated to fans shouting, "Dee-fense!" and as one of the Los Angeles Rams' "Fearsome Foursome." But he was more Renaissance man than football stud. Grier played guitar, recorded albums, served as a bodyguard to U.S. Senator Robert F. Kennedy (and took the handgun from Sirhan Sirhan on the night of Kennedy's assassination in Los Angeles), acted, and took up needlepoint, an image completely at odds with that of a rough-and-tumble football player.

Grier admitted that he began needlepoint as a joke after "needling" a friend about the activity, and then crossed gender boundaries when he wrote a book called *Rosey Grier's Needlepoint for Men.*

Grier was a two-time Pro Bowl player and his personality was one of the Giants' assets in the locker room. During his tenure in New York he played in five title games for the Giants.

Yankee Stadium turf. The Giants' defense did rise to the occasion, but too many of Tittle's passes were windblown, and too many of Green Bay fullback Jim Taylor's runs were sprung by a tough Packer offensive line. Jerry Kramer kicked field goals of 26, 29 and 30 yards, and Taylor scored Green Bay's only touchdown on a 7-yard run in a 16–7 victory. The closeness of defeat might have hurt the Giants more than the blowout of the season before. The Giants' only score was produced by special teams on a blocked punt. "Our defensive line made a much-improved stand," said Rosey Grier, "because we knew their offense the second time around. They don't do anything different than anybody else in the league, but they do it so well."

Once again, as Allie Sherman surveyed the disappointed faces in his locker room, he didn't see reasons to make big changes. The offense was the envy of most teams—Tittle had thrown a league-leading 33 TD passes. The defense was solid. A little tweaking here and there, and Sherman saw a group of players ready to defend the Eastern Division crown and return to the championship game. And he was correct.

The Giants looked every bit as good in 1963 as they had in 1962. New York scored 448 points. Tittle threw for a record 36 touchdown passes and the squad finished 11–3. For their third visit to the title game in three years, the Giants faced a new opponent. Unexpectedly, the resurgent Bears had fought off the Packers to win the Western title. Just like old times, the championship game pitted the Giants against the Bears.

During the week leading up to the December 29 title encounter in Chicago, analysts figured the game would be a battle between the Giants' high-scoring offense and the Bears' stingy defense. Once again, nobody reckoned with the elements. It has known to be wintry in Chicago at the end of December and this was one of those times. Frustrated by high winds in New York the year before when Tittle's prowess as a thrower was blunted, the Giants endured a replay. The temperature at game time in Wrigley Field was 11°F and the wind was roughly 15 mph. Fingers unprotected by gloves suffered. Tittle's accuracy suffered most of all. It was a game nearly devoid of offense. Tittle completed 11 of 29 pass attempts and threw a damaging five interceptions. Bears' quarterback Billy Wade wasn't any

Jimmy Patton moves in for a tackle on Bears halfback Ron Bull in the league championship game on December 29, 1963. The Giants lost 14–10.
NFL/Getty Images

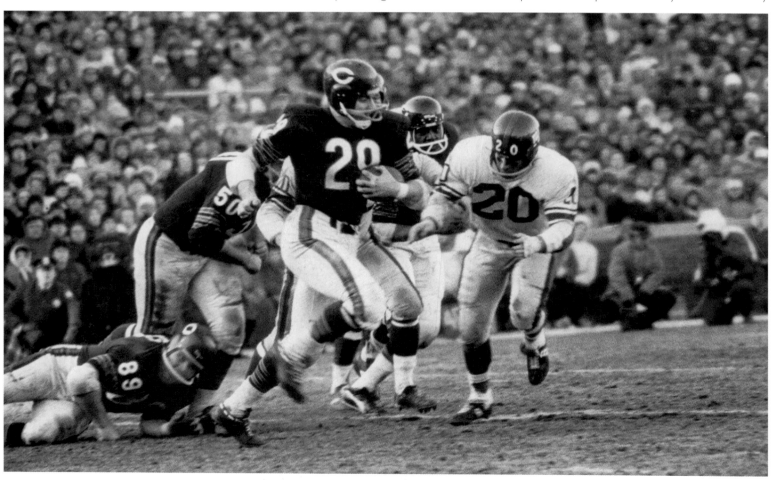

sharper with 10 completions in 28 tries.

The biggest ground-gainer was the Giants' Morrison with 61. But the biggest hero was Wade, who scored on two 1-yard quarterback sneaks. The Bears prevailed, 14–10. The Giants were emotionally crushed. They had failed to win the NFL title in three straight visits to the championship game, and they were zero-for-five in repeated close calls since 1958.

What those New York men who had made pro football special in the nation's largest city could not know was that this was the end of the run. The window of opportunity had closed. The veteran units who had won so often and done so much for the sport while wearing Giants blue had peaked out. The 1964 season would set the Giants on a very different course from what they had known for nearly a decade.

It seemed impossible that the Giants would fall so quickly and so far over a single off-season. But the Giants of 1964 were a parody of their old selves. The record was 2–12–2 in the first 16-game regular-season. The defense surrendered 399 points and all of a sudden the offense couldn't score. Y.A. Tittle had always looked old. Now he played old. From setting a league record for touchdown passes in a single season to being unable to move the team downfield was a gap of more than 100 yards. Tittle threw just 10 touchdown passes and 22 interceptions.

Gifford had retired. Grier had been traded to the Los Angeles Rams. Injuries disrupted plans. Most significantly, the Giants had simply gotten old all at once. It was hard to believe and hard to swallow. It was definitely time for new blood.

With their first-round pick in the 1964 draft, the Giants selected one of the greatest screwballs in NFL history. Joe Don Looney, a supremely talented, speedy battering ram from the University of Oklahoma, was 6 feet 1 inch and 230-pounds of muscle. He was also pretty much the brother from another planet. Looney broke rules and skipped practice at will, demonstrating the same lack of discipline that caused him to flunk out of the University of Texas. He indulged in oddball behavior, such as walking around in the nude. He later investigated eastern religions and died in 1988 in a motorcycle crash. The Giants were searching for help and Looney provided jaw-dropping distractions. He threatened the life of a Giants public relations man who came to his dorm room in training camp without even turning around to see who it was, and he attempted to ax into small pieces a new tackling dummy that he bounced off. Looney lasted with the team until 1966.

The Giants of 1965 finished a mediocre 7–7, but the record implied a restoration and first step back to prominence. It was not. The Giants of 1966 had the

worst record in team history, finishing 1–12–1. It was a relief when the team finished 7–7 for the next two years in a row, but it was not the pace of improvement being sought.

In the midst of the up-and-down performances and alongside the intense focus he had to apply to personnel decisions as the old guard faded and new players were needed, Wellington Mara experienced the trauma of losing his older brother Jack to colon cancer. This was also the era when the upstart American Football League not only competed for

Real football. Sometimes playing in the mud returns players' thoughts to the game's roots. Giants guard Mickey Walker (64) and tackle Rosey Brown (79) look like they want a shower more than anything else in this November 1964 game in St. Louis against the Cardinals that ended in a 10–10 tie. *Herbert Weitman/NFL/Getty Images*

Fullback Joe Don Looney had all the talent in the world, but he defied coaches routinely and frequently got into trouble during a colorful but brief stay with the Giants.
Bob Gomel/Time Life Pictures/Getty Images

Frank Gifford had just stepped off a plane in Hawaii when he learned of Jack's death. He turned around immediately and flew back to New York for the funeral at St. Ignatius Loyola Roman Catholic Church. "His religion was his strength," wrote *New York Times* sports columnist Arthur Daley, a friend of Jack Mara's. "He was a good man, kind, generous and thoughtful."

Allie Sherman had experienced as much success in his first three years leading the Giants as just about any other head coach in history. He was confident the team would turn things around quickly. Sherman and Wellington Mara brought out bandages to staunch the bleeding and attempted major surgery to save the patient.

The Joe Don Looney experiment was a stunning failure. The Giants did not have psychiatrists among their assistant coaches and nothing short of heavy duty analysis would have brought the player and the organization together. They started over again at fullback by drafting Tucker Frederickson, the brilliant Auburn University star, No. 1. This was a sound selection, although his glamour quotient did not match that of the New York Jets' No. 1 choice that year—Joe Willie Namath.

"Broadway Joe" led the Jets to a Super Bowl triumph and helped bring about the merger of the American Football League with the NFL, while Frederickson's pro opportunities were thwarted by repeated injuries. His career was limited to six seasons and he was a solid player, but no savior. Years later, after surgery on his knees and problems with arthritis, Frederickson was looking at possible hip replacement surgery. "You wake up in the morning and sometimes you wonder if it was worth it," he said. "Football is not for the knees and back."

As his own body began to evidence tell-tale signs of collapse in 1964, Tittle was periodically relegated to the bench. Backup quarterback Gary Wood, a rookie from Cornell, sought to date Tittle's daughter. That's when the 38-year-old Tittle knew it was time to retire.

The memory of how speed could jump-start an offense and define a defense was fresh in the minds of Giants' administrators and when they planned their rebuilding, they overturned rocks in the quest for fast runners. Henry Carr was a gifted athlete at Arizona State University who won gold medals in the 200-meter dash and the 4 x 400-meter relay at the 1964 Olympics in Tokyo. You couldn't get any faster than that. The Giants chose Carr and made him into a safety, figuring he wouldn't be beaten by the long pass.

Carr had been a running back at Arizona State. He was a little rusty as a rookie in 1965 and had to decipher how to back-pedal almost as fast as striding forward. "It's coming back to me," Carr said after three

players and kick-started salaries, but also went head-to-head in New York with the Jets. Jack Mara, team president for 31 years, died in June 1965 at the age of 57, leaving Wellington as the last of the triumvirate that had ruled Giants' business since 1925. Jack had kept watch on the finances all of those years. Now Wellington had to do it all and there was a lot on his plate.

First-round Draft Choices of the 1960s

1960	Lou Cordileone	G	Clemson
1961	Bruce Tarbox[1]	G	Syracuse
1962	Jerry Hillebrand	LB	Colorado
1963	Frank Lasky[2]	T	Florida
1964	Joe Don Looney	FB	Oklahoma
1965	Tucker Frederickson	HB	Auburn
1966	Francis Peay	T	Missouri
1967	Louis Thompson[3]	T	Alabama
1968	Dick Buzin [4]	DT	Penn State
1969	Fred Dryer	DE	San Diego State

[1] No 1st-round pick, 2nd round.
[2] No 1st-round pick, 2nd round.
[3] No 1st-round pick, 4th round.
[4] No 1st-round pick, 2nd round.

years away from the game. "Running backwards was the hardest thing I had to do. I didn't realize a defensive back has to make moves just like an offensive end." The Carr experiment was called off after three years—the Giants said he adapted on foot, but never became the tackler he needed to be.

Also in 1965, the Giants obtained Carl "Spider" Lockhart. Carr was a fourth-round pick. Lockhart was not taken until the 13th round out of North Texas State. Lockhart played 11 seasons and was a two-time Pro Bowl choice. When things were falling apart around him, Lockhart was a defensive leader in the 1960s. Emlen Tunnell was coaching the secondary players and he loved Lockhart's style of playing receivers tight. "Skinny, that's the way to play it, just like a spider," Tunnell said. And that's how Lockhart came to be nicknamed "Spider."

Lockhart, who played at only 175-pounds, intercepted 41 passes in his career and was an accomplished punt returner. He gained a reputation as a hard-hitter, and as a guy who would play with minor injuries. Lockhart was close personal friends with adhesive tape and other wraps, but he played hurt. "It's my job," he said. "Mr Mara pays me to play football and I know of no other way to earn my salary than to give 100 percent."

The Giants did not sneer at speed wherever it was to be found. Free agent Clarence Childs, from Florida A&M, made the team with a splash in 1965. He averaged a league-leading 29.0 yards per kickoff return, and ran one back 100 yards for a touchdown against the Minnesota Vikings. Tried on offense, Childs caught 11 passes. Moved to the defensive side, under the tutelage of Emlen Tunnell Childs developed into one of "Emlen's Gremlins" in the secondary. "I don't care where I play as long as I play," Childs said.

The infatuation with fast runners brought Homer Jones onto the Giants' radar screen when the 6 foot 2 inch, 215-pound receiver was matriculating at Texas Southern. He ran the 100-yard dash in 9.3 seconds and the 220-yard in 20.5 seconds. New York liked those stopwatch readings. After some tutoring, Jones was ready for a full-time job in 1965 when he grabbed 26 passes. For the next four seasons he caught between 42 and 49 passes and distinguished himself as a game-breaker. In 1967, Jones averaged 24.7 yards a catch and scored 13 touchdowns, both marks leading the NFL, and he averaged a league-high 23.5 yards a catch the next season.

Jones was nowhere near the goofball that Joe Don

FRANK GIFFORD
RUNNING BACK, RECEIVER, DEFENSIVE BACK
1952–60, 1962–64

Coming from California, graduating from the University of Southern California, acting in movies and modeling in advertisements gave Frank Gifford a pretty-boy image with his new Giants teammates when the club made the all-around back its No. I draft pick in 1952.

What the hardscrabble linemen and growling linebackers did not know was that the true Gifford background had been glossed over by his handsome looks and All-American status. Gifford hardly grew up with a silver spoon in his mouth. More likely it would have a jackhammer or some other hand tool of the proletariat. Gifford's father was a roughneck in the California oil fields and the family moved from place to place based on his jobs.

Gifford was born in 1930 in Santa Monica, but by the time he reached high school his family had lived in 47 towns. That lifestyle provided neither stability for a youngster, nor any type of school continuity. Gifford was not a particularly avid student and figured he was destined to live a similar nomadic life.

The kindness of coaches who recognized his athletic ability and focused him on maintaining acceptable grades changed Gifford's life. From a potential roustabout he became America's golden boy at USC and has remained in the nation's limelight for a half century.

Not only was Gifford a star on the football field, he developed Hollywood contacts and made frequent small appearances in movies. Making movies was his college summer job. After he retired, Gifford became a well-known sportscaster, most prominently as the low-key host on *Monday Night Football* refereeing the back-and-forth barbs tossed by "Dandy" Don Meredith and Howard Cosell, but also handling other sports and Olympic events. In one of life's second acts, Gifford's marriage to

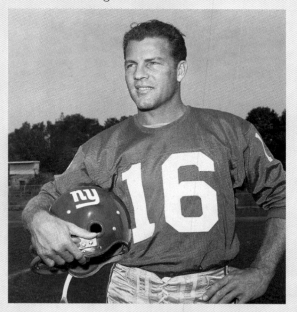

Hall of Famer Frank Gifford was an all-around star for the Giants in the 1950s and 1960s, running the ball, throwing, and even playing defense before gaining fame as a broadcaster on Monday Night Football.
Bettmann/Corbis

Kathie Lee, long-time hostess of the *Live with Regis and Kathie Lee* television talk show, was nearly as high profile as his football career.

Gifford initially felt resentment from older Giants veterans. "I'd get a thumb in the eye here, an elbow in the ribs there," Gifford said. "They also had their little cliques and I didn't belong to any of them."

What none of those Giants realized was that Gifford would out-last them and demonstrably eclipse them in fame and achievement. Gifford, who was married to his college girlfriend and had a two-year-old son, actually bonded with owner Tim Mara's 16-year-old grandson Timmy more than other players. Later, Wellington Mara, who was Gifford's presenter at the Pro Football Hall of Fame in 1977, said he was like a son.

Gifford bounced between positions. In his 1952 rookie year, Gifford threw a few passes, caught a handful of passes, periodically rushed, and played defensive back. He also ran back kicks and punts. By the time he retired in 1964, Gifford had gained 3,609 yards on the ground, caught 367 passes and scored 78 touchdowns. In all, he gained nearly 10,000 yards.

Gifford's first of seven selections to the Pro Bowl came in 1953—on the defensive side of the ball. The next year he was an all-star on offense. In 1956, he was the Most Valuable Player in the NFL.

What Gifford's New York teammates discovered soon enough was that (even though he once had an audition to play a movie Tarzan), he had as deep-seated a determination to win at football as they did. Gifford forged a close relationship with quarterback Charlie Conerly—the two roomed together on road trips. Gifford liked to joke that when he first saw the gray-haired, leather-faced Conerly he thought he was a coach. Gifford was also tight with halfback Kyle Rote from the beginning. "Kyle was one of the few Giants to be nice to me during my rookie year and we've remained friends ever since," Gifford said years later.

Gifford played a more significant role in the offense as the Giants first crumbled, then rebuilt in the latter part of the 1950s. He said the 1956 championship thrashing of the Bears raised the consciousness of the New York public about the team.

On November 20, 1960, Gifford was the victim in one of the most talked-about plays in NFL history. Running across the middle of the field early in a game against the Philadelphia Eagles after a catch, Gifford was leveled by a brutal, blind-side tackle by linebacker Chuck Bednarik. Bednarik, a future Hall of Famer and the last of the league's two-way players who played 60 minutes, was nicknamed "Concrete Charlie." He jumped up from the hit that caused a fumble and pumped his fist in the air.

Suffering from a deep brain concussion, Gifford lay flat on his back on the turf not moving. Gifford was unconscious and was carried off on a stretcher. Players and fans grumbled and seethed, anger directed at Bednarik for what they were certain had to be an illegal hit and for his insensitivity in apparently celebrating Gifford's injury. The situation worsened after a stadium security guard died of a heart attack and his body lay covered near Gifford on another stretcher in a locker room. Word spread falsely that Gifford had died.

"Hell, I wasn't anywhere near death," Gifford insisted later. He said he doesn't remember Bednarik's hit, only what he has seen on replays. Although the myth of Bednarik's coldness persists, the reality was that Bednarik did not revel in Gifford's injury. He later said he was happy because the Eagles got the ball. In fact, rather than being cold-hearted and ignoring the incident, Bednarik sent flowers to Gifford in the hospital, called to check on him and apologized for hurting him. Gifford said he was never angry at Bednarik because the play was a clean hit.

Gifford was severely injured. He missed the rest of the season and did not play in 1961 at all. He made a stirring comeback in 1962, moving to wide receiver full-time, and was a member of the 1962 and 1963 Eastern Division championship teams before retiring in 1964.

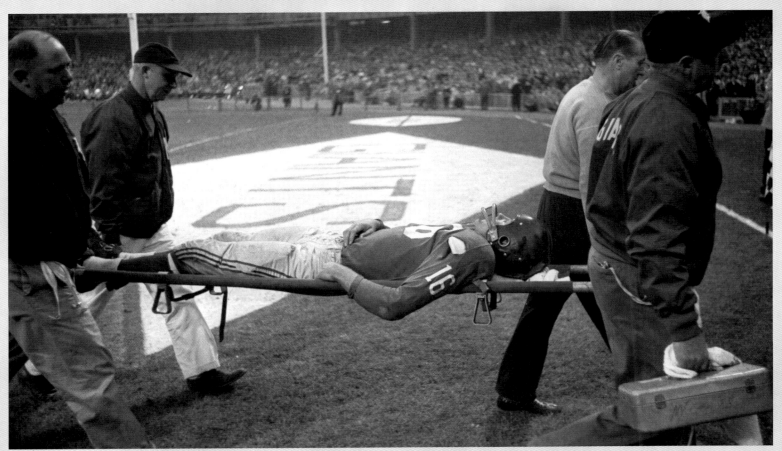

Frank Gifford is carried off the field on a stretcher after he was injured during a wicked tackle by Philadelphia Eagles' linebacker Chuck Bednarik in November 1960. At one point, whispers spread to the team that the unconscious Gifford had died in the locker room. The player sat out a year, but made a comeback in 1962. *Bettmann/Corbis*

Looney was, but he prided himself on being different and was sometimes seen as the class clown. He said his nickname was "Homer Q" and that the Q stood for question mark. The speed Jones exhibited on the track was just as real on the football field. Quarterback Earl Morrall once explained that Jones could out-run a 70-yard pass he had thrown. "There is no way I can overthrow Homer," Morrall said. "I just throw the ball as far as I can and hope he'll have to go get it rather than wait up for it."

Defensive back Carl "Spider" Lockhart was one of the stalwarts of the secondary and one of the Giants' most reliable players during the gloomy years of the mid to late-1960s.
NFL Photos/Getty Images

While the Giants were tinkering, moving new faces in and out, almost rebuilding, and then falling backwards, one player contributed to a revolutionary change in pro football. After two seasons with the Buffalo Bills, Pete Gogolak joined the Giants in 1966 and stayed for the rest of his career through the 1974 season. The Hungarian-born Gogolak, who attended Cornell, was the first pro kicker to use the soccer style approach from the side for extra points and field goals, instead of the head-on step forward.

Not only was Gogolak a full-time kicker (and took abuse for it), he and his brother Charlie, who joined the Redskins in 1966 out of Princeton, demonstrated that the new way of kicking was more accurate. Soccer-style booters took over the job and no one uses the straight-ahead style any longer. Because the brothers were smaller and not particularly muscular, as well as speaking with an accent, their success was sometimes ridiculed. Full-time players didn't think of them as true football players. Some made fun of their speech patterns and other foreigners who followed them with remarks like "I keek a touchdown." Pete Gogolak actually kicked a lot of extra points and field goals in the pros—some 863 points. "It's difficult for any specialist to feel like part of a team," Gogolak said. "He doesn't run plays. He doesn't get into the scrimmage. He doesn't have to go to meetings. He's on the fringe. He isn't really a part of anything until he produces on the field."

The Giants were not bereft of talent in the 1960s, but they were bereft of championships after the old team turned over. At the height of his success with those three Eastern crowns, Allie Sherman was signed to a ten-year contract. Things went sour much more quickly than that. During the worst of times, when the Giants couldn't post a winning record for five years, fans grew more vociferous about wanting change. Whereas once Sherman was applauded as a genius, Giants fans turned on him, chanting loudly and repeatedly, "Goodbye, Allie!" After the 1968 season Wellington Mara said goodbye to Sherman, too. He replaced him as head coach with long-time favorite Alex Webster.

"I think we can finish 10–4 this season and win our division," Webster predicted. Not quite. The Giants finished 6–8 in 1969 under Webster.

1960s NEW YORK GIANTS YEAR BY YEAR

Year	Record
1960	6–4–2
1961	10–3–1
1962	12–2
1963	11–3
1964	2–10–2
1965	7–7
1966	1–12–1
1967	7–7
1968	7–7
1969	6–8

Homer Jones (45) was a dashing receiver with a knack for adding big yards to the play after a catch. Here, he is driven out-of-bounds after a 5-yard gain by Washington's Rickie Harris (46) in a crazy Redskins' 72-41 victory. *Bettmann/Corbis*

THE 1970s
A DECADE OF DESPAIR

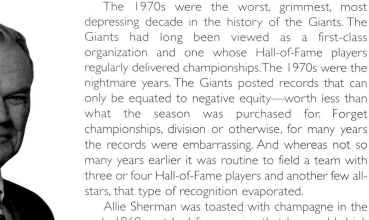

6

Owner Wellington Mara spent his whole life working for the Giants, through good times and bad. *Ross Lewis/NFL Photos/Getty Images*

For most of the 1970s the Giants were like a student repeatedly taking the SATs and hoping the score would one day be high enough to obtain eligibility for college. But the numbers always came up short.

The 1970s were the worst, grimmest, most depressing decade in the history of the Giants. The Giants had long been viewed as a first-class organization and one whose Hall-of-Fame players regularly delivered championships. The 1970s were the nightmare years. The Giants posted records that can only be equated to negative equity—worth less than what the season was purchased for. Forget championships, division or otherwise, for many years the records were embarrassing. And whereas not so many years earlier it was routine to field a team with three or four Hall-of-Fame players and another few all-stars, that type of recognition evaporated.

Allie Sherman was toasted with champagne in the early 1960s, yet had fans praying that he would drink motor oil by the end of the decade. When the Maras searched for a replacement coach they didn't look far. They definitely didn't think out of the box, or the family.

Fullback Alex Webster was a proud member of the Giants' roster from 1955 to 1964. His clutch play spanned the glory years of both decades. When the fans' cries of "Goodbye Allie!" grew too loud, the club turned to Webster to breathe fresh air into the team.

Wellington Mara's explanation for why he fired Sherman was simple. "I just didn't think we were winning enough football games," Mara said. It usually comes down to that when there is transition on the sideline. Sherman was still collecting on a 10-year contract, and Mara said Sherman would assume some front office position. "He and I will be the highest paid spectators at Giants' games this year," Mara said.

Webster had minimal coaching experience, but he was loved by the fans, and was an easy-going sort who would provide a fresh face to the franchise. However, Webster may have been too nice a guy to lead a team of 40 men of disparate personalities in the long run. Yet, in his first year, 1970, the Giants finished 9–5. It was the first above-.500 season since 1963 and the owners and fans believed a corner had been turned.

The comparatively looser style of Webster's guidance seemed to help. So did the harnessing of quarterback Fran Tarkenton's talents. Or perhaps unharnessing, since Tarkenton was still the bold scrambler he had been with the Minnesota Vikings. The 6 foot, 190-pound Tarkenton, who was named Francis Asbury Tarkenton after a Revolutionary War missionary, was a novel addition to the NFL when he was drafted out of Georgia in 1961. He was a quarterback with a strong arm who could lead his team down the field by passing, but he had quick feet, and an instinct that allowed him to avoid being sacked in the pocket. The NFL had turned to stay-at-home quarterbacks, but Tarkenton understood he could be more effective if he was not restrained. He could pass on the run and he could manufacture gains from broken plays. Some observers just couldn't stand that,

"Consider VIP standing for Versatility Inevitably Personified."
—*Giants' publicity director Don Smith, on Joe Morrison.*

and despite his Hall-of-Fame career, Tarkenton was criticized for not standing still.

Tarkenton came over from Minnesota in 1967 and stayed through the 1971 season when he went back there, and while he always shined, the 1970 season gave him his best opportunity to win. That year Tarkenton threw for 2,777 yards and 19 touchdowns and ran for 236, a per-carry gain of 5.5. "Quarterbacks run in every game," Tarkenton said in a moment of sensitivity to suggestions he should leave the running game to the halfbacks. "I suppose no one will say that a scrambler can win a championship until I win one. Sure I'd rather stay in the pocket and give myself time to throw, but if I'm being rushed, my pattern isn't developed yet and I see 10 yards open up the middle, I'll go. Most quarterbacks don't run because of the risk of injury. But if scrambling helps our offense, then I scramble."

As it so happened, the Giants never got close to a championship with Tarkenton, but it is doubtful scrambling had anything to do with that. The Giants did not surround him with the type of talent needed to reach the playoffs.

The Giants thought future Hall of Famer Fran Tarkenton (shown here in 1967) would solve their problems at quarterback. *Bettmann/Corbis*

Right: Old reliable. Long-time Giants mainstay Joe Morrison poses on May 5, 1972, at Monmouth College in West Long Branch, New Jersey. *NFL Photos/Getty Images*

JOE MORRISON
Running back, receiver
1959–72

For a while it seemed as if do-everything Joe Morrison might play forever. Morrison joined the Giants in 1959 and didn't retire until 1972. It seemed as if he had as much longevity with the franchise as the Maras, spanning the era of a title game against the Colts, through the glory years of the early 1960s, the bad years of the 1960s and into the reign of coach Alex Webster, his one-time backfield mate.

Morrison was no average Joe. He stood 6 feet 1 inch and weighed 215-pounds and he played wherever his coach of the moment thought was most advantageous. That was sometimes halfback, sometimes fullback, sometimes flanker, sometimes wide receiver and sometimes if a coach woke up on a certain side of the bed, it was as a special teams player.

Morrison, who stepped in immediately as head coach at the University of Tennessee-Chattanooga upon retirement, rushed for 2,474 yards, caught 395 passes and averaged 21.3 yards a kickoff return. In all, he scored 65 touchdowns for the Giants, behind only Frank Gifford as a position player. Morrison was never the No. 1 option as a runner or receiver, but was always a major contributor even if coaches didn't really know where to use him on any given Sunday.

Allie Sherman once said Morrison might play quarterback if the starter got hurt, and Morrison replied, "Why not?"

"No doubt about it," Sherman said, "Joe is as close to being the complete ballplayer as you can get."

Fran Tarkenton holds the sculpted bust in his likeness about to be put on display at the Pro Football Hall of Fame.
Bettmann/Corbis

After the glimmer-of-hope 1970 season, the Giants immediately plummeted to the depths of the 1960s in 1971. Webster was still coach. Tarkenton was still quarterback, but the team was 4–10. Impatience grew and Tarkenton was shipped back to the Vikings. For the first time in team history, since the founding of the franchise in 1925, not a single member of the team was named an all-star. That was a "how-low-can-you-go?" moment.

For a while, life under Webster improved again. In 1972, the Giants recorded their highest scoring game ever, dismembering Philadelphia, 62–10 and they put together an 8–6 record. Was this a fluke? Was it truly the indication of a new start that was going to restore luster? Actually, it was a last gasp of good news for years. The Giants were headed down the drain fast. The swap of Tarkenton back to Minnesota for Norm Snead did not pay off, except for Tarkenton himself, who led the Vikings to three Super Bowls.

Tarkenton finished his career with 342 touchdown passes while throwing for 47,003 yards, and when the defenses couldn't catch him, he piled up 3,674 yards rushing. Most telling was his 5.4 average gain, better

Whether it was fading back to pass, as he does against the St. Louis Cardinals in this 1971 game, or scrambling for a first down, Giants' quarterback Fran Tarkenton always made things happen.
Bettmann/Corbis

than almost all running backs who took handoffs as frequently as Tarkenton kept the ball.

Tarkenton was one of the NFL's all-time greats and was enshrined in Canton in 1986. Snead was a good player and more of a classic-sized quarterback at 6 feet 4 inches and 215-pounds. He graduated from Wake Forest and joined the Washington Redskins in 1961. He was an established NFL thrower after spending a decade with Washington, the Eagles and Vikings by the time he joined the Giants in 1972. Snead's 60.3 completion percentage led the league that year and he was a pro for 16 seasons, tossing 196 touchdowns. Snead was durable, but he was not the answer New York was looking for at the time. "I played whether I was hurt," Snead said. "I enjoyed all of the cities I played in and all of the people I played with." And he played with plenty of them, going on from the Giants to San

"Outmoded thinking and irrelevant. How can anyone say which type of quarterback can win and which can't?"
—Hall-of-Fame quarterback Fran Tarkenton, responding to charges he scrambled too much.

Francisco, before finishing up with one final year back in New York in 1976.

One of the other milestones of 1972 was the end of the Joe Morrison era. Morrison was one of the most underestimated players in Giants' history. He joined the team in 1959, played against the Colts, during the good times of the 1960s, and just kept expanding his role. He went from backup to jack-of-all-trades, at various times being employed as a halfback, fullback, end, flanker and kick returner. He was never the fastest guy on the team, nor was he the biggest at 6 feet 1 inch and 215-pounds, but was just fast enough and big enough to surprise opposing tacklers. He represented the good spirit of the good times that couldn't conquer the bad times, but displayed class in how to put up with them. Morrison was 36 when he retired to take the job as coach at the University of Tennessee-Chattanooga, and despite his longevity really hadn't thought about giving up his playing days. The instant transfer to coaching attracted him, though. "Retirement never entered my mind until this came up," Morrison said, as he moved on to Tennessee from New York. "I'll miss my teammates, sharing those moments in the dressing rooms before games, the day-to-day locker room stories. But I have no regrets."

The up-and-down tenure of Webster ended in New York after a 2–11–1 season in 1973 that indicated to the higher-ups that progress was not being made. Webster had not come into the head coaching job cold. He was Sherman's offensive coach during the last two years of his old mentor's tenure. During Webster's playing days, the Giants' public relations department once put out a press release praising his clutch running plays. The lead sentence read, "Leave it to Alex." After five years as head coach, though, neither he nor Mara wanted to leave things to Alex anymore.

Webster had never been desperate to coach the

In their quest to find a permanent answer to their quarterback question, the Giants tried Norm Snead (16), who had some memorable games, though not in this 1972 loss to the Detroit Lions.
Clifton Boutelle/NFL Photos/Getty Images

THE MEADOWLANDS

The Giants didn't have a place to call their own until they were nearly 50 years old. From 1925, when the team was founded, through 1955, the Giants played in the Polo Grounds, home of the baseball Giants. From 1956 until 1973, the Giants played in Yankee Stadium, home of the baseball Yankees.

The football Giants were tenants (and some said second-class citizens), borrowing the stadiums for less than a dozen days a year for exhibitions and home games. For part of 1973 and all of 1974, plus the 1975 season, the Giants were forced to find another home. Yankee Stadium was undergoing renovations and the Giants played at the Yale Bowl and then Shea Stadium.

At last, in 1976, when all of the moving vans were parked, the

Giants for the first time had a football stadium of their own. It was located in East Rutherford, New Jersey, on the other side of the Lincoln Tunnel from Midtown Manhattan. It was pleasing to have the "Giants" lettering scripted across the end zones, but some fans howled that the Giants had sold out their real home, abandoning New York for the Garden State.

Angry fans asked, "Why don't you just change the name to the New Jersey Giants?" The Giants were not about to do that—they still identified with New York, and had no plans to alter their ties with the city. The Giants were definitely keeping the white lettering of "NY" on the sides of their blue helmets with the traditional red stripe.

Left: The gleaming new field of Giants Stadium in the Meadowlands Sports Complex in East Rutherford, N.J., right after its completion in 1976.
David Seelig/Getty Images

Below: An October 1997 view of Giants Stadium during a game between the Cincinnati Bengals and the New York Giants.
Charles E. Rotkin/Corbis

Much was made of how the Meadowlands really was a sort of meadowland, a spanking new construction sprouted from swamp land away from residential areas and hotels, restaurants and the like. The legend surrounding the disappearance of famed labor leader Jimmy Hoffa at the time of construction put his body in concrete somewhere in the stadium's walls or underground, perhaps in an end zone. *Sports Illustrated* joked that if true that would give new meaning to the punting expression "coffin corner" kick. There was never proof to support such allegations, though no evidence of Hoffa's body has been found, either at midfield or anywhere else in the world.

Unlike the Polo Grounds or Yankee Stadium, the new field sported artificial turf. The Meadowlands was actually a sports complex, with an NBA basketball arena included in the neighborhood, as well as a horse racing track, and the football team's building was officially Giants Stadium. The shiny new stadium had a capacity of more than 80,000 and it opened for the team on October 10, 1976. Consistent with the club's overall play during the decade, the Giants lost to the Dallas Cowboys that day, 24–14.

Giants. He had tremendous respect for Sherman and recognized that Sherman had a far greater understanding of complex football dynamics than he did. Webster did not have to be told the end was in sight after the disappointing 1973 season. The Giants had raised hopes in the exhibition season by winning all six of their pre-season games, but when the whistle blew for real they accomplished little. After his fifth year in charge, Webster resigned. He telephoned Mara to inform him of his decision the night before he made his own public announcement at a luncheon that was not scheduled for such a newsy purpose. He had quietly informed his teenaged daughter of his plans, too, and she said, "It's about time."

As one of the clan, one of the men who had jump-started the recent glory days, Webster was proud of being a Giant and worked energetically to make the Giants into winners again. Given that he was reluctant to coach in the first place, he was not interested in a long-term contract. Each season he met with Mara to discuss an extension, a one-year extension, and that's how he worked until the end.

The players who knew Webster the longest, in some cases even playing beside him, as well as serving under him, were sad to see him depart, not only from the Giants, but from football (he owned a restaurant and developed other business interests outside the game). "It was a Utopia situation," center Greg Larson said. "Players always talk about having a coach who will treat you like men, and when we finally get one we let the guy down. It's not his fault. But he's shouldering all the blame. That's how he is."

If Giants' fans thought the return to regular winning seasons was going to be as simple as replacing the head coach, they were delusional. The Giants' magic seemed to have vanished all at once with the retirement or trading of the famous group that led the team in the late 1950s and 1960s. The team had lost its groove and didn't know how to regain it. Draft choices flopped, acquisitions didn't pan out. The mighty Giants were mired in mediocrity—and that was in a good year.

Bill Arnsparger earned his early coaching spurs with Ohio State, University of Kentucky, and Tulane University before moving into the NFL in 1964 with the Baltimore Colts. He also coached with the Miami Dolphins before the Giants tapped him to succeed Webster as the new coach for the 1974 season. Arnsparger was itching to run his own team and his work with the Dolphins solidified his standing around the league. When Miami won the Super Bowl after the 1972 season, going 17–0, defensive coordinator Arnsparger was praised for overseeing the "No-Name Defense."

Opposite: Rugged Giants defensive end George Martin was not expected to be a major contributor, but he fooled the experts and turned into a 14–season regular between 1975 and 1988.
Jim Turner/NFL Photos/Getty Images

"That's the best criteria there is for a defensive player's talent— quarterback sacks."
—*defensive end George Martin.*

No one could fault Mara for looking outside the Giants' family this time. Arnsparger seemed to have the credentials. He was unlucky enough to take over the team's leadership, though, at a time of turmoil, when the Giants were car-pooling from stadium to stadium. This was the period when Yankee Stadium was being renovated and The Meadowlands was being constructed. Within just a few seasons, the Giants shuttled from Yankee Stadium to the Yale Bowl to Shea Stadium to The Meadowlands.

It was an unsettled period in club history. By agreeing to jump to New Jersey when The Meadowlands was built, the Giants were accused of abandoning their fan base. Mayor John Lindsey talked of going to court to prohibit the Giants from using the words "New York" in the team name. Many fans were angry because they wouldn't have the same seats their families had held for years at Yankee Stadium. Others were angry because they had no use for New Jersey and didn't want to trek through the Lincoln Tunnel to see games. By then, many fans were just plain angry because the Giants kept losing.

Giants' Stadium also became home to the New York Jets and over the years has hosted the New Jersey Generals of the ill-fated World Football League, college football games, Pope John Paul II, Pele's final soccer game, World Cup soccer, and numerous high-profile concert events played by Bruce Springsteen and the E Street Band, The Grateful Dead, Madonna, The Eagles, The Rolling Stones, U2, Billy Joel and Elton John, among others.

The shift to The Meadowlands was beneficial to the Giants in almost every way. They were the primary tenants, not secondary renters. They got a share of concession and parking revenue. And the words "Giants Stadium" were emblazoned on the building. Also included were 72 luxury boxes, signifying the wave of the future. "We're moving, but we're not leaving," said Wellington Mara, meaning New York. "Each stadium was the most famous of its era, but every family dreams of the day when it can move into its own home and go away from its in-laws, no matter how great the in-laws have been to live with."

No one ever mistook George Steinbrenner for Wellington Mara's father-in-law, but the average fan got it. It was all about greener pastures and that green was the color of money. To say that New York City officials

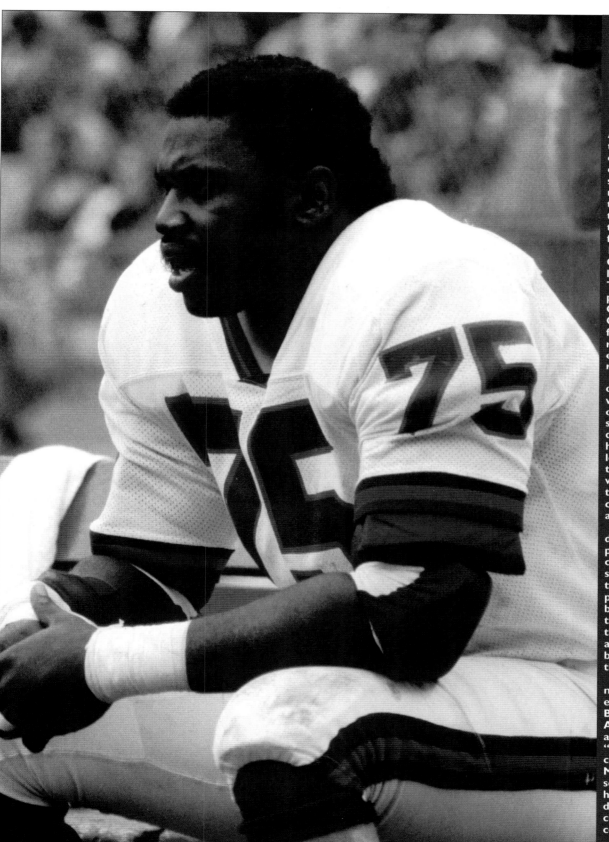

GEORGE MARTIN
Defensive end
1975–88

As much as NFL teams try to reduce the annual evaluation and drafting of collegiate players to a science by weighing and measuring them, by testing them psychologically, timing their speed and cataloguing their power, the effort is far from foolproof. That's why 11th round draft picks like George Martin can produce long and fruitful pro careers. The 6 feet 4 inch, 245-pounds defensive end from Oregon was felt to be an OK player, but didn't even figure to make the final roster in 1975, never mind emerge quickly into a regular.

Martin was an overachiever who by hard work made himself into an outstanding player. Through sheer will and determination he polished his talent, absorbed all lessons and during the trying times of the 1970s, when the Giants fielded few teams to be proud of, they could always point to Martin as a special guy.

Through 14 seasons as a defensive lineman Martin played in 201 games, contributed 46 quarterback sacks and scored seven touchdowns. The latter was particularly impressive because normally the only time defensive ends touch the ball is when they thrust a beefy paw into the air to bat away a quarterback throw.

Martin was one of the most popular Giants of his era and was presented the Byron "Whizzer" White Award, the NFL's prestigious acknowledgement for "service to his team, community and country." Martin taught Sunday school, worked with handicapped and mentally disturbed children, was a chapel leader and a consultant on drug abuse.

HARRY CARSON
Linebacker
1976–88

At the beginning of his career when he came out of South Carolina State in 1976, Harry Carson thought he had blundered into Alice's Wonderland. The Giants were close to bottoming out during the grimmest period in franchise history. For a while, eventual Hall-of-Famer Carson was a lonesome 6 foot 2 inch, 237-pound hero.

Quality players were in short supply as the Giants bumbled through a 3-11 season during Carson's first year. Over the next couple of years, the Giants heard their share of boos from fans who wondered where all of the stars went.

Carson excelled as a linebacker, making nine Pro Bowls, and helped develop pride in a linebacker group that morphed into the best unit on the team. He stuck around long enough—13 seasons through 1988—to become part of a Super Bowl championship team. Carson, who acquired a reputation as the best run-stopping linebacker in the league, led the Giants in tackles six times. On a Monday night football game against the Green Bay Packers in 1982, Carson burnished his image nationwide by making 25 tackles.

Carson's talent helped him outlast most of his contemporaries from the sad old days of the 1970s. As an elder statesman among younger players, though, he once joked that he got sick of telling stories about the past. "It gets to be a pain after a while because you want to forget those days," Carson said. "I was just playing for myself when the team wasn't doing well."

Linebacker Harry Carson put up with a lot of losing before New York turned things around and he let some of his anger out during this 1983 game against the Philadelphia Eagles.
John Iacono/Sports Illustrated/Getty Images

"I've practically eliminated a lot of stuff from my memory. Golf balls being thrown, apples, oranges, tickets being burned, 'Fifteen Years of Lousy Football.' Being the Rodney Dangerfields of the NFL."
—Hall of Fame linebacker Harry Carson, after the Giants improved from terrible to champs during his career.

were ticked off was an understatement. NFL Commissioner Pete Rozelle had to testify before Congress to justify the move. Crossing the state line was more than a state of mind to New Yorkers, but Rozelle said that the distance from Times Square to Yankee Stadium in the Bronx was 6.6 miles and the distance from Times Square to The Meadowlands was 6.9 miles. "The same fans will have tickets," Rozelle said. "Some will have a somewhat longer bus ride, but others will have a shorter ride."

It would have been possible to play the Giants' regular season at Yankee Stadium before the renovations began in 1973, but the Yankees asked the Giants to leave right then. So the Giants played two home games at Yankee Stadium to end their tenure on the premises before moving to the Yale Bowl in mid-season. New Haven, Connecticut was a bit farther away than The Meadowlands so it was hardship travel for fans for the next season-and-a-half.

The Giants made many good memories at Yankee Stadium, winning the 1956 NFL championship, participating in the "greatest game ever played," and putting together their three-year stretch of Eastern

Conference titles in the early 1960s behind Y.A. Tittle and Del Shofner and a defense so rugged it brought the full-throated "Dee-fense!" roar from dedicated fans.

But like many marriages, this one ended in divorce and there were lingering bitter feelings for a while as the Giants became homeless, then vagabonds, before Giants Stadium was available for occupancy.

After nearly 30 years of use, in 2005 it was announced that The Meadowlands' Giants Stadium would be replaced by a new one next door. The planned $800-million-plus home of the Giants (the price is going up) calls for 82,000 seats, 217 luxury boxes, and is scheduled to open in 2010. In 2008, the Giants continued playing home games in the first Meadowlands stadium as construction began in the parking lot.

Arnsparger's first try produced a 2–12 record, almost identical to the record that drove Webster into retirement. Everyone felt things had to get better, and they did, but the 1975 record was just 5–9. If that was the right trend, the 1976 season demonstrated that continued progress would be hard-won. The Giants finished 3–11. Arnsparger did not even make it through the season. After a 0–7 start he was ousted and the reins were turned over to John McVay. The one thing that could be said about the second half of the 1976 campaign was that it wasn't nearly as ugly as the first half. The Giants went 3–4 under McVay.

Beside his college background, McVay had been head coach of the Memphis Southmen of the World Football League in 1975 as the upstart league went belly-up, another doomed challenge to the NFL that played its way into bankruptcy. His old friend Arnsparger rescued McVay, hiring him as an assistant coach for the 1976 season, with neither of them even slightly aware that their roles would change dramatically during the autumn.

Going 3–4 under McVay at the tail end of the season was enough to make the Giants giddy and he was rewarded by being kept on to lead the resurrection that everyone felt was sure to follow, starting in 1977. Not that there was any true evidence of the likelihood of that, other than wishful thinking.

For some unknown reason (too much lead in the paint at offices, too much arsenic in the mashed potatoes in the commissary), the Giants had gone brain dead on draft day as the decade dawned and the infusion of new talent was virtually nil. Not only did the team fail to restock wisely through the draft as the team faltered and provided prime selection positions, the hierarchy committed the cardinal sin of trading away the club's No. 1 pick three times during the decade.

That made it difficult to see how the Giants could get to there (championship contender) from here

Linebacker Harry Carson poses with his bust after his induction into the Pro Football Hall of Fame in 2006.
Matt Sullivan/Reuters/Corbis

New York Giants head coach Alex Webster in 1970.
NFL Photos/Getty Images

Even when the Giants had poor results, they had high quality linebackers. Brad Van Pelt, dropping into pass coverage against the Detroit Lions in a 1974 game, was one of them. *Clifton Boutelle/NFL Photos/Getty Images*

(bottom feeder). Few picks made the roster and fewer picks made an impact. Although there was no number one choice in 1973, No. 2 pick Brad Van Pelt was a winner, becoming a long-time all-star linebacker. Buried much lower in the same draft was a gem. Brian Kelley at No. 14 became another mainstay in the linebacker core. Interestingly, in 1976, still a third linebacker and destined for a Hall-of-Fame career, Harry Carson was chosen in the fourth round. It was hard to believe that the Giants could only analyze the abilities of linebackers, but they kept striking out at other positions.

With Tarkenton and Snead in the rear-view mirror, the Giants were desperate to fill the slightly important position of quarterback. Who was going to be the field leader? Might it be 1976 12th-rounder Jerry Golsteyn out of Illinois? Perhaps the man of the hour would be fifth-round 1977 pick Randy Dean from Northwestern? Or maybe everyone would rally around 1974 fourth-rounder Carl Summerell from East Carolina? Or just maybe the answer was none-of-the-above. Unfortunately for McVay, that turned out to be the case.

Dick Shiner had come and gone earlier in the 1970s, mostly as a backup to Tarkenton. Summerell hung around for 1974 and 1975, Golsteyn stuck from 1976 to 1978, and Dean loitered on the roster from 1977 to 1979, but none are listed as among the team's all-time greats.

With all of the distractions off the field, with the departure from Yankee Stadium and the stadium-hopping regimen, Wellington Mara, who had long been the major voice on personnel matters, brought back former all-star defensive end Andy Robustelli to be director of operations. This was a departure from normal procedures with New York after relying on Mara as de facto general manager for so long. The title did not go to Robustelli, but much of the responsibility did. It was an acknowledgement from on high that things needed to change. Of course, Robustelli's first significant move was hiring Arnsparger, so the one-time cornerstone of the defense was not an overnight sensation in his new job.

This flurry of activity took place in 1974, but one more notable occurrence was registered in October of that season. The Giants acquired Craig Morton from the Dallas Cowboys. Morton had been a pro since 1974 and had bounced back and forth from the starter's job to the bench, to alternating with Roger Staubach in Dallas. In 1974 he actually played on the Giants and Cowboys twice each, but rejoined the Giants in 1975 and spent three seasons as the first-string quarterback.

Morton, who had starred at the University of California, did not have his best seasons with New York, but he offered more stability and know-how at the key position than did the parade of rookies. Morton was an NFL quarterback for 17 years and threw 183 touchdown passes. He added professionalism to the lineup.

Not that Morton had loads of fun with the Giants. He lived through the unhappy, brief Arnsparger era. "It was just a horrible bad team, bad conditions," Morton said. "Great guys, but bad teams. We had fights and

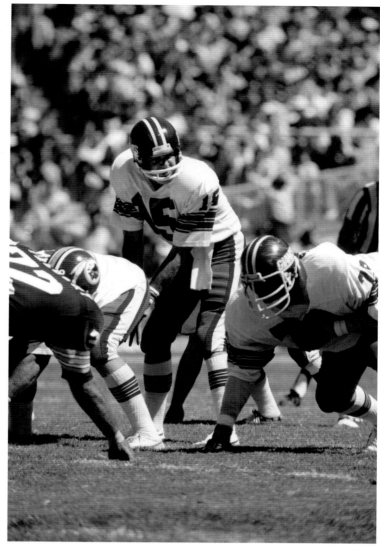

unrest and it was horrible. We were just bad and the press was just unmerciful, horrible on us. Bill Arnsparger . . . didn't handle it well at all because they were really on him. One day he was like Captain Queeg, standing there with all of the change in his pockets, running through that, and wouldn't stop."

While the Giants were trying to figure out why there was no quarterback under the Christmas tree for them year after year, they did develop a pretty impressive running attack in the early 1970s. His name was Ron Johnson. Johnson was the genuine article, the type of player who would be an asset on a championship team. Too bad for him he was with the Giants. His older brother Alex was a major league baseball player and batting champion. The 6 feet 1 inch 205-pound Ron, a former Michigan star, not only caught 48 passes and rushed for 1,027 yards for the 1970 Giants, but his performance marked the first time

in team history that anyone had broken the 1,000-yard barrier.

"That was the highlight of my career," Johnson said. "It was huge to be the Giants' first 1,000-yard rusher as far as what doors it opened to me. I was just totally overwhelmed by how everyone got so excited by that." Johnson did it again—breaking his own team mark—with a 1,182-yard season in 1972.

Although Johnson was the most prominent star on the offense in 1970, he said the rest of the team wasn't exactly on the same page under the laid-back Webster. "Those guys didn't give 100 percent and ruined the team," Johnson said.

One of the other winners on the Giants in the 1970s was tight end Bob Tucker. Tucker was a powerful 6 feet 3 inches, 230-pounds overachiever who attended tiny Bloomsburg State. He caught 40 passes as a rookie and 422 in an 11-season career. He was one

Above left: Brian Kelley, shown here in 1978, helped make the Giants' linebacker core the NFL's best during his era.
Jim Turner/NFL Photos/Getty Images

Above: Quarterback Craig Morton spent nearly 3 of his 18 NFL seasons with the Giants. Here he calls signals during a 1976 game against the Washington Redskins.
Diamond Images/Getty Images

Above: Running back Ron Johnson was a two-time Pro Bowler in his six seasons with the Giants. He's shown here wearing the unfamiliar uniform of the National Football Conference during the Pro Bowl at Los Angeles Memorial Coliseum in 1971. *Darryl Norenberg/NFL Photos/Getty Images*

Above right: Tight end Bob Tucker added an exciting dimension to the Giants' passing attack during his time with the team between 1970 and 1977.
NFL Photos/Getty Images

guy who could be counted on when the Giants were trying to fit the other pieces together to rebound. Tucker and Johnson bonded, and Johnson said he used to rely on Tucker's tough blocking to make big holes. "I would kid him coming out of the huddle to make sure that he took out the defensive end," Johnson said.

Tucker had intended to be a center when he enrolled at his small college in Pennsylvania, but for some reason the school was loaded with guys who liked to hike the ball. He opted for tight end to make an impact on the offense. He felt that Arnsparger was in over his head as the overall coaching boss. Although he respected Arnsparger's smarts on D he bemoaned the deterioration of the Giants under Arnsparger's command. "Arnsparger dismantled the offense and defense and he wanted to coach

everything," Tucker said. "He once even sent in a call for a quick kick on third and long. We became a drab, meaningless entity."

The Giants kept stockpiling those hard-hitting, prideful linebackers who didn't like to lose one bit, and the chief of that unit was Harry Carson. Carson graduated from traditionally black South Carolina State, halfway under radar, but he imposed his will on the league for 13 seasons starting in 1976. Carson was 6 feet 2 inches, 237-pounds, and a well-muscled package of dynamite. A lineman in high school, he studied NFL stars Willie Davis and Deacon Jones for style. Then he got shifted to linebacker, which led him to the Hall of Fame. "It was the players I followed," Carson said of the role models he studied while growing up in Florence, South Carolina. When he

wasn't playing football, Carson said he was outside playing all day long, often cowboys and Indians using a stick for a gun. When fans asked what his most satisfying moment in football was, he said, "I tell them I get the most satisfaction just out of being here, playing football in the NFL."

Carson played in nine Pro Bowls and was voted into the Hall of Fame in 2006. During the 1970s, like the Giants' administration, the fans, and other players, he was frustrated. It wasn't until later, in the 1980s, that Carson's efforts were rewarded and he felt vindicated.

The star linebacker was one of the many witnesses pained by what might have been the worst moment in team history. In a 1978 game against the Philadelphia Eagles, the Giants had the game sewn up with seconds left and possession of the ball.

Quarterback Joe Pisarcik followed the instructions of the coaches and handed off the ball to fullback Larry Csonka. The handoff was never completed. The ball rolled to the ground and Mr. Goodhands Herman Edwards, an Eagles' defensive back, scooped up the ball and ran it into the end zone for the winning touchdown. The play left Giant players morose, the ownership aghast and the fans furious.

It was the culmination of years of losing play and botched opportunities. Soon after, at a home game, some fans rented an airplane to soar overhead, flying a banner reading, "15 Years of Lousy Football—We've Had Enough." It was the fans' way of saying "We're mad as hell and we're not going to take it anymore." Sure enough, they did say that. Fans inside Yankee Stadium began chanting "We've

When good-hands man Bob Tucker was in the Giants' lineup it meant trouble for the other team. Here Tucker scores a touchdown after a reception against the St. Louis Cardinals in 1973.
Herbert Weitman/NFL Photos/Getty Images

The worst play of all time

There is no official ranking, but what was probably the worst single nightmare of a play in NFL history befell the Giants on November 19, 1978. Some 70,318 witnesses at The Meadowlands saw defeat snatched from the jaws of victory with a suddenness that was impossible to imagine.

New York took a 17–6 lead into the fourth quarter of a game against conference rival Philadelphia Eagles for a potential season-closing playoff run. The Eagles narrowed the lead to 17–12, but the Giants controlled the ball in the final minutes.

The infamous play, cursed as "The Fumble," occurred when New York faced a third down at its own 28-yard-line needing two yards for a first down with 31 seconds left. The obvious call was for quarterback Joe Pisarcik to take a knee and let the clock run out. However, assistant coach Bob Gibson called a handoff to fullback Larry Csonka.

Players in the huddle opposed the unnecessary risk, but Pisarcik had been lectured before for changing plays, so he went along. Pisarcik's handoff to Csonka was bobbled. The ball came loose, and Eagles defender Herman Edwards scooped up the fumble and ran it 26 yards for the winning touchdown.

The day after the crushing 19–17 loss Gibson was fired, and 100 fans burned tickets and mailed them to Wellington Mara.

"That's the most horrifying ending to a ballgame I've ever seen."
—Coach John McVay, after a Giants' fumble run back for a touchdown in the last seconds cost the team a win against the Eagles in 1978.

The sight of Philadelphia cornerback Herman Edwards (46) scooping up a Joe Pisarcik fumble and running it back for a touchdown with 20 seconds remaining to give the Eagles a 19–17 victory over the Giants on November 19, 1978, at Giants Stadium was one of the most demoralizing in team history. A win seemed assured for the Giants until they made the ugly mistake. Eagle fans called the sudden turn-around "Miracle at the Meadowlands."
Edwin Mahan/NFL Photos/Getty Images

ny 1970s ny
NEW YORK GIANTS
YEAR BY YEAR

1970	9–5
1971	4–10
1972	8–6
1973	2–11–1
1974	2–12
1975	5–9
1976	3–11
1977	5–9
1978	6–10
1979	6–10

had enough!" after the plane circled the stadium. Mara got the message and took action. After the 1978 season, which ended with a 6–8 record, Mara hired George Young, a complete outsider, to take control of all personnel matters and rebuild the Giants. The 1979 season was his first and he held onto the role for 19 years. One of the first major shakeups was the replacement of McVay with former Alabama star and five-year Baltimore Colt Ray Perkins as the new coach.

Perkins was a no-nonsense coach who might be the only one frowning in the audience of a stand-up comic's show. His first season did not produce much of a change in the record—6–10 again—but Perkins set a fresh tone. There weren't going to be many chuckles in training camps. It was going to be more like boot camp.

The last year of the decade also turned up the finest No. 1 draft pick of the era. When the Giants announced the selection of an unknown quarterback from little-known Morehead State University in Kentucky, fans who came out for the draft show booed. Their judgment was wrong. The top pick was Phil Simms and the arrival of Simms in 1979 marked the beginning of the end of a depressing era in Giants' football history.

Above left: Ray Perkins, arms folded, seemed like the long-term answer as head coach when he was hired in 1979, but he quit after the 1982 season to coach Alabama, his alma mater.
Andy Hayt/Getty Images

Left: Giant fans booed rookie quarterback Phil Simms in 1979 when he was selected in the first round by the team out of Morehead State, but he became a star Super Bowl quarterback.
NFL Photos/Getty Images

THE 1980s
BACK TO THE TOP

Scott Brunner (12), handing off to running back Rob Carpenter (26) during the Giants' 38–24 loss to the San Francisco 49ers in the 1981 NFC divisional playoff game in 1982 at San Francisco's Candlestick, was one of the many temporary hires the Giants used at quarterback as they searched for a new star.
Arthur Anderson/NFL Photos/Getty Images

A novel by Richard Farina was called *Been Down So Long It Looks Like Up To Me*. For a decade-and-a-half that fictional title could also have described the Giants' winding path through the NFL seasons. But under the sharp-eyed vision of coach Ray Perkins, that began to change. Perkins laid the foundation for improvement with the 6–10 season of 1979 and then in 1980 and 1981, the Giants finished 8–6 and 9–7. In 1981 the Giants even returned to the playoffs.

They won the National Football Conference wild card game, 27–21, over the Philadelphia Eagles. The last time New York had been in the playoff hunt there was no such thing as a wild card game. The NFL really had passed the Giants by for a while. The Giants lost their next playoff game, 38–24, to San Francisco, but the team had shown potential, making fans and owners happy.

The year, 1982, was the first time a Monday night football game was broadcast from The Meadowlands—the Giants lost to the Packers. But 1982 was a season destroyed by labor unrest. A player's strike cost six games. Everything was out of rhythm and the final record was 4–5. It was pretty much a wasted season.

Concurrently, a shocking college football development had implications for New York. Paul "Bear" Bryant had taken his record 325 victories and walked off into the sunset, retiring from the University of Alabama and then even more stunningly, died a month after season's end in early 1983.

Perkins was among the legion of loyal alumni players and he was offered the chance to succeed the legend. Perkins had done an admirable job leading the Giants, producing their best teams in 20 years. But his heart lay in Dixie and he quit to lead the Crimson Tide.

For the first time in a while, the Giants lost a coach they wanted to stay. New York needed a coach to continue the work Perkins started. Perkins was a stern leader, and a disciplinarian. There was no comedy channel on his cable package. The replacement Giants' coach, Bill Parcells, was more bombastic, just as strict, but he could be sarcastic and clever simultaneously. He also had an eye for talent and soon would be spoken of as one of the best coaches in the NFL.

Parcells was a Jersey guy, from Englewood, just

Bill Parcells, shouting instructions to his players at training camp in Pleasantville, New York, in 1983, proved to be the coaching savior the Giants had sought since the 1960s.
Bruce Bennett Studios/Getty Images

"If it wasn't for the law of gravity he wouldn't have been able to hit the ground with the ball."
—Owner Wellington Mara on how nervous quarterback Phil Simms was at the beginning of his career.

Yelling on the sidelines in a 1985 playoff game against the San Francisco 49ers, Giants coach Bill Parcells was the man who took the team to the promised land of winning the Super Bowl.
Ronald C. Modra/Sports Imagery/ Getty Images

across the border from New York in Bergen County. His first college head coaching assignment was at the Air Force Academy in 1978 after years of holding down assistants' jobs at Hastings, Wichita State, Army, Florida State, Vanderbilt and Texas Tech. Perkins hired Parcells as defensive coordinator in 1979, but after a year Parcells left for the New England Patriots. He was back in New York just in time, running the defense, when Perkins jetted off to Tuscaloosa.

Parcells was thrilled. The Giants was the team he had followed when he was a kid. "I grew up a Giants' fan and I recall being as young as 10 and watching the New York Giants Football Huddle on television with Marty Glickman," Parcells said. He said he was even in attendance on the snowy day at Yankee Stadium when Pat Summerall kicked that classic 49-yard field goal to beat the Browns.

Everything was in place for a resurrection. Phil Simms was maturing at quarterback. Lawrence Taylor had added an amazing dimension to a ball-hawking defense. The new coach was familiar with the personnel and had commanded the outstanding defense. And promptly, it all fell apart. The Giants finished 3–12–1 in 1983. A few highlights included

Giants' linebacker Lawrence Taylor turned into a Hall of Famer and was one of the greatest pass rushers of all time.
Al Messerschmidt/Getty Images

kicker Ali Haji-Sheikh scoring 127 points and Butch Woolfolk rushing for 857 yards. But Simms was injured and missed most of the year and that made a huge difference. The results even shook up the implacable Parcells, reducing his swagger a bit. "Some changes are needed and we are going to make some," Parcells said.

No more Mr. Nice Guy for Parcells. After that showing, Parcells tightened up the rules and the reins. He was tougher on the players, demanding more, insulting them if he felt it was necessary. He knew if he didn't pull things together in a hurry his long-sought NFL head coaching job would go pffft.

Parcells had a voice that could be measured on the Richter scale. He shouted at players often and at some players regularly. For various reasons he wanted to make examples out of them for the rest of the team— and in front of the rest of the team. He also recognized who could take the verbal harangues and who could not. One whipping boy was tackle Brad Benson. "Every single day," guard Billy Ard said. "Bill yelled at guys he

Place kicker Ali Haji-Sheikh attempts a field goal in the Giants' 16–13 victory over the Los Angeles Rams in the 1984 NFC Wild Card playoff game in 1984.
NFL Photos/Getty Images

"I had that (nickname Whitey) growing up and it never left me. As a youth my hair was white. My dad used to say, "Son, don't get in trouble. They'll be able to find you."
—Quarterback Phil Simms.

knew he could yell at. He would yell at me once and that would shake me up for six months. So if he got after me once a year, that was a lot." Ard said every day Benson would comment in the locker room about how Parcells lit into him during practice and promised he was going to let him have it back. One day, Ard said, Benson complained because Parcells did not yell at him. That made him worry that the coach didn't care about him anymore. That was probably just how Parcells wanted the big tackle to think.

Simms was the linchpin of the success in a 1984 season that brought a first-round playoff win over the Los Angles Rams. Simms threw for a career high 4,044 yards and 22 touchdowns in a season that served as his coming-out party.

Simms and Parcells were not always buddy-buddy. But Simms said he appreciated Parcells' bluntness and compared his honesty to what a father would tell a son that he needed to know. Parcells did not want the quarterback getting a swelled head, nor did he want him to get too down. "He'd walk by and say, 'Just because you completed a few passes you think you're a hero,'" Simms said. "He'd downplay it. But after a bad game, he'd tell you some things you did well and reinforce that. The best thing about Bill is that he does talk straight. It's cut and dried. He doesn't give you a pat on the back to console you. When you stink, he tells you."

If Parcells was not going to hand out gratuitous, feel-good compliments, Simms at least knew he had general manager George Young watching his back. Young put his own reputation on the line by making Simms the No. 1 pick in 1979 when no one else in America saw it coming. Young had squirmed through the Simms learning process and injuries.

When Simms began heating up in 1984 and it was clear that he was on his way to his best season, Young spoke up. "We like Phil because he is a classic, drop-

Right: After a revolving door at quarterback, Phil Simms turned into the most prolific passer in team history and won the Most Valuable Player award in Super Bowl XXI.
George Rose/Getty Images

PHIL SIMMS
Quarterback
1979–93

Giants fans present for the 1979 NFL draft booed when the team chose quarterback Phil Simms with its No. 1 choice because they didn't know who he was. That was a little bit like getting jeered at birth.

It took time, persevering through challenges, and overcoming injuries, but Simms made those fans recant. By the time Simms retired in 1993 he had a universal stamp of approval for not only his grittiness and record-setting passing, but for leading the Giants to the Super Bowl.

In 1984, Simms set a club record, throwing for 4,044 yards. In all he passed for 33,462 yards and 199 touchdowns. It was not a smooth ride for the thrower from Lebanon, Kentucky, but when he was swatted to the ground by debilitating injuries or circumstances, he always got back up.

Simms had numerous highlight games, but his signature moment occurred in Super Bowl XXI when he completed 22 of 25 passes, and his clutch toss to receiver Phil McConkey set up the touchdown that propelled New York to victory over Denver. "Simms-to-McConkey" became the phrase of the era.

Known for practical jokes, Simms once placed raw fish under the hoods of teammates' cars when they were in meetings. When they turned on the heaters the smell permeated everything.

"I'm so dumb I didn't figure it out for a day-and-a-half," said backup quarterback Matt Cavanaugh. "He's always had that sick mentality where he thinks a prank a day helps things go good."

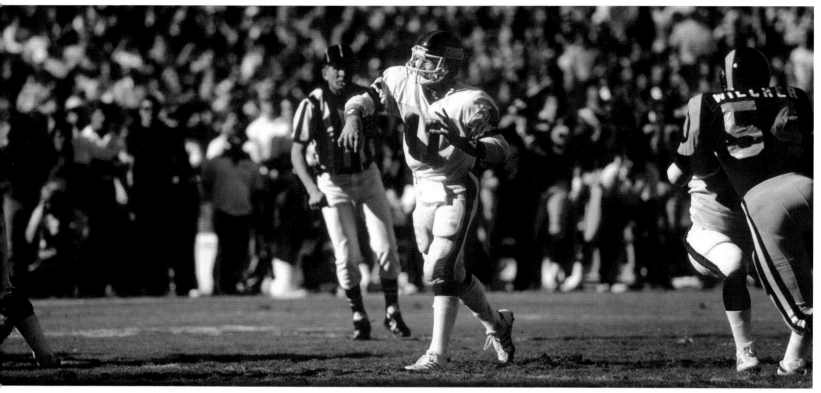

Quarterback Phil Simms throwing against the Los Angeles Rams in a 16–13 Giants victory in 1984, was a money player, more accurate than ever when the stakes were high.
NFL Photos/Getty Image

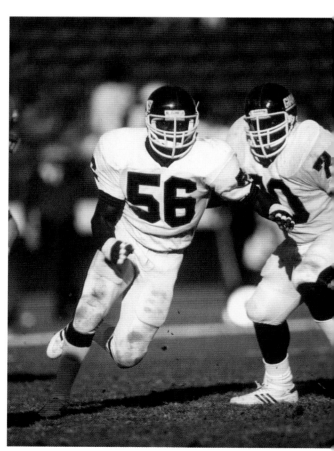

One of the most nightmarish sights for a Giants opposing quarterback was linebacker Lawrence Taylor on the loose coming at him.
Al Messerschmidt/NFL Photos/Getty Images

back passer and he has the artillery piece (aka a strong arm)," Young said. "He also has intelligence and courage. We thought of him as having Pro Bowl potential without any major failings. And the only failing he has had is being unfortunate."

Simms was as aware as anyone else that much of the Giants' progress rested on his arm. It was 1981 when Simms proclaimed, "It's time for the Giants to get dividends from me." It took a little bit longer.

While the Giants were waiting on Simms, and mixing and matching to create a reliable offense, the defense seemed ready-made. Part of that was Parcells' work as ex-defensive coordinator. When the Giants drafted Lawrence Taylor with their No. 1 pick in 1981, some members of the team wondered why. It was not a slur on Taylor's ability, it was an opinion based on the feeling that New York had greater needs. Linebackers Harry Carson, Brad Van Pelt and Brian Kelley were already in place. What did the Giants need with another linebacker?

The two philosophies that NFL teams adopt, and sometimes alternate as they enter each year's draft of college talent is whether or not they should draft to fill specific needs or if they should draft the best athlete available regardless of position. The Giants took the best athlete available.

The decision produced a near-mutiny. Taylor was about to be blessed with a contract paying him more than the veterans—he was asking for $750,000 a year. There was a threatened walkout and the atmosphere was tense. When Taylor signed, he joked that he was going to like New York because it had more TV stations than North Carolina and he had just watched *The Three Stooges*. "I like them," he said.

It didn't take very long before skeptics understood Young's reasoning. The three incumbent linebackers may have felt a little bit like "The Three Stooges" when they realized how good Taylor was. Taylor was stupendous, and the adoption of a 3-4 defensive set allowed all four linebackers to start. Regarded by some

as the greatest linebacker who ever lived, Taylor was a wild-card player. He went wild and dealt the cards to the offense, disrupting game plans and what seemed to be good ideas at the time.

Football is sanctioned violence and Taylor's demeanor spoke as loudly as his results—"I'm going to rip you limb from limb." In his autobiography, Donnell Thompson, a tackle on the North Carolina defense recounted how Taylor's on-field persona translated off the field. "Lawrence had a short fuse," Thompson said. "Pity anyone who yelled something derogatory about the Tar Heels while Lawrence was walking down

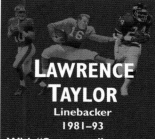

LAWRENCE TAYLOR
Linebacker
1981–93

With "Superman" as a nickname there is a lot to live up to. Lawrence Taylor did so with speed, power, instincts and a ferocity that frightened opposing players as he mangled their bones and muscle. His flaw was thinking he was Superman off the field and Taylor's addiction to cocaine was his Kryptonite.

In a pro career that began when he was drafted No. I out of North Carolina in 1981, Taylor was a sensation, his combination of strength and speed in a 6 feet 3 inches, 240-pounds package made him a nuclear weapon as the Giants' foremost linebacker until 1993. Taylor recorded 132.5 sacks and won election to the Hall of Fame in 1999.

New York running back Lee Rouson said Taylor was nervous before games because "he was scared he wasn't going to be the best football player on the field that day." Few brought such relish to the pursuit of the ball in a career repeatedly honored by superlatives, including ten Pro Bowl selections. In 1986, a season during which Taylor notched 20 sacks, he was chosen Most Valuable Player in the NFL. While still in college, Taylor was nicknamed "Filthy McNasty."

Taylor said when he burst in on a quarterback he thought of something else before sacks—stealing the pigskin. "I'd go after the ball," he said. "I'd tackle with one hand and go after the ball with the other. Of course I wanted sacks, but defensive players get paid to give the offense the ball."

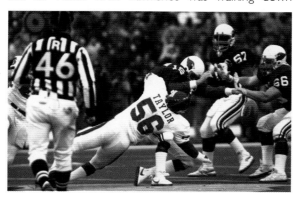

Above left: Demonstrating what a superior force could be, Lawrence Taylor ran amok against the Minnesota Vikings in a 1989 game, recording seven solo tackles, two assists, and two and a half sacks. *Jim Turner/NFL Photos/Getty Images*

Above right: Quarterbacks could run from Lawrence Taylor, but they couldn't hide. This sack of St. Louis Cardinals quarterback Neil Lomax in a 1984 game caused a fumble. *John Iacono/Sports Illustrated/Getty Images*

Below: Here lowering the boom on Dallas quarterback Gary Hogeboom in 1985, Lawrence Taylor's hard hits made him a Hall of Famer. *John Biever/Sports Illustrated/Getty Images*

**"I had to know where the ball was going before it got there."
—Brian Kelley, on not being as fast as his fellow linebackers.**

Franklin Street. Lawrence would run to the car and chase the guy down and whip his ass. Then there was the time during a pool game at Mayo's when I looked up and saw Lawrence take a bite out of a glass and start chewing it. I'm like, 'You're out of your mind.'"

Taylor was on his way to a Hall of Fame career during which he recorded 132.5 sacks in 13 seasons. He may not have eaten glass with the Giants, but he did munch on quarterbacks. When he wasn't a wrecking ball on the field, Taylor was in danger of wrecking his life and career by partying, ingesting drugs and alcohol, driving too fast and staying up all night. He packed for road trips in advance and stayed out right up to team flights. He was friendly with his defensive buddies, but Taylor did not make friends across the line of scrimmage.

"I don't think people realize the destructiveness he brought to the game," said 49ers star defensive back Ronnie Lott. "I'd never seen that kind of nastiness, all out, 100 percent, for four quarters. He was gonna come after you and he was gonna punish you."

The disappointment of 1983 was swiftly buried.

The No. 1 pick in the Giants' 1984 draft was yet another linebacker, Carl Banks, and while he did not create the same hullabaloo (positive or negative) as Taylor, Banks was a classy, tremendous player.

Banks came to New York bearing the nickname "Killer." It was not as ominous as the story about Taylor's glass-chomping, nor did the appellation relate to anything Banks did on the field. When he was a kid he worked in a cemetery. He was also a spelling bee champion, so he could have been called a "Killer Bee." Banks, who played for Michigan State, was surprised just how clued in Giants' fans were. They knew everything about all of the players and that impressed him, whether they were using the information to cheer or boo. "They're unique in that they have an unparalleled knowledge of the game, of its players, where they come from, and what was expected of them," Banks said. "They'd recite stats. You could hear them from the stands."

In 1985, pundits projected the Giants as a potential Eastern Division champion and a team likely to go deep into the playoffs. New York finished 10-6 and lost twice to the Cowboys and in overtime to the Eagles. But they were peaking and did qualify for the playoffs.

During the regular season, a Giants' player was once again involved in one of the more grisly tackles publicized by television in NFL history. The first time, in 1960, Frank Gifford was knocked unconscious by

Three tough members of the Giants defense during a 1987 practice: linebacker Lawrence Taylor (56), nose tackle Jim Burt, (64), and linebacker Carl Banks (58).
Bettmann/Corbis

Chuck Bednarik. This time, on November 18, 1985, a Giants defender delivered the punishment. Redskin quarterback Joe Theisman was steamrolled by linebacker Lawrence Taylor. His right leg bent underneath him and shattered, with a bone sticking through the flesh.

Theisman, a former Notre Dame star, was the NFL's Most Valuable Player in 1983. On the play, Taylor smacked into Theisman on a blitz and fell on his leg. The contact broke the tibia and fibula. Theisman was taken off the field on a stretcher and never played again, becoming a successful broadcaster. "I heard, 'Pow. Pow,'" like two muzzled gunshots," Theisman said. "It was my leg breaking. The pain was beyond description." Theisman said Taylor called him in the hospital that night to check up on him. Neither man would watch the taped replay of the play. It was a gruesome result to a legal hit, and voters in an ESPN poll called it the NFL's "Most Shocking Moment in History."

In their first playoff game the Giants triumphed 17–3 over San Francisco. In the second round they were whipped by the Chicago Bears, 21–0. The Bears were the team of destiny that season. Behind Jim McMahon, Walter Payton, and a phenomenal defense they lost just one game and took home the Super Bowl trophy.

That game also showed a nationwide TV audience one of the NFL's all-time bloopers. With the score 0–0, New York punter Sean Landeta was well back from the center for the snap, near the Giants' end zone. When

the ball reached his hands, he did as he always did, dropping the ball and raising his right leg like a high-stepping Broadway dancer. Only this time foot and ball did not connect for the kick. Landeta whiffed on the boot, creating a fumble. Bear Shaun Gayle scooped up the ball and ran it 5 yards for a touchdown. "One mistake can overshadow five months of pretty good playing," Landeta said in a marvelous understatement. "I guess I was the fall guy." Later, Landeta said the wind

Punter Sean Landeta (5) is about to punt, but he whiffed on the ball when he lowered it. The embarrassing miscue enabled the Bears to score an easy touchdown during the Giants' playoff 21–0 loss to Chicago in 1986 at Soldier Field.
Jerald Pinkus/NFL Photos/Getty Images

Washington Redskins quarterback Joe Theisman fumbles after being hit by linebacker Lawrence Taylor during the Redskins' 17–7 loss to the Giants in 1981.
Nate Fine/NFL Photos/Getty Images

MARK BAVARO
Tight end
1985–90

When the 6 feet 4 inches, 245-pounds Mark Bavaro was a rookie tight end in 1985 after making his mark at Notre Dame, he let his muscular physique and blocking do his talking. They spoke volumes and the fourth-round draft made an impact immediately with 37 catches.

As he grew more comfortable with the organization, everyone believed Bavaro would open up in the locker room. He never did. He was often described as the strong, silent type who did all of his talking on the field, but he spoke up to protest a nickname. "I don't like to be called Rambo," Bavaro said. He also added that he didn't like reporters. Bavaro's 66 catches his second season made him a star.

Quarterback Phil Simms loved throwing to Bavaro and admired his bullish methods downfield after the catch. Bavaro's style was on display during an exhibition game against the Pittsburgh Steelers after Simms zipped a pass to him.

"I threw that pass to him when I saw the blitz coming," Simms said. "I knew it was a touchdown because I knew he had only one guy to beat and I knew he'd run that guy over. And he did. You come to expect certain things of Mark."

Talking football philosophy was not one of them. Bavaro answered most questions with single words or whispered short phrases, but none of it was bragging. "I don't stand out. I just try to play my hardest every game," he said. "That's my job."

Mark Bavaro looked like a model, and was a quiet locker room presence, but when he was in full Giants uniform he was a fierce tight end.
Ronald C. Modra/Sports Imagery/Getty Images

took the ball out of his hands. It was a haunting mistake for the ages, but Landeta played 16 years in the NFL and averaged a notable 43.6 yards a kick.

Nobody thought the Giants would beat the Bears, but Parcells saw the game as a missed opportunity. Playoff elimination in such a thorough manner would not happen again, Parcells pledged. It didn't. One year later the Giants blitzed the league, finishing the regular season 14–2 and owned the month of January. They crushed the 49ers, 49–3, they handled the Washington Redskins, 17–0, and then in the Super Bowl in Pasadena, California, they out-lasted Denver, 39–20. The triumph represented New York's first NFL championship since 1956.

During the regular season Simms posted 3,829 yards and 22 touchdown passes. On October 13 versus the Cincinnati Bengals, Simms turned in a remarkable game. He attempted 62 passes, completed 40 and notched 513 yards gained. All three of those figures remain team records. Tight end Mark Bavaro caught 12 passes that day.

Complementing the passing game was an excellent rushing game. Joe Morris was a 5 feet 7 inches, 195-pounds workhorse who starred for Syracuse, but had spent 1982, 1983, and 1984 trying to convince the New York coaches that he deserved more playing time. In 1985 he got it. Morris dashed for 1,336 yards and scored 21 touchdowns, or 126 points, while tucking the ball under his arm 294 times from scrimmage. The double-edged explosiveness changed the dynamic of the team and coupled with the No. 2 ranked defense in the league made the Giants too formidable for most teams.

Morris, who scored bonus points for the small men in the sport, piled up 181 yards rushing against the Redskins on October 27 and then did it again, collecting 181 yards rushing against the Dallas Cowboys on November 2. "It was quite a week for me," Morris said. "I also scored two touchdowns in each game. It was easy

Running back Joe Morris helped the Giants balance their attack by providing good speed out of the backfield while still handling the tough up-the-middle action.
George Gojkovich/Getty Images

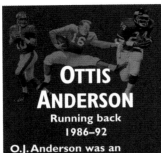

OTTIS ANDERSON
**Running back
1986–92**

O.J. Anderson was an insurance policy who added juice to the Giants' offense when they needed it, first during their 1986 run to the Super Bowl championship. Anderson, a 6 feet 2 inches, 220-pounds power back, had been the top rusher for the St. Louis Cardinals, topping 1,600 yards one season, but the Cardinals felt he was wearing out and had no more use for the former University of Miami star.

Anderson was a fill-in during brief appearances in 1986, useful to spell regular Joe Morris. Most felt Anderson was playing out the string in a career that began in 1979, but before the end of the decade Anderson had unexpectedly once again become a 1,000-yard rusher.

The Giants had been left out of the Super Bowl sweepstakes since the big game began in 1967. They did not qualify for the first time until 1987, after their 14–2 regular season of 1986. Giants' general manager George Young called the pursuit of the Super Bowl "the run for the roses," borrowing the phrase from the Kentucky Derby. When he traded for Anderson, it represented adding another quality player. "If you're going to try for the roses, you try to get someone who can help you (get there)," Young said.

Giants' center Bart Oates loved adding the big-bodied runner. "When I think of Anderson, I think of a running back who's tough, bounces off people, runs over people," Oates said. "I'm sure he'll add a big spark to the offense."

He did.

for me to give my all because I was so sick of losing."

The 1985 season paved the path for 1986. The performance in the playoffs showed the Giants what they could be and Parcells reminded them every week as they marched into the playoffs. This was a new team with a new outlook that had been painstakingly fit together by Young, starting with Perkins and finishing with Parcells who polished the crew into a title contender.

The Giants simply demolished the 49ers, but had to adapt to the quirkiness of the conditions against the Redskins. It was a very windy day, with gusts up to 35 mph that made passing challenging. The combination of

> **"He's got some speed nobody knew about. He visited the Fountain of Youth."**
> **—Linebacker Carl Banks, on resurgent running back Ottis Anderson.**

Ottis Anderson was brought to New York merely for backfield insurance, but the running back found renewed life and became a Super Bowl MVP for the Giants.
Anthony Neste//Time Life Pictures/Getty Images

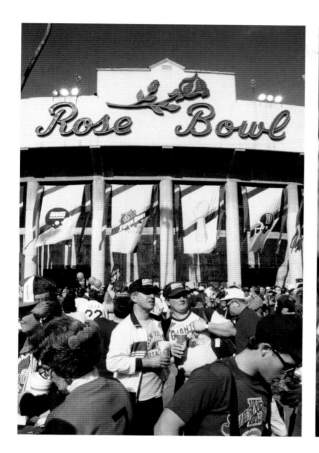

Far left: No better place to be. Giants fans gathered outside the Rose Bowl share their enthusiasm before Super Bowl XXI in Pasadena, California.
George Rose/Getty Images

Left: A fan holds a sign in support of her favorite team the New York Giants, during Super Bowl XXI against the Denver Broncos. The Giants topped Denver, 39–20.
George Rose/Getty Images

a solid running game and a voracious defense made it possible to adjust successfully. The Giants ran up all of their points in the first half.

The Super Bowl was a contest for a half. Denver, led by Hall of Famer John Elway, led 10–9 at intermission, but the most important series didn't show up on the scoreboard. The Broncos had a first-down on the Giants 1-yard-line, but a New York goal-line stand kept Denver out of the end zone, preventing the accumulation of a bigger lead. Banks singled out the goal-line stand as part of the bigger picture of winning the Super Bowl as his best moment in sports. "They had first-and-goal at our one," he said. "On third down I made a tackle for a one-yard loss. It was the turning point in our whole season and obviously, that game."

Guard Billy Ard took home a humorous Super Bowl anecdote. Standing on the sideline at the Rose Bowl for the national anthem, Ard realized he was next to sports artist Leroy Neiman. Ard relayed later that he told Neiman to put him into his painting. Neiman replied, "You've got to win that game." A few months later, a woman he knew at an art gallery telephoned him and told Ard that she had a Leroy Neiman painting and he was quite visible in it. The focus was actually of Simms fading back to pass, but Neiman had included linemen blocking for the quarterback. "All I can tell you

is that Leroy Neiman stuck me right in the middle of that freaking picture because I asked for it," said Ard, who immediately purchased it for $3,000. "He threw me in there, big No. 67, in the middle of the picture. It's my pride and joy. It's my Super Bowl moment."

In the locker room, some of the players were poised to drench Wellington Mara in a celebratory shower. It wasn't that he didn't appreciate the sentiment, but he asked Harry Carson for permission to take off his shoes and jacket. The Giants let him do it and then soaked him. Winning Super Bowl XXI was a milestone in the history of the Giants' organization. One of the oldest clubs in the NFL, they were situated in the largest city in the country, but until that moment, before 101,000 fans in the Rose Bowl, the Super Bowl era had passed the Giants by. It was an important victory, showing the devoted fan base that the franchise could still record memorable achievements that weren't linked to the days of yesteryear.

"Without a doubt, the entire 1986 season will be one that I'll always remember," said Simms, who was the game's Most Valuable Player. "Not just because of what happened, but also because of the way things happened. There were some games we won that we might not have won in other seasons, but because of the way the Giants played as a team—and because we

Super Bowl XXI
January 25, 1987
at the Rose Bowl, Pasadena, California
Attendance 101,063
New York Giants 39, Denver Broncos 20

	1	2	3	4	Final
Broncos	10	0	0	10	20
Giants	7	2	17	13	39

Den—Karlis, 48-yard field goal

NY—Mowatt, 6-yard pass from Simms (Allegre kick)

Den—Elway, 4-yard run (Karlis kick)

NY—Safety, Martin tackles Elway in end zone

NY—Bavaro, 13-yard pass from Simms (Allegre kick)

NY—Allegre, 21-yard field goal

NY—Morris, 1-yard run (Allegre kick)

NY—McConkey, 5-yard pass from Simms (Allegre kick)

Den—Karlis, 28-yard field goal

NY—Anderson, 2-yard run (kick failed)

Den—Johnson 47 pass from Elway (Karlis kick)

seconds of NBA games. And the Gatorade bath turned into such a trademark that when the Giants visited the White House after winning the Super Bowl, players turned a Gatorade bucket over the head of President Ronald Reagan—though it was filled only with popcorn. That was brave enough rather than risking Secret Service intervention for soaking the leader of the free world.

Professional sport is very much a seize-the-moment activity. The Bears were so dominant in 1985 that everyone believed they would repeat the next year. But that Bears group never returned to the Super Bowl. Whether because of trades, age, injuries or coaching changes, windows of opportunity slam shut swiftly. In 1987, prognosticators could see no reason why the Giants would not be in the mix to win again.

were building something solid all year long—the season became something special."

It was during the 1986 regular season that the Giants devised a new form of victory celebration that proved more popular than the Wave and is still commonly used. Defensive lineman Jim Burt was the first to pour Gatorade over the head of coach Bill Parcells to mark a triumph. Linebacker Harry Carson kept it up, win after win. "The reason why I had to keep doing it was because everybody knew that Bill was superstitious," Carson said. "We were winning, so I kept giving him this shower."

The maneuver turned into the most famous sideline victory celebration since Boston Celtics coach Red Auerbach lit his victory cigars in the closing

But the season was again afflicted with labor unrest requiring the use of replacement players for three games and one game was called off altogether. The defense was softer than it had been, allowing 312 points. At one time or another, 11 starters were injured. The Giants finished 6–9. No one saw that coming.

After his slow career start, Joe Morris was the man in the Giants' backfield. In 15 games he rushed for 1,516 yards and carried 341 times. Simms remained in fine form, throwing 17 touchdowns in the reduced schedule. But overall, it was a lost year. Different teams respond differently to distractions. The 1986 Giants were totally focused on the goal of reaching the Super Bowl. In 1987, while the Giants were busy trying to cope with celebrity, at the same time, their sport was falling apart, antagonizing the fans who loved them.

Linebacker Harry Carson douses coach Parcells with the traditional bath of Gatorade as the team clinched the 1987 Super Bowl with a 39–20 win over the Denver Broncos.
Getty Images

Giants linebacker Carl Banks (58) meets Denver running back Gerald Wilhite (47) for a tough tackle in Super Bowl XXI.
Gin Ellis/NFL Photos/Getty Images

SUPER BOWL XXI

The Giants played in six NFL championship games between 1956 and 1963, winning one. They did not appear in another playoff game for 18 years and it took until January 25, 1987 for them to compete for—and win—another title.

In-between, the National Football League and the American Football League merged and the NFL created a new championship playoff procedure and a title game that came to be known as the Super Bowl. Once the power of the Eastern Division, the Giants ran through several generations of players, and fans ran through several generations of patience, before New York reached its first Super Bowl.

The 1986 Giants recorded a superb 14–2 regular-season record, and then crushed the San Francisco 49ers in their playoff opener, 49–3, when defensive tackle Jim Burt knocked 49er quarterback Joe Montana unconscious with a hit. In the next round, the Giants shut out the Redskins, 17–0. That set up a Super Bowl match with the Denver Broncos and the Giants emerged as 39–20 victors. It was their first league crown in 30 years.

It was a moment greatly savored. Wellington Mara, 70, had lived to see it, 61 years after the franchise was founded by his father. "I always said the Giants would make the Super Bowl," Mara said. "I just didn't know if I'd still be around."

These Giants were guided on the sidelines by a gruff, hard-nosed coach named Bill Parcells, on offense by quarterback Phil Simms, who won the game's MVP award, and the hungry, annihilating defense was led by linebacker Lawrence Taylor.

A reporter asked Taylor when he knew he was ready to breathe fire on the Broncos. "When you feel like slapping your mama," he said. Taylor got to slap around Denver quarterback John Elway a little bit.

Phil McConkey was the unlikeliest Giant hero that season. McConkey was a 5 feet 10 inches, 170-pound wide receiver. He played at the Naval Academy and then served five years in the Navy, flying helicopters. In 1984, as a 27-year-old rookie he stuck with the Giants and returned punts and kickoffs. He brought an exuberant style to the team and Parcells loved his kamikaze dedication. At the start of the Super Bowl in Pasadena, California, McConkey led the team onto the field waving a white towel to rev up the crowd.

In the game, McConkey was a 150 mph version of his usual self, catching a key pass from Simms in the third quarter on a flea flicker that went for 44 yards. He was upended on the Denver 1-yard-line, but the Giants pushed the ball in for a critical touchdown. McConkey also scored on a 6-yard pass. The funny part was that McConkey believed he was going to score for sure on the first catch, thinking, "My God I'm going to get a touchdown in the Super Bowl!" Then he was tackled. His actual touchdown was more touch-and-go, with McConkey scoring after a Simms pass deflected into the air off tight end Mark Bavaro's hands.

The Broncos led 10–7 after one quarter and 10–9 at the half. In the locker room, the Giant leaders were vociferous and forceful. They were convinced they were the better team and virtually ordered their teammates to play like it. The third quarter decided the game when New York ran up 17 points and 161 yards. Denver made a move to come back with 10 points in the

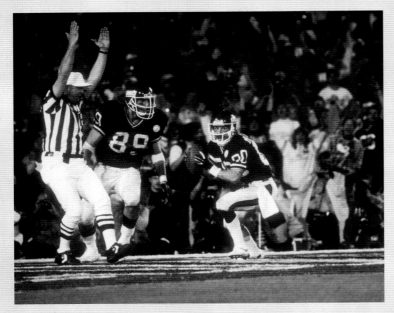

The phrase "Simms-to-McConkey" resonates in the minds of Giant fans because of their connection in the 1987 Super Bowl when quarterback Phil Simms and receiver Phil McConkey combined for a 44-yard gain on a tricky flea flicker play against the Denver Broncos.
Steve Dykes /Allsport/Getty Images

fourth quarter, but the Giants piled on 13 more.

Afterwards, Parcells called the first big McConkey catch the game-changing play. "When we hit the flea flicker," he said, "we really had a tremendous volume of momentum. We were dominating the third quarter pretty well. Once we hit that one and got the touchdown, I knew we would be hard to beat."

When the game ended, Giants' players—especially those who had invested years in the team's turnaround from patsies—exulted in the victory. Some drank champagne, some partied all night, and some said they still couldn't believe that they were world champions. Jim Burt said he wandered around the team's hotel lobby mingling with fans.

"Some of them didn't get to sleep, either," Burt said. "We're the world champions. We deserve to be because we worked so hard. And besides that, we blew these guys out."

A day after the game, McConkey was still stunned and admitted he had no idea how long the feeling would last "because I've never done this before."

Mara had served in the Navy during World War II and had a special fondness for McConkey. When Mara first met McConkey, the player said the boss called him "lieutenant." The more McConkey achieved, the higher his rank progressed. When he made the team, McConkey said, "Mara promotes me to commander. In 1985, I'm up to captain. We get in the playoffs and I keep getting these promotions. We win the Super Bowl and he's calling me admiral."

The post-victory celebration continued at Giant Stadium in The Meadowlands when 25,000 people feted the team on a 13°F day that was chilled even more by a strong wind. The sometimes bizarre party included appearances from Tiny Tim, who had no tulips to tip-toe through on a wintry day, Professor Irwin Corey, the babbling comic, and the playing of "The Beer Barrel Polka." New Jersey Governor Thomas Kean hailed the team as the first champions representing the Garden State even though the team was still referred to as the "New York" Giants. Kean could pretend, but nobody had forgotten that.

The final score, Giants 39, Broncos 20, was displayed on the stadium scoreboard and the song "We Are The Champions" was played. That selection made sense.

Years later, linebacker Harry Carson, who had suffered through many of the bad Giants' years, reflected on becoming a world champ. "The end of Super Bowl XXI was the realization of a dream for me and every football player who has ever strapped on a helmet," Carson said.

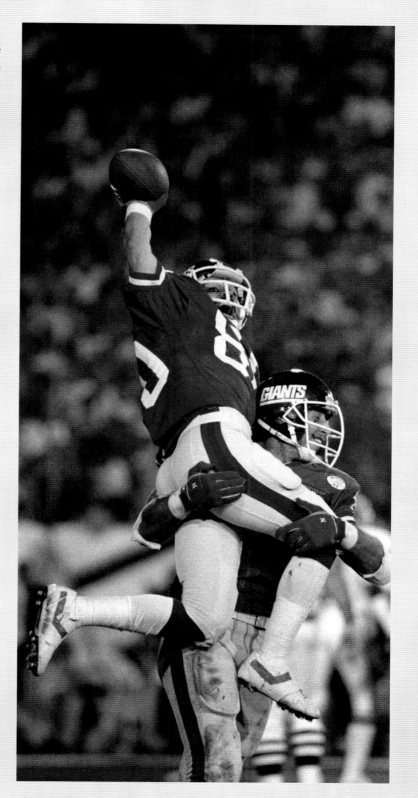

Unheralded receiver Phil McConkey's great game in the 1987 Super Bowl, including catching a deflected pass for a touchdown in fourth quarter, gave teammates like Mark Bavaro reason to celebrate. *Bettmann/Corbis*

Main: Going limp. Bronco Quarterback John Elway looks like a rag doll in the hands of linebacker Lawrence Taylor in a fourth quarter end zone play that the referee is whistling dead.
Bettmann/Corbis

Above: Rose Bowl, home of UCLA, and one of the most famous stadiums in the country, was the site of Super Bowl XXI on January 25, 1987.
Al Messerschmidt/Getty Images

Below: Giants quarterback Phil Simms (11) picked apart the Denver secondary by completing 22 out of 25 pass attempts for three touchdowns.
NFL Photos/Getty Images

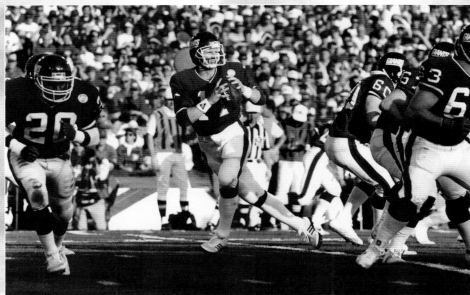

Quarterback Phil Simms (11) sets
the Giants offense against the
Denver Broncos defense.
Gin Ellis/NFL Photos/Getty Images

Running back Joe Morris runs
upfield.
Gin Ellis/NFL Photos/Getty Images

Raul Allegre (2) kicks a New York extra point.
Vernon Biever/NFL Photos/Getty Images

Ottis Anderson (24) bursts into the end zone to give the Giants a short-yardage touchdown.
Gin Ellis/NFL Photos/Getty Images

LEONARD MARSHALL

Defensive end
1983–92

Leonard Marshall was one of the largest guys on defense when he played between 1983 and 1994, weighing in at 295-pounds at times for the Giants. He also stood 6 feet 3 inches and offensive blockers did not enjoy being assigned to prevent Marshall from sacking the quarterback.

Marshall, however, enjoyed manhandling the offensive linemen who were not as strong. "All I think about is how I'm going to beat the living bleep out of this guy for 60 minutes," Marshall once said.

Marshall was a monster in the trenches, a former Louisiana State star that as a pro became an all-star player and was voted the NFL's lineman of the year for 1985. Marshall definitely had the admiration of his peers. "Leonard Marshall is a great football player," said Hall of Fame teammate Lawrence Taylor.

Not since Sam Huff did a Giant defensive player seem to so relish the collision of worlds when the ball was hiked. Marshall said he inspired himself by humming songs as he tackled. Although he did not specify his greatest musical hits list, Marshall could have jotted down the names of opposing quarterbacks who were on his greatest football hits list.

"It is scary," Marshall said of his capability to do harm. "It is intimidating. You have to find a way to diffuse your anger."

It was up to the other guys not to make Marshall too angry. Marshall recorded 79.5 sacks for the Giants before moving on to the Jets in 1993.

"They're [opponents] holding me and nobody is doing anything about it. I tell the officials about it and they tell me to mind my own business. Hey, it is my business."
—Defensive end Leonard Marshall.

The 1988 Giants did revive. Morris rushed for 1,083 yards, his third Giants' 1,000-yard year. Receiver Lionel Manuel made his presence felt with 65 catches for 1,029 yards. The team was riding a 10–5 record and was in a close race for the division title entering the season's last week, but a 27–21 loss to the Jets not only knocked the club out of first place, but knocked them out of the playoffs altogether.

By 1989, the Super Bowl victory was too far in the rearview mirror to see without craning the neck. Parcells was all about going forward, anyway, and he was determined to fix the New York flaws and problems. In 1989 the Giants finished 12–4 and won the NFC East. Simms again threw for more than 3,000 yards and the defense was repaired, holding opponents to about 100 points fewer than the offense scored. Taylor contributed 15 sacks. Defensive end Leonard Marshall, who had 15.5 sacks in 1985, terrorized quarterbacks, too. And Carl Banks was often the first man in on the tackle.

All looked peaceful on the western front—until the first-round playoff game against the Los Angeles Rams actually began. The Giants were swept out of the playoffs by a 19–13 overtime loss. The end of the season felt empty. Marshall had been superb in the Super Bowl with two sacks and a forced fumble. He was aging, but he wanted one more moment of glory with the Giants before retiring. It wasn't much to ask for, he felt. "I'd like to win another Super Bowl, maybe two," Marshall said. "I'm not greedy." He was also prepared, like Parcells, to keep on trying.

Left: Defensive tackle Leonard Marshall of the New York Giants knows who is No. 1, signaling his feelings to the world after New York out-played Denver, 39–20, in Super Bowl XXI at the Rose Bowl. *George Rose/Getty Images*

Right: New York Giants fans in the stands cope with disappointment during the Giants' 19–13 overtime loss to the Los Angeles Rams in a playoff game on January 7, 1990. *Al Messerschmidt/Getty Images*

1980s NEW YORK GIANTS YEAR BY YEAR

Year	Record
1980	4–12
1981	9–7
1982	4–5
1983	3–12–1
1984	9–7
1985	10–6
1986	14–2
1987	6–9
1988	10–6
1989	12–4

CHAPTER 8
THE 1990s
SUPER-DUPER AGAIN

(Left to right) New York Giants coach Bill Parcells, owner Wellington Mara, and NFL commissioner Paul Tagliabue, after New York beat the Buffalo Bills in Super Bowl XXV in Tampa in 1991.
John Biever/Sports Illustrated/Getty Images

There are coaches for teams and coaches that make teams. Bill Parcells succeeded at both for the Giants. He presided over a rebuilding, and re-patched the crumbling brick works when needed, so that the Giants won two Super Bowls on his watch.

The spotlight is brighter in New York than anywhere else and the city is often called the media capital of the world. Nothing occurs under the radar and everything that is reported is magnified beyond reasonable perspective.

So every time Parcells criticized a player —and he would loudly express his feelings —it seemed as if the entire world was screaming. When the Giants played well it was as if they were the greatest team in the history of the world. Parcells made his reputation as a great coach in New York between 1983 and 1990, yet half the time he was employed by the Giants it seemed he was looking elsewhere.

For a man who seemed to cope with and set aside pressure in his own way, Parcells might well have been unable to really control the outside forces. He often spoke of health issues and eventually of exploring other NFL opportunities where he could be both coach and general manager. Such conversations were sideshows, but except when there were circumstances out of his control, from player-owner labor wars to injuries, Giants teams under Parcells were winners. "Bill Parcells is the best coach the Giants ever had," said Tim Mara, the grandson of the team founder with the same name. He may have been right.

In an NFL that worked to ensure parity, the Parcells' Giants entered the 1990s with one Super Bowl victory from the end of the 1986 season, and consistent playoff teams with records of 10–6 and 12–4 in the last two years of the decade. With quarterback Phil Simms at the controls, veteran Ottis Anderson and rookie Rodney Hampton leading the ground game, and a defense still led by "Superman" Lawrence Taylor, the Giants had all of the ingredients to pocket a second Super Bowl championship.

The regular season proved optimists right. The Giants manhandled almost all opponents and by mid-

Raul Allegre (2) of the New York Giants kicks a field goal with quarterback Jeff Hostetler holding during a game at Giants Stadium. *Larry French/Getty Images*

Phil Simms (11) at the line of scrimmage during a game against the 49ers as center Bart Oates (65) makes the snap. *Anthony Neste/Time Life Pictures/Getty Images*

December were established as the best team in the league. Then, on December 15, 1990 Simms broke his foot in a game against the Buffalo Bills. When he limped to the sideline a giant questionmark was injected to the Giants' previously smoothly operating system. Backup quarterback Jeff Hostetler had been a star once upon a time at West Virginia, but had spent more than six full seasons essentially twiddling his thumbs. No one knew how he would perform.

Hostetler was on a mission to show that he had been worthy of more playing time all along, and over the last two games of the regular season he played more like a seasoned veteran than an inexperienced retread. He was cool facing the rush, completed most of his passes, and generally looked as if he had been a general waiting to take control of the army for a long time. "I've played behind a quarterback who is very talented and who had never had serious injuries," Hostetler said. "How can you prove yourself when you don't get to play? It's not been hard to convince myself that I'm not a second stringer. It's been hard to convince others."

Simms had been behind the steering wheel for 90 percent of what shaped up as potentially one of the Giants' greatest seasons of all. Abruptly, he was forced out and a guy who had been rotting on the bench for

BART OATES
Center
1985–93

Bart Oates, the 6 feet 3 inch 265-pound rookie from Brigham Young University, took just two games in 1985 to establish himself as the full-time starting center for the Giants.

Oates never budged for eight years, and few members of opposing defenses could budge him, either. Oates was a stalwart on the New York line as the team grew into a Super Bowl contender and champion.

One of the big, strong guys who make an offensive line work smoothly, Oates also had the proper temperament to play for coach Bill Parcells. When the boss shouted, which he did a lot, Oates never took it personally, seeing much of what Parcells did as a performance.

"That's one thing about playing for him," Oates said. "If you can't take it, tough. He's just your typical, cynical guy from the Northeast who never gives anybody any credit. It's all an act. He'll come into the locker room and rant and rave, but it's just like a lawyer making his closing argument—a lot of it is acting."

Like few before or after him, Oates immersed himself in helping out in the community. He served as a member of the board of directors of a foundation at a New York hospital, worked with a county youth program for troubled youths, conducted anti-drug seminars for the New Jersey State Police, and served as a spokesman for charitable organizations seeking cures for cerebral palsy and lupus. He also earned a law degree from Seton Hall.

Although the Giants won this game, 31–7 over the Rams, it was not always easy sailing for quarterback Phil Simms, here being decked by linebacker Kevin Greene of Los Angeles.
Mike Powell/Allsport/Getty Images

so long he had practically changed colors like an over-ripe piece of fruit was in his slot. Ready or not, like it or not, it was Hostetler's time.

The Giants crushed the Chicago Bears in their first playoff game, but Hampton broke his leg and was finished for the year. Then they out-lasted the San Francisco 49ers, 15–13, on five Matt Bahr field goals to advance to the Super Bowl against the AFC champion Bills. It didn't matter if Hostetler was the second coming of Sammy Baugh or not—everyone knew if the Giants were going to contain Buffalo's explosive, Jim Kelly-led offense the defense had to play at its peak.

The Giants' defense of the period played angry, aggressive and intelligently, with great athletes manning key positions. Defensive coordinator Bill Belichick, who later attained fame as the architect of the New England Patriots' multiple Super Bowl-winning teams, was the godfather of that group. Regardless of how well-stocked the positions were, the player who

constantly and routinely stepped up to create roars in The Meadowlands and fear in foes, was Lawrence Taylor. Taylor posted 10.5 sacks that season.

The 1991 Super Bowl was scheduled for Tampa. When the Giants bested the 49ers, Taylor said he was running up and down the team plane excitedly calling everyone he knew in Florida to announce, "This is L.T. We're comin' down there to kick ass."

The game was being played concurrently with the Gulf War under the direction of the first President George Bush. It was physically half a world away, but mentally omnipresent. The nation was in a patriotic frenzy and Whitney Houston's singing of the national anthem garnered tremendous attention. So did the news that terrorist threats had been made in connection with the game and that FBI sharpshooters were deployed around Tampa Stadium.

Several times over the years Taylor had said aloud—and to Parcells—that he was certain they would win at least two Super Bowls together. This was the second chance. When the pre-game hullabaloo began, Parcells told his players not to believe anything attributed to him in the media. His psychological plan was to build up the idea that Buffalo was unstoppable. The Bills were favored, at least partially because of the Giants' injuries and partially because they had scored 95 points in two playoff games, including crushing the Los Angeles Raiders, 51–3, in the AFC title game.

Naturally, Hostetler was a huge object of attention before the game. His was a fresh face on the national stage, a feel-good story of a guy living the moment after emerging from obscurity. He was digging the scene, not acting overwhelmed by it at all. "I'm sure I'll feel some butterflies before kickoff," he said, "but right

When Phil Simms got hurt, backup quarterback Jeff Hostetler rallied the Giants into the Super Bowl. Here, "Hoss" celebrates Matt Bahr's game-winning field goal against the 49ers in the NFC Championship Game in January 1991.
George Rose/Getty Images

now I feel the best I've felt the whole time since I've been starting."

The championship game was a slugfest. Buffalo did run a dangerous offense, but the Giants' secret was ball control, keeping the Bills off the field as much as possible, while New York ate up yardage and clock. Hostetler was just right as the field general, but the man of the hour was O.J. Anderson. The aging running back bashed his way to 102 yards and a touchdown. At no time did the Bills' offense look awed by the New York defense, but they were itching for more opportunities.

The game remained close and some say it was the best Super Bowl ever played. As the clock ran down, Buffalo marched toward the New York end zone. The

Bills got a last at-bat, so to speak. In one of the most famous "almosts" in NFL history, Buffalo kicker Scott Norwood attempted a 47-yard goal. The ball sailed wide right and the Giants exhaled. Final score, New York 20, Buffalo 19.

"Winning Super Bowl honors is as good as it gets," said Anderson (MVP), who had been in the league for 11 years and was 33 years old at the time. "It was important to me because of what it represented at that time, the impact the Gulf War had on it, and the magnitude of that particular game. We weren't given a chance in hell to win the Super Bowl. It's a happy ending to a long story for myself and my teammates."

The Super Bowl triumph and his own outstanding

One of the most famous misses of all time. That's how Scott Norwood's attempt at a 47-yard field goal at the end of Super Bowl XXV is viewed. The Giants held on to beat Buffalo, 20–19, to win the championship in Tampa. *Ronald C. Modra/Sports Illustrated/Getty Images*

day were savored as no other performance in Anderson's career, perhaps because of the grand stage, but also because he waited so long for the moment. In that sense, although his overall career had been much more productive, he was like Hostetler. "I said a long time ago that if I got to play in a Super Bowl, I'd be the most valuable player," Anderson said.

Awash in good feelings, the Giants' organization was proud of its second Super Bowl crown. It was a high point, and although Wellington Mara and George Young knew there were problems percolating to the surface, they also wanted to enjoy the results for a bit.

The respite did not last long. This time when Bill Parcells talked about fixing his health problems and

taking a break from coaching, he was serious. Parcells walked away and New York needed a new coach. The player least happy about the departure was probably Lawrence Taylor, who blasted team administrators for "allowing" Parcells to go.

Ray Handley had met Parcells years earlier, working as an assistant coach for him at the Air Force Academy. He had been with the Giants since 1984 as an offensive assistant coach when he was promoted to replace Parcells for the 1991 regular season. His first act dealing with the players as boss took place in a mini-camp and Handley admitted he felt "a little strange" in his new role. Unfortunately, things stayed pretty strange.

The refrigerator was full. Handley had double the

It was hard going for Buffalo running back Thurman Thomas every time he took a handoff and went up against the gang of Giants tacklers in the 1991 Super Bowl.
Getty Images

1991 SUPER BOWL XXV

Most of the ride back to the franchise's second Super Bowl was sweet and bump-free. The Giants started the 1990 season 10–0 and were on glide control on their way to finishing 13–3 as champs of the NFC East.

After fine-tuning the roster following the Super Bowl XXI victory, the Giants were ready to provide coach Bill Parcells with his second world title. The defense was superb, holding foes to 211 points. Phil Simms looked as sharp as ever.

Through 14 games Simms was supremely efficient. He threw for 2,284 yards and his touchdown to interception rate was exceptional, with 15 touchdowns against four interceptions. Things had been going too well. On December 15, with two regular-season games remaining, Simms broke a bone in his right foot in a loss to the Buffalo Bills. For the Giants it seemed that the loss of the game was not nearly as painful as the loss of Simms.

Suddenly, New York was a team of hand wringers. Parcells turned to Jeff "Hoss" Hostetler to fill in for Simms. Including reserve squad time and injuries the former West Virginia star had mostly hung around the Giants' bench for six seasons-plus. The 6 feet 3 inch, 215-pound Hostetler did not attempt more than 39 passes in any year. He was busiest serving on the scout team, impersonating the upcoming opponent's quarterback.

Throughout his entire career, until Simms went down with the injury, just about all Hostetler had done was wait, wait, wait, for a chance to play. Now he had it and Hostetler emerged as the story of the late season, the playoffs and the Super Bowl. Simms could not recover in time to play, so offensive leadership was turned over to the hungry Hostetler.

Planning on a Super Bowl return, the Giants and Hostetler had two weeks of regular-season play to adapt to the change in signal-caller. They won both of the games. Hostetler completed 47 of 87 passing attempts for three touchdowns and threw just one interception. The team felt pretty good about itself again. Hostetler performed so well that before the playoffs reporters even asked Parcells if the new guy was going to get a chance to be the starter the next year.

Predictably, Parcells blew up at the question, saying it was not something he was going to give a moment's thought to until the season ended. Not even Hostetler was thinking that far into the future. "There's no use bringing that up right now," he said. "I'm not looking at it that way. I've just taken each week one week at a time."

The cliché was accurate. The Giants were due to open the playoffs against the Chicago Bears and it was time to see how the backup would perform under pressure. Quite well, as it so happened. New York pummeled the Bears, 31–3.

That was step one. From there the Giants took on the San Francisco 49ers, the defending Super Bowl champs of Joe Montana and Jerry Rice who had wrecked the Denver Broncos 55–10, in Super Bowl XXIV. In the NFC showdown the Giants' defense was in charge and New York prevailed, 15–13, to advance to the Super Bowl.

"He waited his turn and then he made the most of it," said Matt Cavanaugh, who was Hostetler's backup by the time the Super Bowl began.

The Giants met the Buffalo Bills on January 27, 1991 in one of the most compelling of Super Bowls. These were the Bills of Jim Kelly, Thurman Thomas, and Bruce Smith, a team that reached four Super Bowls and yet walked away without a trophy. The Giants, using their backup quarterback, controlled Buffalo's dominating offense just enough to win 20–19. In the most tense finish to a Super Bowl, Bills' kicker Scott Norwood missed a potential game-winning 47-yard field goal wide right at the buzzer.

New York's winning points had come on a 21-yard field goal by Matt Bahr minutes earlier. He had booted five field goals to beat the 49ers in the NFC title game. "One of things about kicking the game-winner is that it's very much like being a golfer," Bahr said. "You know when you've hit the ball well as soon as it's off your foot."

Hostetler threw one touchdown pass. The Giants won their second Super Bowl and a career backup quarterback had led them to the title. It was the second field goal for Bahr that day, in a game that was close all of the way. Buffalo led 12–3 and the Giants led 17–12 in the third quarter.

Rather than reach down for fancy plays, the Giants physically dominated the game. On offense New York ate up 40 minutes and 33 seconds of a potential 60 minutes of possession time. That was a Super Bowl record. Without the ball Buffalo couldn't score. New York was able to hold onto the ball so long because running back Ottis Anderson bullied his way across the line of scrimmage for yard after yard. He totaled 102 yards and one touchdown and was named MVP of the game.

With Hostetler at the helm, the Giants were 5–0, counting two regular-season games and three playoff games. He shrugged off any pressure and did what the team needed. "You're not going to see a situation more dramatic than that," said Giants' center Brad Oates. "From almost virtual anonymity to stardom. It was a storybook finish for Jeff."

Hostetler's road to the limelight had been a long one. He was so far down the depth chart some years the only thing he did was hold for extra points. Occasionally, he would be called upon for weird duty.

"Before I had thrown my first NFL pass, I had caught one," Hostetler said. "I had carried the ball. And I had blocked a punt. Not many quarterbacks can say that."

And not many quarterbacks can say that they led a team to a Super Bowl championship.

Left: A ticket for Super Bowl XXV.
NFL Photos/Getty Images

Above: The New York Giants take the field for the start of Super Bowl XXV against the Buffalo Bills at Tampa Stadium in Tampa, Florida, in January 1991.
Mike Powell/Getty Images

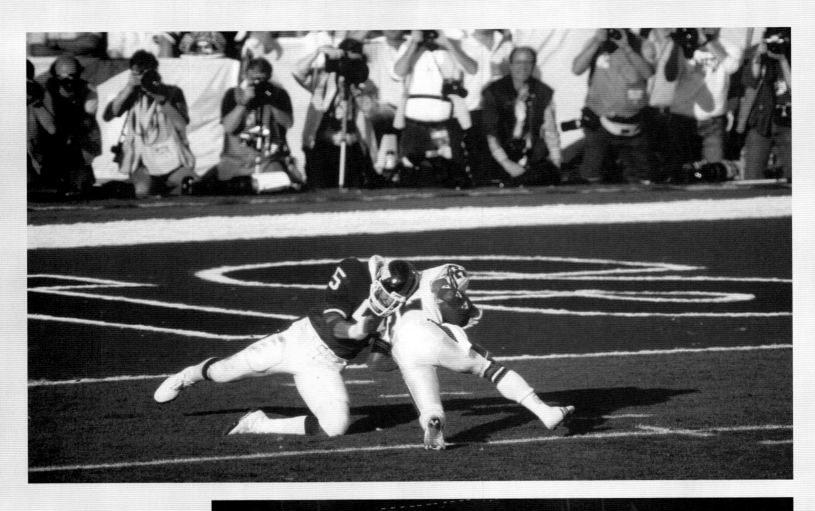

New York's Gary Reasons defends the end zone against the Buffalo Bills during Super Bowl XXV.
Focus on Sport/Getty Images

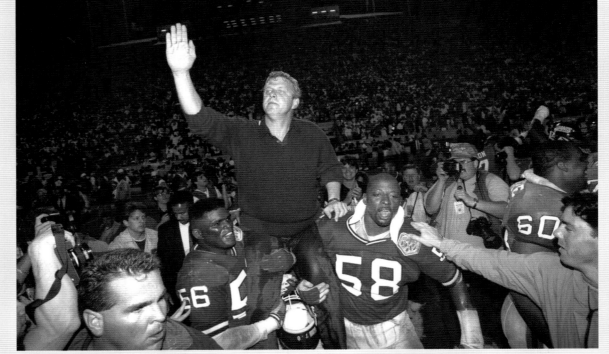

In time-honored tradition, Giants players Lawrence Taylor (56), and Carl Banks (58) parade coach Bill Parcells around on their shoulders after defeating the Bills.
Mike Powell/Getty Images

Right: Super Bowl XXV Program cover.
NFL Photos/Getty Images

Giants wide receiver Stephen Baker catches a 14-yard touchdown pass in front of Buffalo Bills cornerback Nate Odomes during Super Bowl XXV.
NFL Photos/Getty Images

"**The New York press didn't like him because he wouldn't talk to them, but he was actually very fair about that. He didn't talk to me for two years, either.**"
—*General manager George Young on enigmatic tight end Zeke Mowatt.*

talent needed at some positions. He just had to make the right personnel decision. Would he start Phil Simms at quarterback again or give the Super Bowl winner, Jeff Hostetler, a chance? Would he allow Rodney Hampton to blossom in his second season, or could workhorse Ottis Anderson still play every day?

The running back situation was resolved quickly enough in training camp. Hampton was a young prospect coming into his own and he was ready to fly. Anderson's best years were behind him and he was best used for spot duty. Hampton was the man.

Quarterback controversies are the most common important personnel matters that drive coaches batty. The quarterback is the most visible player on the field, playing the most important position. Historically, it is also said that players do not lose their starting jobs because of injury. Simms had been playing just about the best football of his life when he got hurt during the Super Bowl stretch run. Much to Simms' surprise, Handley threw open the job. "It's a carnival," Simms said at training camp at Farleigh Dickinson University. "People think it's funny. Do you really think they care who plays? I think the average fan really doesn't care who's under the helmet —just go out there and make us happy."

Ultimately, Handley tapped Hostetler on the shoulder and told him he was going to be the main guy in 1991. Hostetler had waited a long time to hear that news. Although the thrower completed 62.8 percent of his passes in 12 games, Hostetler never ignited things in the playoffs. He threw just five touchdown passes against four interceptions as the offense slumbered. Starter or no starter, Simms contributed eight touchdown passes in six games. The defense faltered and the Giants went from champions to 8–8 post-season TV watchers.

The next year, when the Giants finished 6–10 under Handley, it was adios Ray. A major contributing factor to the disintegration was the serious injury suffered by Lawrence Taylor. Taylor had toyed with the idea of retirement at the end of the 1992 season, but when he tore his right Achilles tendon on November 8 in a game against the Green Bay Packers, many believed he would have no choice.

Opposite: It used to be that winning football coaches got thrown in the shower. In recent years, they get a Gatorade bath, and so coach Bill Parcells was drenched by his players as the last seconds ticked off the clock in Super Bowl XXV. *Bettmann/Corbis*

Above: An aerial view of the packed house at Super Bowl XXV on January 27, 1991, in Tampa. The New York Giants defeated the Buffalo Bills before 73,813 fans at Tampa Stadium. *Al Messerschmidt/NFL Photos/Getty Images*

Above left: Running back Ottis Anderson was almost unstoppable for the Giants in their heart-stopping 20–19 victory over the Buffalo Bills during Super Bowl XXV. *George Rose/Getty Images*

Below left: Quarterback Jeff Hostetler just gets this pass away for the Giants as he is being hit by Bills linebacker Cornelius Bennett during Super Bowl XXV. *Rick Stewart/Getty Images*

Below: Just doing his job. Giants linebacker Carl Banks (58) dives to tackle Buffalo wide receiver Andre Reed (83) in the second quarter of Super Bowl XXV at Tampa Stadium on January 27, 1991. *George Rose/Getty Images*

"I didn't know that I'd lost it."
—Quarterback Phil Simms, responding to a question on whether or not he thought he would regain his starter's job.

Taylor jumped in the air and got a hand on a Brett Favre pass. Thinking he could catch it for an interception Taylor didn't see a Packer about to hit him. As he lay on the ground he said it felt as if his ankle was on fire. He began to cry and shouted, "My career is over!" At first Taylor refused to be taken off the field on a cart, but he couldn't walk and had to accept the ride. Taylor did not want to end his career as a wounded player. So he endured a painful and lengthy rehabilitation in order to be available for the 1993 season and go out on his own terms.

The Giants were in the market for another coach and they went after a bigger NFL name. Dan Reeves, who as a player had been an overachieving running back for the Dallas Cowboys, always seeming to make clutch plays, and had taken the Denver Broncos to three Super Bowls, topped the list. Reeves took over for 1993 and restored some dignity. The Giants went 11–5 in the regular season and won a playoff game over Minnesota before being slaughtered, 44–3, in the next round by San Francisco.

Dignity was at issue in Taylor's final campaign. He returned strong enough and healthy enough to make 36 tackles and add six sacks to his final total of 132.5. It was not his finest season, but neither did Taylor limp away. His last game was the wipeout on January 15,

Above: Linebacker Lawrence Taylor yells as he is looked at on the turf after injuring his right Achilles' tendon when he blocked a pass by Green Bay Packers quarterback Brett Favre in a November 1992 game that could have ended his career. Taylor made a one-year comeback after healing the injury.
Mark D. Phillips/AFP/Getty Images

Left: Quarterback Phil Simms watches the action next to Giants coach Ray Handley during an October 1992 game against the Los Angeles Raiders at Los Angeles Memorial Coliseum. *Andy Hayt/Getty Images*

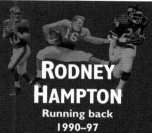

RODNEY HAMPTON
Running back
1990–97

When the Giants picked 5 feet 11 inch, 221-pounds Rodney Hampton out of Georgia with their No. 1 selection in the 1990 draft, they expected big things. He delivered. Although injuries cut short his career, in eight seasons he rushed for a then-team record 6,897 yards and cracked the 1,000-yard barrier five times. Hampton scored 14 touchdowns in 1992 and four times also caught at least 24 passes.

Hampton became established as one of the top runners in the league and long-time star Ottis Anderson was proud to see it. "I kind of brought him up, in a pro football sense," Anderson said. "Bill (Parcells) asked me to take him under my wing, show him the ropes, tell him how to do things, how to act, what was expected."

Hampton, whose career-high rushing game was 187 yards against Dallas in 1995, still ranks near the top of the Giants all-time rushing play lists. His four touchdowns in a game against New Orleans in 1995 is the team record.

At the end of his career, after knee surgery slowed him, Hampton was still popular with New York fans. When he returned to the lineup after a long absence, spectators at The Meadowlands chanted, "Rod-ney! Rod-ney!"

Unable to make the same types of cuts from the backfield as he had in his prime, in 1997 Hampton volunteered to play another position. "I can adapt to any situation," he said. "Different coaches, different situations. That's the one good thing about me."

Above: Giants running back Rodney Hampton races down the sideline alongside New Orleans Saints safety Vince Buck in the first quarter of their September 1995 game at Giants Stadium in East Rutherford, New Jersey. Hampton had 149 yards rushing and four touchdowns as the Giants won 45–29. *Stan Honda/AFP/Getty Images*

Below: Quarterbacks Jeff Hostetler (15), Phil Simms (11), and Jeff Rutledge (17) listen to coach Bill Parcells on the sideline against the Los Angeles Rams during a 1989 game in California. *NFL Photos/Getty Images*

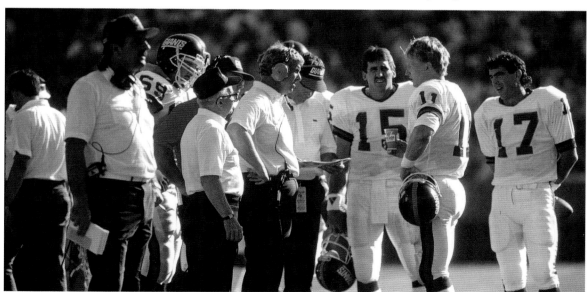

50 percent up for sale

From the moment the Giants were founded by bookmaker Tim Mara in 1925, until the Super Bowl championship of January 1991, the team remained solely in the hands of the Mara family. It was the family business.

Tim Mara turned over the daily operations to his sons Jack and Wellington decades earlier when they were boys. When Tim died, the team was owned 50-50 by his sons. When Jack died, his ownership stake passed into the hands of his son, also named Tim. From the late 1970s, the relationship between Wellington and Tim deteriorated, and this affected Giants' business.

Their disputes degenerated into a feud and they could not even agree on the hiring of a new coach. In 1978, NFL Commissioner Pete Rozelle intervened and ordered the men to clean up the shop. He brokered the arrangement by which George Young became general manager.

Less than two months after the Giants won Super Bowl XXV over the Buffalo Bills in Tampa, Florida, Tim Mara finalized the sale of his share of the team, or 50 percent, to Robert Tisch, a New York millionaire and the former postmaster general, for $75 million.

The deal marked the end of an era of 100 percent family ownership. Wellington Mara retained his 50 percent, but the parting with his nephew (they were not speaking) was bitter and sad. Wellington and Tisch hit it off well, and the new partnership worked out fine for the team.

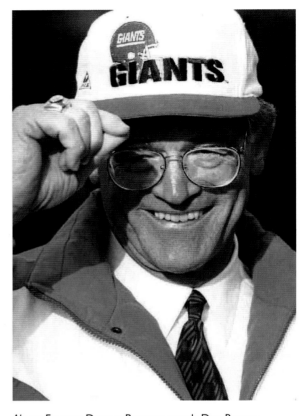

Above: Former Denver Broncos coach Dan Reeves advertises his new affiliation by putting on a team cap after being named head coach of the New York Giants on January 26, 1993.
Mark D. Phillips/AFP/Getty Images

Below: Giants quarterback Phil Simms in action against the Washington Redskins in 1993.
Damian Strohmeyer/Sports Illustrated/Getty Images

1994 in that playoff defeat to the 49ers. "I've been to the Super Bowl, I've been to the playoffs, I've been able to do things that not a lot of people have done," Taylor said. "I've been a dominant force and I've earned the respect of players and people in general around the country. I deserve the rest."

Between Jeff Hostetler and injuries, it was unlikely that anyone ever believed Phil Simms would become the full-time Giants' starting quarterback again, but in 1993 he did just that under Reeves. It was a last hurrah for a player who turned 39 during the season. Simms played in all 16 games, completed 61.8 percent of his passes for 3,038 yards and 15 touchdowns. It was a season worthy of kudos.

An elbow injury during the 1992 season looked as if it had finished Simms. He played in just four games and when a sportswriter asked that if by writing that Simms had thrown his last pass for the Giants he would be wrong, Simms did not discourage the prose.

"No, you can go ahead and write that," Simms said. "It's probably the truth." Instead, just like Taylor, he recovered and got himself healthy enough to start again. "They'll probably have to tear this uniform off me someday," Simms said.

He could not have imagined how close to the truth that observation was. After his very solid 1993 performance Simms wanted to play one more year. However, due to salary cap considerations the Giants cut him loose. The unexpected parting meant that Simms left with bitterness over the way he had been treated. After 14 seasons, Simms retired with 199 touchdown passes.

There was a lot of transition. Taylor retired. Simms retired. Carl Banks went to the Redskins in 1993. Pepper Johnson went to Cleveland in 1993. Leonard Marshall went to the Jets in 1993.

One of the most exciting, fresh, all-around players added to the Giants' roster was Dave Meggett. An explosive runner, the 5 feet 7 inches, 190-pounds Meggett was drafted in the fifth round in 1989. For six years he served as a deadly weapon for the Giants in several roles. Meggett ran back punts and kickoffs and handled the ball out of the backfield. He was at his

> **"To see some guys play hard three plays out of 54, and you know that person is better than that, it's very frustrating."**
> **—Linebacker Pepper Johnson calling out his teammates.**

most dangerous in the open field, running back at least one punt for a touchdown in five seasons.

Meggett had been a high school quarterback. He said he chose that role because the school in Charleston, South Carolina, was loaded with skilled players at other positions. As a freshman in college, he played defensive back for Morgan State before transferring to Towson State. Meggett made the Pro Bowl quickly and his value was measured by his versatility and his all-purpose yards. He went from making $75,000 in salary to more than $1 million a year, something that flabbergasted him. "You've got to be more mature about a whole lot of things," Meggett said. "You've got to be more responsible as far as temptation is concerned. I try to be discreet about a

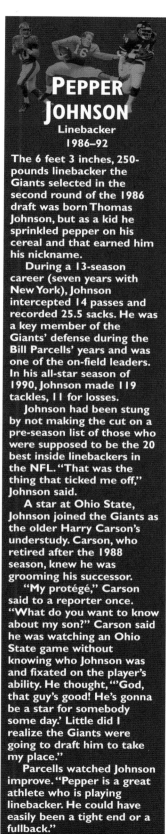

PEPPER JOHNSON
Linebacker
1986–92

The 6 feet 3 inches, 250-pounds linebacker the Giants selected in the second round of the 1986 draft was born Thomas Johnson, but as a kid he sprinkled pepper on his cereal and that earned him his nickname.

During a 13-season career (seven years with New York), Johnson intercepted 14 passes and recorded 25.5 sacks. He was a key member of the Giants' defense during the Bill Parcells' years and was one of the on-field leaders. In his all-star season of 1990, Johnson made 119 tackles, 11 for losses.

Johnson had been stung by not making the cut on a pre-season list of those who were supposed to be the 20 best inside linebackers in the NFL. "That was the thing that ticked me off," Johnson said.

A star at Ohio State, Johnson joined the Giants as the older Harry Carson's understudy. Carson, who retired after the 1988 season, knew he was grooming his successor.

"My protégé," Carson said to a reporter once. "What do you want to know about my son?" Carson said he was watching an Ohio State game without knowing who Johnson was and fixated on the player's ability. He thought, "'God, that guy's good! He's gonna be a star for somebody some day.' Little did I realize the Giants were going to draft him to take my place."

Parcells watched Johnson improve. "Pepper is a great athlete who is playing linebacker. He could have easily been a tight end or a fullback."

Pepper Johnson (52) emerged as one of the many stars who roamed the middle of the defense for the New York Giants through the years, holding down a linebacker spot from 1986 to 1992.
NFL Photos/Getty Images

whole lot of things that I do. I have to because of the fact that whatever I do it's going to be zeroed in on because I'm zeroed in on Sundays."

Meggett averaged 12.7 yards per punt return in 1989. He caught 50 passes in 1991. He rushed for 329 yards in 1993. The object of the game was just to get the ball into Meggett's hands some way. "When we've asked him to do something he's always come through,"

1990s Key Draft Picks

1990   Rodney Hampton, running back, *first round*
Mike Fox, defensive end, *second round*

1991   Corey Miller, linebacker, *sixth round*

1992   Phillippi Sparks, cornerback, *second round*
Aaron Pierce, tight end, *third round*
Keith Hamilton, defensive tackle, *fourth round*
Kent Graham, quarterback, *eighth round*
Dave Brown, quarterback, *supplemental draft*

1993   Michael Strahan, defensive end, *second round*
Marcus Buckley, linebacker, *third round*
Jessie Armstead, linebacker, *eighth round*

1994   Tommy Lewis, receiver, *first round*
Thomas Randolph, cornerback, *second round*
Jason Sehorn, safety, *second round*

1995   Tyrone Wheatley, running back, *first round*
Scott Gragg, tackle, *second round*

1996   Cedric Jones, defensive end, *first round*
Amani Toomer, receiver, *second round*
Roman Oben, tackle, *third round*
Danny Kanell, quarterback, *fourth round*

1997   Ike Hilliard, receiver, *first round*
Tiki Barber, running back, *second round*
Brad Maynard, punter, *third round*

1998   Shaun Williams, safety, *first round*
Joe Jurevicius, receiver, *second round*

1999   Luke Petitgout, tackle, *first round*

Giants' coach Dan Reeves said.

Meggett added an extra dimension to the Giants' production. Fans always get revved up by a touchdown return and the fact that Meggett was a smaller than normal football ball of fire just added to his appeal. "He's a real weapon," said Bill Parcells, who needed to be convinced. "One of those rare players who always seem to be on the verge of making a big play."

Despite his moment in the sun, Hostetler was an ex-Giant by 1993 when he was off to the Raiders. And with Simms in retirement, the Giants entered a period where quarterback juggling was the latest midway game. Dave Brown was drafted in 1992 out of Duke, and was not asked to do anything more taxing than watch film until 1994.

For three seasons Brown, at 6 feet 5 inches and 220-pounds, looked the part of modern-day quarterback. He ran up 2,536, 2,814, and 2,412 yards

Dave Meggett, who was an all-purpose yard-gainer for the Giants as a running back and kick returner, on the sidelines during a 1993 game against the Washington Redskins. *Tom Berg/NFL Photos/Getty Images*

Above: Touchdown! Giants receiver Amani Toomer lunges into the end zone for a score as he shakes off coverage from Dallas Cowboys defender Ken Hamlin during the January 2008 playoff game won by New York, 21–17. *Michael Ainsworth/Dallas Morning News/Corbis*

Below: Defensive Back Jason Sehorn was selected by the Giants in the second round of the 1994 draft. He went on to lead the team in interceptions in 1996 and 1997. *Geiger Kraig/Corbis Sygma*

in a row, but in two of his three starting seasons Brown threw more interceptions than touchdowns. The Giants did not see him as a long-term answer.

The draft did offer long-term answers in key positions, though. Amani Toomer was drafted with the No. 2 pick in 1996 out of Michigan, and more than a decade later is still a fixture in the Giants' lineup. The wide receiver was eased into the lineup. He caught just one pass as a rookie and his production climbed only incrementally. But in 1999 Toomer caught 79 passes for 1,183 yards. He definitely belonged.

"They had no plans for me," Toomer said. "The only thing that kept me active and kept me playing was the fact that I returned punts." He tried to maintain his confidence and periodically would tease quarterback Kent Graham, most of the time the backup for Brown, to look for him on routes. "Throw me the ball," Toomer teased Graham. "I'll make you famous." As it turned out, the joking comment might have come true. Only Graham was playing elsewhere by the time Toomer became a regular.

As some prominent Giants on defense began showing their age, the team plucked replacements in the draft. In 1993, New York grabbed cornerback Jason Sehorn out of the University of Southern California.

The lightning fast and athletic Sehorn was an anomaly, at one time the only Caucasian cornerback in the NFL. Teammates nicknamed him "Species" for his athleticism. Sehorn, who was married to actress Angie Harmon, proposed to her on *The Tonight Show* with Jay Leno. Sehorn was briefly an actor, but settled in as a TV football commentator after retiring in 2004.

Sehorn, however, wasn't even the best defensive player the Giants selected in the 1993 draft. A higher pick was 6 feet 4 inches, 280-pounds Texas Southern defensive end Michael Strahan. Strahan was the new Lawrence Taylor, the run-stopping, sack-creating immovable object of the defense. He was on his way to a career during which he would eclipse Taylor's team records for lifetime sacks with 141.5, and for a season with 22.5. The season mark was a league record, too. He was a disrupter, a defensive force, like the best of his predecessors, who had to be accounted for in the game plan by opposing coaches.

It did not take very many years before other teams were double-teaming Strahan every time he lined up. It was a self-preservation move, an effort to keep their quarterbacks alive and ambulatory a little bit longer. "I've seen tackle-guard, tackle-tight end, tackle-back, tight end-back, and worst of all, tackle-tight end-back," Strahan said. "The game plans are different. I'm not getting as much action as far as the run. I kind of enjoy playing the run, so it takes a lot of self-control to not

> **"I didn't hate it (New York City). I was scared of it. The only time I left my room was when somebody came to pick me up."**
> —*Defensive end Michael Strahan, after being drafted in the second round out of Texas Southern in 1993.*

get angry when that gets taken away from you. I guess it's a matter of respect."

New York also wanted to instill such a sense of foreboding into opposing defenses, too, and the 1997 selection of Tiki Barber in the draft transformed the offense. Barber, who played for the University of Virginia alongside his identical twin brother Ronde (who joined Tampa Bay as a defensive back), became the Giants' greatest running back of all time.

Articulate, friendly, speedy and powerful, Barber was a force on the field and a popular face off of it in a celebrity-crazed New York. He had a wide smile and a shaved head and was instantly recognizable. The Giants had never had such an all-around talent as Attim Kiambu Hakeem-ah "Tiki" Barber at their disposal. At 5 feet 10 inches and 205-pounds Barber could rip off big runs and catch passes with incredible shiftiness. "He has got some burst and some wiggle to

Giants running back Tiki Barber (21) breaks free from Eagles defender Damon Moore (43) for a 23-yard run during a game at Philadelphia in September 2000. *Tim Shaffer/ Reuters/Corbis*

him," coach Jim Fassel said early in Barber's career.

Floundering along, perpetually searching for a quarterback who could compare favorably to Phil Simms, the Giants made it to the end of the decade before arriving at a controversial solution. General manager Ernie Accorsi, who took over from George Young in 1998, signed free agent quarterback Kerry Collins to a four-year, $16.9-million deal.

Collins could have modeled for sculptures as the fantasy-sized quarterback. He stood 6 feet 5 inches and weighed 240-pounds, and had a great pedigree, starring for Joe Paterno at Penn State. The No. 1 pick of the Carolina Panthers in 1995, Collins was thrown to the wolves as a rookie. In one of the riskier experiments of the era, the Panthers made him a starter immediately.

Over the next several years Collins showed flashes of greatness and many lapses in judgment. That was just on the field. Off the field, a beleaguered Collins was battling alcoholism, injuries that included a broken jaw, and he made an ill-advised statement that was taken for racism and turned teammates against him. When the Giants scooped up Collins, he had just one true plus on his pro resume. He had led the Panthers to a conference championship game as a fledgling expansion team.

Giants' fans and players were otherwise being asked to take Collins on faith, being told he had learned from his mistakes, overcome his rocky beginning, and would now show off his God-given talent. "You look at the big picture," Accorsi said.

The Giants' big picture was looking for more than a band-aid, however. Reeves was ousted after his 6–10 record in the 1996 season and Jim Fassel was named the new coach. Fassel had a deep background in college coaching and had been the offensive coordinator for the Oakland Raiders, Denver Broncos and the Arizona Cardinals before the Giants hired him as head coach. Fassel produced immediately, with a 10–5–1 record in 1997. There were struggles in 1998 (8–8) and 1999 (7–9), but the Giants were soon remade into contenders after that down period.

After a shaky start with New York, Collins played some of the best football of his life. He was after a fresh beginning and while few people would choose the limelight of New York, with its demanding fans and insistent tabloid media for a comeback, Collins felt he could handle things. In 1999, during his first season with the Giants, Collins figured he was in the right place at the right time. "I feel like I'm a completely different person than I was a year ago at this time," he said. "I feel like I've come full circle."

So had the Giants.

1990s NEW YORK GIANTS YEAR BY YEAR

Year	Record
1990	13–3
1991	8–8
1992	6–10
1993	11–5
1994	9–7
1995	5–11
1996	6–10
1997	10–5–1
1998	8–8
1999	7–9

Quarterback Kerry Collins surprised fans by claiming the first-string job and leading the Giants into Super Bowl XXXV in 2000.
Geiger Kraig/Corbis Sygma

New York Giants coach Jim Fassel checks out the field at the Meadowlands Complex in September 1997.
Al Messerschmidt/Getty Images

THE 2000s
UNEXPECTED GIFTS

For a while, Jim Fassel was the toast of the town. After he succeeded Dan Reeves as coach, and after the Kerry Collins-at-quarterback-reclamation-project succeeded, the Giants worked their way into a Super Bowl to start the 21st century.

Riding Collins' big arm, a hungry defense, and Tiki Barber's slick ball-carrying, the Giants completed the 2000 regular season with a 12–4 mark, an NFC East divisional championship, and home-field advantage in the playoffs.

The Giants kept the Philadelphia Eagles under control and topped them 20–10, in the first round of the playoffs, which set up a showdown with the Minnesota Vikings. The Vikings had pieced together their most explosive offensive season in team history and one of the highest scoring and demoralizing

Right: Return man Ron Dixon (86) races 97 yards on the opening kickoff for a touchdown during the Giants' 20–10 playoff victory over the Philadelphia Eagles in January 2001.
Jim Turner/NFL Photos/Getty Images

Opposite above: Looking good in blue, Giants quarterback Kerry Collins fades back to pass during a 2001 playoff game against the Minnesota Vikings.
Al Messerschmidt/Getty Images

Opposite below: Quarterback Kerry Collins calls the signals during the 2001 NFC Championship Game at the Meadowlands.
Al Messerschmidt/Getty Images

"When I think 'thunder,' I send in Ron (Dayne) and when I think 'lightning,' I send in Tiki (Barber)."
—*Offensive coordinator Sean Payton.*

offenses in league history. The major question seemed not so much whether or not the Giants could win the game, but what they could do to keep from being blown out.

The absolute, thorough 41–0 dismantling of Minnesota was one of the most unexpected massacres in NFL annals. Barber, who broke his arm late in the regular season, was playing with a soft cast. Before the Minnesota smackdown, he dreamed up a motivational plan for his teammates.

Randy Moss was the leading offensive weapon in the Vikings' arsenal. He was a superb receiver, who also talked a good game. Barber bought a Moss replica team jersey, attached a Super Bowl logo to it and then scrawled a quote from former President Ulysses S. Grant on it reading, "The art of war is simple enough. Find out where your enemy is. Get to him as soon as you can. Strike at him as hard as you can and keep moving on." As far as battle plans go, even if the Giants didn't borrow maps and charts from Grant's days as a Union Civil War general, they brought the attack to the Vikings hard.

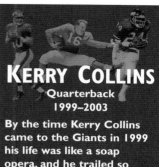

KERRY COLLINS
Quarterback
1999–2003

By the time Kerry Collins came to the Giants in 1999 his life was like a soap opera, and he trailed so much baggage he could have been a spokesman for North American Van Lines.

It was not a pretty picture. Collins had been an all-star quarterback for Penn State, but in what was probably an ill-advised plan, the expanding Carolina Panthers decided they and Collins would grow together and made him the starter as a rookie in 1995.

Collins was alternately good and bad. His tribulations were compounded, though, by what later was revealed as a harsh battle with alcoholism. At times Collins was called a quitter and was accused of making a racist statement. By the time the Giants acquired the 6 feet 5 inch, 240-pound player, NFL experts saw him as a bust.

Instead, after coping successfully with his personal problems, and under the guidance of coach Jim Fassel, Collins was rejuvenated. He led the Giants to a 12-4 season in 2000 and into the Super Bowl. In 2002. He threw for 4,073 yards, the team record for a single season, and in five seasons ranked third on the all-time passing yardage list behind only Phil Simms and Charlie Conerly. "I got a tremendous opportunity here in a lot of ways," Collins said, "not only from a football standpoint, but from a personal standpoint, to get my life back in order. I owe them a lot for that."

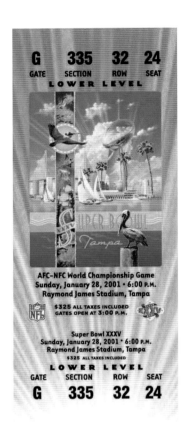

A prized ticket for Super Bowl XXXV.
NFL Photos/Getty Images

Although the Giants had performed well enough to win 12 games and sweep through the early rounds of the playoffs, they had not always looked like a coolly operating machine. There had been criticism of their failings. Taking exception to that season-long picking at the Giants, owner Wellington Mara tweaked critics after New York pummeled Minnesota. "Today we proved that we're the worst team to ever win the National Football Conference championship," Mara said. "I'm happy to say that in two weeks we're going to try to become the worst team ever to win the Super Bowl."

During the press conferences leading up to the big game, Collins' turnaround from the scrap heap to the Super Bowl and all of his life's difficulties were dissected. Collins was composed and revealing as he outlined his problems with alcohol, starting when he was 13 and evolving into binge drinking. "My drinking wasn't every day, or every other day," he said. "But when I drank, I didn't stop. That loss of control is the main crux of my alcohol dependency. Confusion, angst and anger came to the fore. Alcohol fueled it. I am proud to be standing here. I'm proud of where I've been and I'm proud of where I'm going."

Alas, for the Giants, two weeks later, in contrast to Mara's hopes, they were going nowhere, creamed by the Baltimore Ravens, 34–7 in Super Bowl XXXV. The Ravens boasted of fielding the best defense ever, and if that impossible-to-gauge statement was accurate, at the least they demonstrated that their defense was the king of the turf at the time.

As seemed to happen regularly with the Giants, as soon as they reached the Super Bowl, things soured quickly. The 2001 season in no way resembled the magical ride of 2000. New York finished a disappointing 7-9. Howard Cross, an institution at tight end after 13 seasons, retired with 201 catches.

Focus wasn't on the Giants as much that season, however. Everything changed in America because of the September 11, 2001, terrorist attacks. With the

Giants running back Tiki Barber fights off defensive back Tony Parrish during a 39–38 loss to the San Francisco 49ers in the 2003 NFC Wild Card Playoff.
Joseph Patronite/NFL Photos/Getty Images

Coach Tom Coughlin watches from the sideline during a 23–22 loss to the Cincinnati Bengals on December 26, 2004, at Paul Brown Stadium in Cincinnati.
Scott Boehm/Getty Images

ny

Notable Giants' Statistics, 2000–08

Tiki Barber's 1,000-yard Seasons

2000	1,006
2002	1,387
2003	1,216
2004	1,518
2005	1,860
2006	1,662

Eli Manning's 300-yard Games

2005	352 vs. San Diego
2005	344 vs. Seattle
2006	312 vs. Philadelphia
2006	371 vs. Philadelphia
2007	312 vs. Philadelphia
2007	303 vs. Atlanta

70-Catch Seasons

2000	78	Amani Toomer
2000	70	Tiki Barber
2001	72	Amani Toomer
2001	72	Tiki Barber
2002	82	Amani Toomer
2002	74	Jeremy Shockey
2005	76	Plaxico Burress
2007	70	Plaxico Burress

deaths of thousands, and fear and depression engulfing the city at the World Trade Center twin towers, New York was a deeply wounded place. Football was played, but was not nearly as important.

The Giants played a Monday night game in Denver the evening before the attacks, losing to the Broncos, 31-20. The NFL suspended the next week's games while the nation caught its breath and tried to begin a long recovery process. That meant the Giants did not play again until September 23, in Kansas City, and did not play again at home until September 30, against New Orleans.

Giants' players, like other athletes, actors and celebrities, volunteered to help firefighters and rescue workers by bringing them food and drink and simply trying to cheer people up. The scene at all professional sporting events highlighted patriotism, sometimes in the forceful, extra singing of "God Bless America" in addition to the national anthem. It was a tumultuous time when football shrunk in importance and the Giants' home city was distracted by significantly weightier matters.

Giants' owner Wellington Mara had been with the team on December 7, 1941, when Pearl Harbor was bombed. He was with the team on November 22, 1963, when President John F. Kennedy was assassinated, and he was still with the team when terrorists crashed airplanes into the World Trade

Above: Quarterback Eli Manning passes during a January 2009 game against the Philadelphia Eagles.
Drew Hallowell/Getty Images

Center another 38 years later. JFK was murdered on a Friday and the NFL did not cancel its weekend games. It had been harshly criticized for that lack of sensitivity. Mara remembered that well and he had no desire to see the NFL make the same mistake twice. "The same feeling is here," Mara said after 9/11, in stating that the games should not be played. "The players are human, especially our players and the Jets, because they can just look out and see that smoke."

Bouncing back in 2002, the year Collins passed for his team a record 4,073 yards, New York finished 10–6, good enough for the playoffs. In a tense, dramatic game, the Giants fell in the first round to the San Francisco 49ers, 39–38. That was the last high point of the Fassel reign. The next season it was as if all the nuts and bolts rusted at once. The Giants were out-scored 387–243, they went 1–7 in home games, and finished 4–12.

Fassel was out and the mess was not going to be sopped up with a single towel, as former Jacksonville Jaguars coach Tom Coughlin discovered in his 6–10 first season. That made for a long 2004. There was also

considerable friction between Coughlin and the press and some players. Coughlin was a do-it-my-way-or-hit-the-highway type. He had an abundance of rules and intended to stick with them. Some players felt they were being treated like high schoolers instead of grown men and bristled.

Things quieted down when the Giants finished 11–5 in 2005 and qualified for the playoffs once more. Kicker Jay Feely set a team record with 148 points. Even though New York was trampled 23–0, by Carolina, there was improvement for the franchise in an otherwise sad season.

On October 25, 2005, Wellington Mara, face of the club for decades, and with the team from its inception, died of cancer at age 89. He had been involved with the team since 1925, or since he was a 9-year-old boy. He had out-lasted his father and brother, and unfortunately the nephew that sold his 50 percent of the team.

Mara had been a pioneer owner when the Giants were a pioneer team in the NFL in the days of leather helmets and limited forward passing. He had helped shepherd his team through times of challenge and

Widow Ann (wearing sunglasses) is flanked by her sons John (left) and Chris (right) and other family members, as Wellington Mara's casket is carried into St. Patrick's Cathedral for a funeral mass on October 28, 2005, in New York City. Mara, who was 89 when he died, had owned the Giants since 1930.
Stephen Chernin/Getty Images

Above: Tight end Jeremy Shockey lands on his neck after catching a pass against the Chicago Bears at Soldier Field in December 2007. *Scott Boehm/Getty Images*

Below: Derrick Pope of the Miami Dolphins tackles Giants tight end Jeremy Shockey during the NFL Bridgestone International Series game at Wembley Stadium on October 28, 2007, in London, England. This was the first-ever regular-season NFL game to be played outside of the United States. *Al Bello/Getty Images*

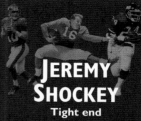

JEREMY SHOCKEY

Tight end
2002–2007

The big tight end lived up to his name. Jeremy Shockey provided shocks on more than one front when he joined the Giants in 2002 as a No. 1 draft pick out of the University of Miami.

The first shock was how good Shockey was right away. The 6 feet 5 inches, 251-pounds bruiser made All-Pro as a rookie and won the rookie-of-the-year award. The second shock was how he seemed to say anything that came to mind. Sometimes he was refreshingly humorous. Sometimes he was too candid for his own good, with criticism of teammates and coaches.

Shockey was big, strong and swift, a lethal combination given that he also had good hands. He was a dangerous new weapon in the Giants' arsenal and was a four-time Pro Bowl selection by 2006. However, relations between Shockey and the front office, from new general manager Jerry Reese to coach Tom Coughlin, grew tenser. During the 2006 season an upset Shockey told reporters after a loss to Seattle, "We got outplayed and we got out-coached. Write that down." The outburst did not score Shockey any style points with his team.

Not even a five-year contract for $26.4 million, giving Shockey's the richest payout for his position, smoothed the situation and when Shockey battled injuries and the Giants won the Super Bowl during the 2007 season he became expendable and was traded to the New Orleans Saints for two 2009 draft picks.

Shockey gathered 371 passes and scored 27 touchdowns for the Giants.

MICHAEL STRAHAN

**Defensive end
1993–2007**

The gap-toothed smile, the half-inch wide space in the middle of his mouth, is what New York fans will remember when they think of Michael Strahan and his sure-to-be-Hall-of-Fame career as much as they will recall his team record 141.5 sacks.

Heck, Strahan, the 6 feet 4 inches, 280-pounds defensive end, probably smiled at quarterbacks as he crunched them. Strahan, who spent 15 seasons in a New York uniform, culminating with the 2008 Super Bowl title, owns the single-season NFL record for sacks with 22.5. "He put the team above self and that's the greatest thing he did," said Giants' coach Tom Coughlin.

One of the most dominating defenders of his time, Strahan gave the Giants' defense a fresh identity when he was drafted immediately after Lawrence Taylor retired in 1992. As a small-school star from Texas Southern, no one could predict that Strahan would become the superstar he developed into.

Strahan nearly retired one season sooner, but was tremendously glad he stuck it out and was part of the Super Bowl champions' team. After waiting years for a chance to win it all (following a loss in 2001), Strahan's biggest test getting ready for the big game against the New England Patriots, was making game day go by. "It was the longest day of my career," he said. "I started clock-watching...and did things that I hoped would eat up large amounts of time."

And then, with the victory, it became the most satisfying day of Strahan's career.

Showing his trademark gap-toothed grin, Giants defensive end Michael Strahan looks on before a 2006 game against the Eagles at Lincoln Financial Field in Philadelphia. *Jamie Squire/Getty Images*

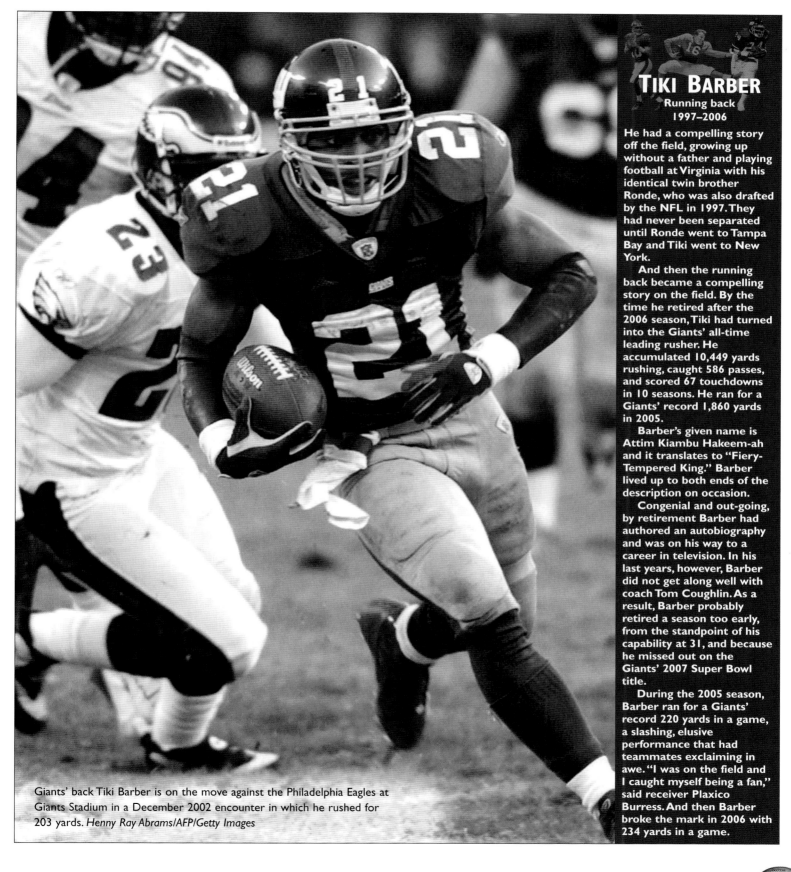

Giants' back Tiki Barber is on the move against the Philadelphia Eagles at Giants Stadium in a December 2002 encounter in which he rushed for 203 yards. *Henny Ray Abrams/AFP/Getty Images*

TIKI BARBER
Running back
1997–2006

He had a compelling story off the field, growing up without a father and playing football at Virginia with his identical twin brother Ronde, who was also drafted by the NFL in 1997. They had never been separated until Ronde went to Tampa Bay and Tiki went to New York.

And then the running back became a compelling story on the field. By the time he retired after the 2006 season, Tiki had turned into the Giants' all-time leading rusher. He accumulated 10,449 yards rushing, caught 586 passes, and scored 67 touchdowns in 10 seasons. He ran for a Giants' record 1,860 yards in 2005.

Barber's given name is Attim Kiambu Hakeem-ah and it translates to "Fiery-Tempered King." Barber lived up to both ends of the description on occasion.

Congenial and out-going, by retirement Barber had authored an autobiography and was on his way to a career in television. In his last years, however, Barber did not get along well with coach Tom Coughlin. As a result, Barber probably retired a season too early, from the standpoint of his capability at 31, and because he missed out on the Giants' 2007 Super Bowl title.

During the 2005 season, Barber ran for a Giants' record 220 yards in a game, a slashing, elusive performance that had teammates exclaiming in awe. "I was on the field and I caught myself being a fan," said receiver Plaxico Burress. And then Barber broke the mark in 2006 with 234 yards in a game.

General manager Ernie Accorsi smiles as he looks over the team he is assembling while watching rookie mini camp at Giants Stadium in May 2006.
Evan Pinkus/NFL Photos/ Getty Images

> **"He's the benchmark for me . . . He always has been."**
> **—Quarterback Eli Manning, on older brother and NFL star Peyton.**

Over the last weeks of his life, several members of the current Giants visited Mara at his home, including Michael Strahan, Tiki Barber and Jeremy Shockey. Shockey, the outspoken tight end, was the only player who routinely called Wellington Mara by his nickname "Duke." The approach fit the brash Shockey's personality and Mara did not mind.

Barber expressed particular fondness for Wellington Mara and appreciated his longevity with the league. Barber said he did not know Mara as well as he would have liked, but got to know him a little bit through his grandsons who acted as Giants ballboys just as he had done so many decades before. "Wellington Mara, for me, was a symbol of everything that was right with the league," Barber said. "Every time the Giants were there as a team, Wellington Mara was there. No exceptions."

The Giants played a game on October 23 and had the next day off. Barber used it to visit Mara for the last time "to say thank you and pay my respects to a great man. He had given me my chance."

Only three weeks after Mara's death, Robert Tisch, his co-owner since 1991, also died from cancer. After the demise of both owners, their sons took over team operations, with things split 50-50 between John Mara and Steven Tisch.

Coming off the 11–5 season, with Eli Manning gaining seasoning since his 2004 rookie year, and firmly entrenched in the quarterback position, there were high expectations for the Giants in 2006. Yet they never came to fruition. There were increased rumblings about Coughlin being on the way out after an 8–8 struggle.

Barber, who rushed for 1,662 yards in 2006, the second-most of his career, announced his intention to retire. He took heat for the timing of his in-season announcement and some felt that despite his performance he was focused on his next career more than his current one.

Also retiring, as he had long planned, was general manager Ernie Accorsi. In January, 2007, Accorsi's assistant and former long-time scout Jerry Reese was promoted. Reese's appointment made him one of the few African-American general managers in pro football history. "I don't take that lightly," said Reese of his ascension. "There are many African-Americans coming along behind me, saying, 'Man, look at Jerry.'" The hiring

aided younger owners. He had even out-lasted the Bears' George Halas. The "Duke" graduated from Fordham University, but only service in World War II drew him away from his beloved Giants. Mara and wife Ann had 11 children and 40 grandchildren. Son John succeeded Wellington as co-owner of the Giants.

Quarterback Eli Manning drafted to be the Giants' long-term leader, points at the line of scrimmage during Super Bowl XLII, February 3, 2008 against the New England Patriots.
Donald Miralle/Getty Images

ELI MANNING
Quarterback
2004–present

It took until 2012 before the younger brother of superstar Peyton Manning and the second son of Archie Manning was anointed as one of the best quarterbacks in the NFL.

Leading his team to eight fourth-quarter comeback victories in the regular season and playoffs, Eli Manning recorded one of the best years ever for a quarterback. He threw for 4,933 yards and 31 touchdowns before carrying the underdog Giants to victory over the New England Patriots in Super Bowl XLVI. It was the second time in five years that Manning had led his team to an upset win over the Patriots and the second time he was voted Super Bowl MVP.

The judgment of former Giants general manager Ernie Accorsi was vindicated. After Manning made it clear he had no desire to play for the San Diego Chargers, who drafted him with the No. 1 overall pick in 2004, Accorsi indicated just about any price was worth paying to obtain Manning.

After much wheeling and dealing, the Giants sent their own high draft picks to San Diego and obtained the rights to the 6 foot 4 inch, 225-pound former University of Mississippi All-American. Although it was not planned to happen so quickly, by the end of his rookie year, Manning was the team's starting quarterback. His on-the-job training was sometimes painful, but Manning maintained a placid demeanor.

"I'm not a screamer and a yeller," Manning said. "I get fired up. I get mad. I get intense."

He was intense enough to win the biggest game of all—twice.

of Reese was even more significant because the Giants historically had featured a very white front office.

Reacting to the turmoil surrounding Coughlin in the .500 season, the Giants also gave him a one-year contract extension. That bought Coughlin time to produce under Reese's administration, although from the time the team gathered in training camp in July, the New York newspapers reported, with varying degrees of insistence, that Coughlin pretty much had to take the 2007 club to the playoffs or else he was going to be the ex-coach.

A long view of New York Giants offense on the field against the Tampa Buccaneers during the NFC Wild Card game at Raymond James Stadium in Tampa, Florida on January 6, 2008. The Giants defeated the Buccaneers 24–14.
Tom Hauck/Getty Images

Coughlin had to know he was under scrutiny and although he did not change his stripes, he allowed a little bit more sunshine to reach his personality. Still, most of his hard-line rules were in force, something that aggravated 15-year veteran Michael Strahan.

Strahan, laid-back by nature off the field, was destined to clash with Coughlin, who would have been equally at home at the paratroop training camp at Fort Bragg. Strahan simply despised the way Coughlin told time. To Coughlin, being on time meant being five minutes early to meetings. To Strahan, being on time meant being on time.

Strahan called Coughlin "psychotic, though not in a dangerous, criminal way. More in a delusional way." The way Coughlin saw the five-minute rule, it was in place to demonstrate how eager the players were to meet. "Eager?" Strahan scoffed. "I couldn't be more eager to

have bamboo shoved up under my fingernails. It was Tom's way of just trying to be a hard-ass. Why? Because he could."

By 2007, Strahan didn't care much about clocks and meetings. He was back for one last season in a Giants' uniform for one reason only. He wanted to win a Super Bowl. Barber had run out of patience and retired young. Strahan's bones were feeling their decade-and-half of hits, but he believed he could suck it up one more time and that if everything went smoothly, the Giants would get another chance at the No. 1 prize in the sport.

That was the optimistic side of Strahan's thinking. People who write previews for pre-season NFL magazines did not envisiage the Giants marching to the Super Bowl. No one even believed they were a sure thing for the playoffs.

New York experienced a strange season. The Giants had a losing record at home, going 3–5, but were 7–1 on the road. That was not a traditional pattern in the NFL, where more often than not the home team holds serve. The Giants began weakly, losing their first two games. There was grumbling. If they started 0–3, there would have been a crescendo of moans from those who felt the season was lost already. But after the slow start, the Giants won six games in a row.

The Giants won some, lost some, but by the time the last game of the regular season rolled around they were 10–5. Although falling to the New England Patriots, darlings of the sport that season as they compiled the first 16–0 regular-season record, the Giants finished in the NFC East at 10–6. They were in the playoffs.

It has long been common wisdom that to succeed in the playoffs and to win the Super Bowl, teams must be commanded by highly efficient, seasoned quarterbacks. There have been exceptions when young, comparatively inexperienced quarterbacks led teams, but they had demonstrated a level of competence and assuredness that didn't worry fans.

At that point, nearing the end of his fourth season, Manning was viewed as an unfinished canvas. His potential had been raved about since day one. He had made big plays and carried the Giants on his broad shoulders. But he also had been guilty of ill-timed interceptions that were costly. He was not yet seen as one of the best quarterbacks in the league, but was regarded as the guy who was not quite there yet.

If there were doubts about how far the Giants could go in the playoffs, especially since they would be forced to play every game on the road, there was a lack of faith that Manning was the man to take them very far into January.

> **"You're the best free agent signing of my career."**
> **—Retiring general manager Ernie Accorsi to receiver Plaxico Burress at the end of the 2006 season.**

It was supposed to be the playoffs of the New England Patriots, a team that looked unstoppable, inevitably crunching AFC competition on the way to the Super Bowl. There the Patriots would find fodder from the inferior NFC, perhaps the Green Bay Packers. It would be a nice going-away present if Brett Favre, presumably in his last season, won one more Super Bowl title, as hopeless as the assignment appeared.

But Eli Manning grew up in the playoffs. From week to week he improved. Always implacable, rarely showing emotion on the field, Manning calmly led the Giants to win after win. In the first round of the playoffs

Kicker Lawrence Tynes (9) of the New York Giants boots the winning field goal against the Green Bay Packers during the NFC Championship game at Lambeau Field in Green Bay, Wisconsin on January 20, 2008. The Giants defeated the Packers 23–20 in overtime to advance to Super Bowl XLII.
David Stluka/Getty Images

the Giants knocked out Tampa Bay in Florida. Manning was the mastermind, completing 20-of-27 passes and throwing two touchdowns. "My thought process was to play really safe," Manning said, "don't force anything. They do a great job of getting turnovers."

The Giants had lost to divisional rival Dallas twice during the regular season and the Cowboys, 13–3, expressed the belief that there was no way New York would beat them in the playoffs either. The Giants won, 21–17, on the road again. Manning tossed two more touchdown passes. "That's what happens with people like that," said Giants' linebacker Kawika Mitchell. "They stick their foot in their mouth and they end up going home early. We're still in the dance and we'll be having some fun while they'll be watching us on TV."

The win earned the Giants a free trip to Green Bay, Wisconsin, where on game day the temperature was minus-1 and the windchill factor was about 25 degrees below zero. In a back-and-forth game that went into overtime and was left for New York kicker Lawrence Tynes to decide on a 47-yard field goal, 23–20, Manning was outside his comfort zone, but played as if he was in it. Manning completed 21 passes for 255 yards and found receiver Plaxico Burress for 11 completions and 154 yards.

No one envied Tynes having the result weighing on his shoulders, especially since he had already missed

(continued on page 164)

Left: Quarterback Eli Manning celebrates after Giants backfield mate Brandon Jacobs scored the go-ahead touchdown in a 2008 playoff game versus the Dallas Cowboys.
Harry How/Getty Images

SUPER BOWL XLII

Only the most optimistic of Giants' fans that had consulted ouija boards or fortune tellers before the season might have predicted the New Yorkers' win in the 2008 Super Bowl. And only those with blind faith would have predicted the Giants would win that Super Bowl once the playoffs started.

Tiki Barber, the greatest rusher in team history, had retired. Defensive end Michael Strahan, the leading sackmeister in team history, had nearly retired and it wasn't clear if his body was in first-rate shape to endure a long, last season. Eli Manning was still learning his trade at quarterback. Coach Tom Coughlin was under siege. Coming off an 8–8 season, a win-or-else mentality hovered over his head.

There was no evidence that the Giants were an all-the-way team after finishing the regular season 10–6. The Giants started the season 0–2. They also trailed by 14 points during their third game. New York rallied for a 24–17 victory over the Washington Redskins, highlighted by a goal-line stand at the 1-yard-line.

"We had already decided there was no way we were going to play that good in the first 58 minutes and let it slip away on the last drive," said defensive end Justin Tuck.

If they had not bounced back to win it's unclear just what might have become of the team. Still, the Giants finished 3–5 at home in The Meadowlands and lost their last four home games in a row. Some years 10–6 teams don't even qualify for the playoffs, but the Giants slipped in. From a distance, they had the look of a team that was just hanging on, not gearing up for a Super Bowl run.

The average record did not buy the Giants any credit with the post-season schedule-makers. All of their playoff games were going to be on the road, however long they lasted.

New York topped Tampa Bay, 24–14, in Florida to win the NFC wild card game. That was the Giants' first playoff win in seven years. Not many of the Giants had played in the second round of any playoffs when the Dallas Cowboys beckoned. "We're coming to work next week," guard Chris Snee said. "That's something we haven't been able to do the last couple of years."

The Giants earned another week of work by topping Dallas, 21–17, in Texas (after losing to the Cowboys twice during the regular season), a triumph that propelled them into the NFC championship game against favored Green Bay. This was supposed to be Brett Favre's swan song, leading the Packers to one more Super Bowl before retirement. The Giants spoiled the day for shivering Wisconsin fans, winning, 23–20 in overtime, and deliriously finding themselves in the Super Bowl in Arizona, instead.

Lawrence Tynes kicked a 47-yard field goal to upset Green Bay in weather calculated as a minus-25 windchill after the defense intercepted Favre. The win was New York's tenth straight on the road, and the Giants were the first NFC team to win three straight road playoff games to reach the Super Bowl. They won the three games, all tight struggles, by a combined 17 points.

"It's Giants' football," New York receiver Amani Toomer said after Tynes' boot. "We want to make sure our fans have some good, healthy blood pressure going into our games."

It was generally believed that New York supporters would need to ingest something quite strong to stomach the match-up that loomed. The Giants had scraped their way to the Super Bowl the hard way. The other team still standing was the New England Patriots.

The Patriots had put together the most dazzling season of any NFL team in history. After blitzing the regular season, 16–0, the first team to do so, behind quarterback Tom Brady's record 50 touchdown passes, the Patriots brushed aside playoff threats and were 18–0. Only the Miami Dolphins, 17-0, had recorded an undefeated Super Bowl-winning season. The Patriots, who defeated the Giants, 35–18, on the last weekend of the regular season, seemed certain to match and eclipse that feat.

What happened on February 3, 2008, however, varied quite a bit from the expected script. The Giants' defense turned in a monumental effort, from Michael Strahan and Osi Umenyiora, to Sam Madison, and others. The explosive New England offense was neutralized by constant pressure on Brady and the Giants kept the Patriots' offense off the field for long stretches.

New York quarterback Eli Manning, in his true coming-out party, was poised and sharp. The running game, behind Brandon Jacobs and Ahmad Bradshaw, ate up time, as well as yardage.

The Patriots scored the go-ahead touchdown with 2 minutes, 42 seconds to play in the fourth quarter, and with the Giants trailing 14–10, it looked as if the Patriots would survive with relief rather than earn a coronation. The Giants came to a crossroads with 1:15 remaining. They had a third-and-five when Manning faded back to pass. The Patriots rush was fierce and defenders grabbed his jersey. Manning spun free, heaved a pass downfield, and culminating in possibly the most remarkable play in Super

"It's the greatest victory in the history of this franchise, without question."
—Giants' co-owner John Mara on the team's 2008 Super Bowl victory over the New England Patriots.

Bowl history, receiver David Tyree leapt, pinned the ball against his helmet and held onto it as he fell to the ground.

"When you see a guy in trouble, you have to break off your route," Tyree said of running back toward Manning.

The miraculous play gave the Giants a first down at New England's 24-yard-line, and soon after, Manning completed a 13-yard touchdown pass to receiver Plaxico Burress. The Giants prevailed, 17–14, and Manning won the MVP award.

"The guys on this team and the run we've made, it's hard to believe," Manning said. "It really is. We knew if we played our best we'd have a chance to beat them. We believed the whole time."

The surprising result produced the New York Giants' third Super Bowl victory in four visits to the big game. "We shocked the world, but not ourselves," said linebacker Antonio Pierce.

The Giants head onto the field through a tunnel lined with team flags for the introduction of teams at Super Bowl XLII between the New York Giants and New England Patriots at University of Phoenix Stadium in Glendale, Arizona.
John Munson/Star Ledger/Corbis

Above: Giants wide receiver Plaxico Burress catches the game-winning touchdown in front of New England Patriots cornerback Ellis Hobbs in the fourth quarter of Super Bowl XLII as New York defeated the Patriots 17–14.
Paul Buck/epa/Corbis

Right: Defensive end Michael Strahan jumps over linebacker Kawika Mitchell and knocks down New England quarterback Tom Brady for a loss of seven yards in the second quarter of Super Bowl XLII.
John A. Angelillo/Corbis

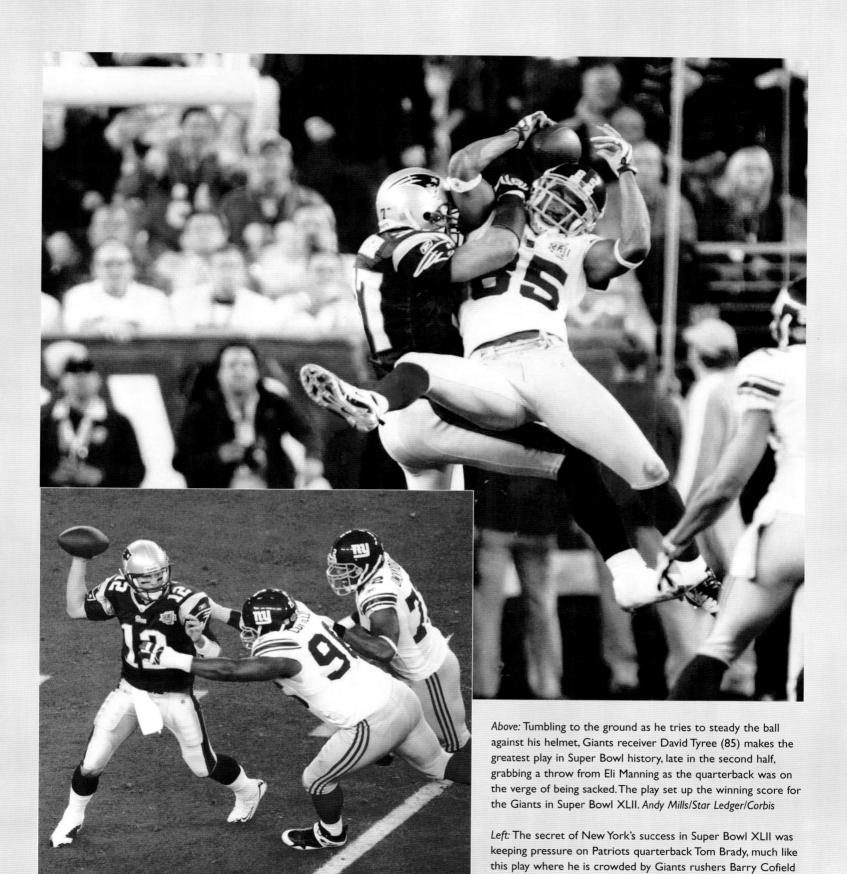

Above: Tumbling to the ground as he tries to steady the ball against his helmet, Giants receiver David Tyree (85) makes the greatest play in Super Bowl history, late in the second half, grabbing a throw from Eli Manning as the quarterback was on the verge of being sacked. The play set up the winning score for the Giants in Super Bowl XLII. *Andy Mills/Star Ledger/Corbis*

Left: The secret of New York's success in Super Bowl XLII was keeping pressure on Patriots quarterback Tom Brady, much like this play where he is crowded by Giants rushers Barry Cofield (96) and Osi Umenyiora. *Tim Farrell/Star Ledger/Corbis*

Giants owner John Mara is a happy guy after his team upset the Patriots, 17–14, to claim the trophy in Super Bowl XLII.
Tim Farrell/Star Ledger/Corbis

New England's perfect season was in tatters. The Giants won four playoff games on the road to capture the title when few thought that they would actually win any of them. "You can't write a better script," said Manning, who claimed the Super Bowl's MVP Award one year after his brother Peyton led the Colts to the crown.

Tyree, the 6 feet, 206-pound alumnus of Syracuse, had been with the Giants since 2003. Burress and Amani Toomer, as well as runners out of the backfield, got far more attention on pass routes than he did. His top season was 2006 when he caught 19 passes. During the entire 2007 season, Tyree, who got into 12 of the 16 games, caught four passes. And then he made the most astounding and outstanding catch in Super Bowl history to rescue the Giants on a third down by trapping a Manning throw against his helmet and saving the ball from hitting the ground. "Some things just don't make sense," Tyree said, "and I guess you can put that catch right up there with them."

GM Jerry Reese wasn't surprised. In every Super Bowl, he said, an unheralded player steps up and makes a difference. Happens all the time and this time the roulette wheel stopped on Tyree's number 85. "You win championships with guys like David Tyree," Reese said. "He just comes to work, does his job, never complains about anything, plays on special teams."

When the Giants won their first Super Bowl, feelings still were still raw about them moving to New Jersey to play at The Meadowlands. This time New York Mayor Michael Bloomberg welcomed them not only with a ticker tape parade through the Canyon of Heroes, but presented the players with a key to the city. Indeed, the Super Bowl champs were popular enough to open just about every Manhattan door with their faces, but it was nice insurance.

The Giants discovered it was good to be the kings, to be considered royalty. Eli Manning, previously in the shadow of brother Peyton, found more sponsors who wanted him to endorse their products, not just appear in commercials alongside Peyton and his famous football father Archie. David Tyree, really a journeyman wide receiver, was offered a book contract.

In big and small ways, the Giants were shown how special their victory was to so many and how becoming champions transformed their identities. Sam Madison, the veteran defensive back who played for historically black Florida A&M, was invited back to his hometown of Monticello, Florida, 35 miles east of the school, that is known as the watermelon capital of the world. "I was grand marshal of the Watermelon Festival parade," a beaming Madison said. "It was a blast." To him, the hometown boy making good, it was

one kick earlier that could have been decisive. When he booted this one through the uprights, Tynes ran right off the field into the locker room. He said he knew he had to make the kick. "I just wanted to get out of the cold," he said.

There would be palm trees and desert in the background, not snow and frigid winds, for the Giants' next game. In the last game of the season, the underdog New Yorkers would meet the Patriots, who had indeed romped through the early rounds of the playoffs and now were a record 18–0. New England, heavily favored to win the Vince Lombardi Trophy, was bucking for the first 19–0 season in NFL history.

For all of their resilience and creativity, for all of the explosiveness of quarterback Tom Brady and receivers Randy Moss and Wes Welker, and for all of their talent, the Patriots never looked like they were their true selves the entire game in Arizona. The Giants played superior defense. The Giants made the big plays. As the game wound down—even with New York needing a miraculous pass from Manning to David Tyree to stay alive and another pass from Manning to Burress to win—most of the millions watching were shocked to feel that the Patriots were lucky to be close. The victory, 17–14, was taut and tense and certainly evidence of the NFL's motto that on any given Sunday, any team can beat any other.

better than being invited to be grand marshal of the Macy's Thanksgiving Day Parade.

Long-time wide receiver Amani Toomer said the only thing unusual that happened to him beyond the expected celebrations, was receiving an unexpected email from an old friend who was in the military, sending congratulations. Toomer had lost touch with the man and didn't know where he was serving. He was under the impression it was top secret. "I heard from a lot of people," Toomer said.

The status of coach Tom Coughlin changed. He was no longer viewed as a coach on a short leash with excessive pressure to perform immediately. He, like Tyree, received a book deal. Although he didn't have much hair, it was a way of letting his hair down a little bit, showing that he wasn't always stiff and unapproachable.

Veteran tackle David Diehl, a 6 feet 5 inches, 319-pounds colossus from Oak Lawn, Illinois, said the 2007 season represented a great run, and a good time was had by all, but as the new 2008 season approached, he expected more respect from the same so-called football experts who made it sound as if the Giants were not going to be in the hunt for the playoffs, never mind another Super Bowl. "They make it sound as if it was all a fluke," Diehl said. "We'll have to show them again."

> **"This team is itching for more. We want more for ourselves, for our team, and our city."**
> **—Linebacker Antonio Pierce, on following up the 2007 Super Bowl season.**

A growing irritation was taking root at the suggestion that somehow the Giants had barely managed to beat four teams on the road, including the apparently predestined greatest team of all time. Coughlin did not sense any letdown in training camp or when the season started. "I don't see any complacency," Coughlin said. "There's a real hunger to win with this group."

On the opening night of the 2008 NFL season, a Thursday night game at The Meadowlands, the Giants met the Washington Redskins. Before the game, the Giants' organization unveiled one last celebration of the season past before moving on to the season at hand.

Kate Mara, grand-daughter of Wellington, who is a singer and actress, sang the national anthem. A group of Giants from the past, all from Super Bowl champion rosters, were introduced with the PA announcer's phrase, "Your Super Bowl Heroes!" The group included Karl Nelson, Brad Benson, Billy Ard, Rodney Hampton,

Eli Manning reacts to his game-winning touchdown pass to Plaxico Burress as the New York Giants defeat the New England Patriots in Super Bowl XLII. *Andy Mills/Star Ledger/Corbis*

Retiring defensive end Michael Strahan and quarterback Eli Manning during the celebration of the Giants' upset victory in Super Bowl XLII.
Tomasso DeRosa/Corbis

Ottis Anderson, Carl Banks, Mark Bavaro and Harry Carson. A huge, silver, float replica of the Lombardi Trophy was wheeled onto the field as fireworks lit the night sky. It seemed as tall as a four-story building. Suddenly, a door opened in the float and out stepped Michael Strahan, gripping the real Lombardi Trophy in his right hand and raising it in a toast to the 80,000 fans. Strahan, now retired, wore his No. 92 Giants' blue home jersey and a wide smile. Fans provided a roaring, standing ovation. "You thought I was never coming back," Strahan said. "But I had to come back to celebrate with the greatest fans by far in all sports."

Then the Giants played ball. Especially on defense, New York looked as formidable as ever, winning 16–7, and jump-starting a new season that took off with an 11–1 record. The attitude was clear: We'll show anyone who thinks that last year was a fluke.

An underdog throughout the playoffs following the 2007 season, the Super Bowl triumph gave the Giants confidence that carried into the 2008 regular season. Still smarting from being underrated, New York wanted to parlay its terrific late-season play into a Super Bowl repeat.

No two seasons are alike, however. Even as Eli Manning was turning in an all-star season and

powerhouse running back Brandon Jacobs rushed for more than 1,000 yards, retirements and injuries weakened the superb Giants defense. Still, a seven-game winning streak in midseason allowed New York to maintain a stranglehold on first place in the NFC East. The team finished with a 12–4 record, tying Carolina for the best record in the conference.

But things quickly turned sour in the postseason. Matched against the division-rival Eagles, the Giants knew they had no easy draw for their first playoff game. They mustered just three field goals by John Carney, plus a safety, and the Eagles won 23–11.

Regrouping, reorganizing, and starting fresh during the offseason, the Giants seemed poised to be a power in the NFC again heading into the 2009 season. They had reached the playoffs in five straight years, and the Giants vowed to make up for the disappointing end to 2008.

There was one huge difference in the Giants lineup, however, resulting from an early-season incident in 2008 that deeply affected the offense and shook up the core of the roster. In late November, while visiting a nightclub, wide receiver Plaxico Burress accidentally shot himself in his right thigh when his own Glock pistol discharged in his pants. Burress was treated and

"I'm not surprised by anything we do. You might see one of us fly one day, you never know."
—Running back Brandon Jacobs on the 2008 team's fast start.

released at a local hospital. Beyond paying the physical price for his poor judgment, Burress was charged with criminal possession of a handgun.

Burress did not have a New York license to possess the gun, and when the news broke, Mayor Michael Bloomberg was incensed and demanded that the star football player receive no special treatment. Burress surrendered to authorities and was released on $100,000 bail. However, the Giants suspended him for the duration of the 2008 season.

The court case dragged on through the offseason, and on April 3, 2009, he was cut by the Giants. Burress—whose behavior had previously been called into question by his former club, the Pittsburgh Steelers—swiftly descended the ladder of celebrity, going from famous to infamous, from Super Bowl hero to unemployed, within a matter of months. On August 20, Burress accepted a plea deal with the district attorney's office and a two-year prison sentence, plus two years of supervised release. His Giants career was over.

While Burress' court case was still going on, the Giants used their first-round pick in the draft to select Hakeem Nicks, a wide receiver out of North Carolina. Although Nicks proved to be an excellent long-term selection, the loss of Burress for the 2009 season hit hard, especially after Nicks sprained his foot in the fourth quarter of the season-opening game.

The Giants began the season 5–0 and were looking as strong as ever, but it was a false impression. The team stumbled over the remainder of the season, losing 8 of their last 11 to finish at 8–8 and out of the playoffs altogether—which had seemed unthinkable at the start of the year.

Defense had been the pride of the Super Bowl champs of 2007 and the 12–4 club of 2008 as well, but defensive coordinator Steve Spagnuolo departed before the 2009 season to become head coach of the St. Louis Rams. So New York's defensive unit was playing under new leadership. Bill Sheridan, who spent four years as linebackers coach, was promoted to defensive coordinator. The transition proved to be rough.

Luck also seemed to desert the Giants in the opener against Washington. Not only was top draft pick Nicks hurt in the game, but on the opening kickoff, the very first play of the season, D. J. Ware, who was both a running back and return man, dislocated an elbow. He would miss half the season.

Nevertheless, the Giants bested the Redskins, 23–17, and a week later, they were the guest

Huddling up to call a play, quarterback Eli Manning (10) gathers his offensive unit during the playoff game against the Philadelphia Eagles in January 2009.
Brian Garfinkel/Icon SMI/Corbis

After back-to-back 1,000-yard seasons in 2007 and 2008, Brandon Jacobs' production declined in 2009 as the team's offense focused more on the passing game. He ran for a season-high 92 yards and scored a touchdown in the Giants' 24–0 win at Tampa Bay in Week 3. *Al Messerschmidt/Getty Images*

opponents of the Cowboys for the debut of that team's new billion-dollar stadium. With the largest regular-season attendance in league history on hand (105,121), the Giants won in a 33–31 thriller.

After opening the season with five straight wins, the Giants showed no obvious hints that they were about to collapse. New Orleans was 4–0 and featured a new acquisition, New York's former star tight end Jeremy Shockey, but it was shocking when the Saints demolished the New York defense in Week 6. New Orleans gained 493 yards and scored seven touchdowns in a 48–27 thrashing.

Further insult came the next week when the Arizona Cardinals bested the Giants, 24–17, with quarterback Kurt Warner, a one-time backup for New York, at the controls. It was all part of a downward

spiral that was low-lighted by a 45–38 loss to the Eagles in Week 8 that knocked the Giants out of first place. In their two games against Philadelphia that season, the Giants surrendered 85 points, a record smudge in the long history of battles with that team.

In the second-to-last week of the season, the Giants played their final game at the Meadowlands after 33 years of calling Giants Stadium home. They lost to the Carolina Panthers, 41–9, and then dropped the season finale in Minnesota, 44–7.

Short memories prompted the New York tabloids to scream that it was time for Tom Coughlin to be canned and raised questions about whether Eli Manning was the right leader for the team.

The defense was the real problem. The Giants allowed 427 points that season and yielded at least

Watching his defense give up 41 points to the Carolina Panthers in the final game at Giants Stadium on December 27 only added to coach Tom Coughlin's disappointments from the 2009 season.
Nick Laham/Getty Images

40 points in a game five times. That poor defensive performance led to the firing of Sheridan and the hiring of a new coordinator, Perry Fewell. Defensive line coach Mike Waufle was also let go and replaced with Robert Nunn. Coughlin kept his job, and so did Manning.

It was apparent that Coughlin agonized over the way the 2009 season played out, although he only briefly touched on the disappointment. The opening of 2010 training camp offered opportunity for a fresh start.

"There is nothing to be said," Coughlin said. "I am excited this year as much as I have ever been excited. I am looking forward to it and have been since the end of the season last year. All you can do is plan and be ready to go on the field as soon as they let us and try to do something about it."

The 2010 season marked the grand opening of the Giants' new home field, MetLife Stadium, a $1.6-billion project with a capacity of 82,566 fans for football. The NFL promptly awarded it hosting rights for the 2014 Super Bowl.

The Giants were energized for the first-ever football game at the new stadium. They defeated the Panthers, 31–18, as Manning and Nicks connected on three touchdown passes.

Always focused on building a formidable defense, the Giants selected defensive end Jason Pierre-Paul out of the University of South Florida with their top draft pick that year and signed him to a five-year, $20 million deal.

The son of Haitian immigrants, the 6 foot 5 inch, 270-pound Pierre-Paul had little awareness of pro football before he became a star. A natural athlete, he didn't play football until his junior year in high school and had little training before excelling in junior college and for one year at South Florida. He declared himself eligible for the draft after his junior year with the Bulls.

"I'm just God-gifted," Pierre-Paul said. "I have talent."

That may sound arrogant, but when the Giants saw him play in person and again on tape, they agreed.

"This guy is a freak of nature," said director of scouting Marc Ross. "He has done things that I haven't seen in scouting—in games. . . . Combination of length and power and speed, just running through people and rag-dolling tackles."

New York was on a mission to return to the playoffs in 2010, and while the road was not easy, it was an off-year in the NFC Eastern Division, with no clearly dominant team. As such, the Giants were in the hunt for the division title all season. They were head-to-head with Philadelphia entering the final weeks, and with three games left in the season, the Eagles drove north on the New Jersey Turnpike to MetLife Stadium for the first time.

It was a game the Giants had to win, and they seemed to have it in hand early, leading 24–3 at halftime. Eli Manning threw three touchdown passes in the first 30 minutes, two to Mario Manningham and one to Nicks. Lawrence Tynes contributed a 25-yard field goal.

Manning threw a fourth touchdown pass in the fourth quarter to Kevin Boss, but Eagles quarterback Michael Vick was engineering a comeback. Philadelphia scored 28 points in the fourth quarter, tying the game at 31–31 as time was running down in regulation. The game seemed certain to go into overtime as the Giants lined up to punt.

The kick sailed through the air to the Eagles' return man DeShaun Jackson, who gathered it in after bobbling, picked up blocking, and sped downfield. To the stunned dismay of the 81,000-plus fans on hand, Jackson took the ball all the way to the house, scoring a touchdown with no time left on the clock. The play gave Philadelphia a 38–31 victory and was termed "The Miracle at the Meadowlands."

Although the Giants and Eagles both finished at 10–6, the Eagles had the tie-breaker by virtue of two regular-season wins over New York, which kept the Giants out of the playoffs once again. Even though the Giants finished two games better than they had in 2009, they didn't feel much better.

One reason was Manning's league-leading 25 interceptions. While he threw for an impressive 4,002 yards and 31 touchdowns, completing 62.9 percent of his passes, the interceptions were costly, including four thrown in a loss to the Green Bay Packers and three in a game against the Cowboys.

"It's like a damn plague," Coughlin said at one point.

Still, he didn't want to rein Manning in and curb his instincts. "You don't want to take that aspect away from him," Coughlin continued. "He's always trying to

Hakeem Nicks established his credentials as a star receiver during the opening game at new MetLife Stadium. Nicks pulled in three touchdown catches in the 31–18 victory over Carolina. *John Iacono/Sports Illustrated/ Getty Images*

make something happen, even if it's something out of nothing, and all I stress with Eli, and with any of them, is to be aware of the circumstances, know the situation, don't put your team in jeopardy." The interceptions were a shortcoming that Manning knew he had to correct going into the 2011 season. Whatever remedy he applied, Manning recorded one of the finest seasons ever by a quarterback and reached a new plateau as team leader. Five times in NFL history have quarterbacks thrown for at least 5,000 yards; three of them occurred in 2011. Manning's total of 4,933 yards ranks sixth on the all-time list.

Most remarkable, however, is how Manning rallied his team week after week to victories after trailing in the fourth quarter. He did so six times during the regular season, in games against the Eagles, Cardinals, Buffalo Bills, Miami Dolphins, Patriots, and Cowboys, and then twice in the playoffs, against the San Francisco 49ers and Patriots.

Previously a run-first team, the Giants had morphed into a throw-first—and most assuredly throw-last— team behind Manning. Fullback Brandon Jacobs was not playing as well as he had in the past, and his

carries and yards per game both were down. Running back Ahmad Bradshaw missed games with injuries, appearing in just 12 after being designated the feature back. It wasn't what Coughlin preferred, but the Giants' first option had become the pass.

While Manning was doing things like passing for 406 yards against New Orleans, the Giants were losing, as the defense once again ranked in the bottom third of the league. The Giants had to beat the local-rival Jets and the division-rival Cowboys in the last two weeks of the season in order to squeak into the playoffs with a 9–7 record.

Virtually nobody expected the Giants to advance far. Then they easily handled the Atlanta Falcons, 24–2, in the first round to earn a meeting with the 15–1 Packers in the divisional round. The defending-champion Packers featured the soon-to-be-named league MVP in quarterback Aaron Rodgers and were the odds-on favorite to repeat as champions. But defying the odds, the Giants led most of the game and were all-conquering in the fourth quarter of the 37–20 victory. Manning outplayed Rodgers, and Bradshaw seemed like his old self again.

Jason Pierre-Paul (90), Kenny Phillips (21), and Justin Tuck (91) converge on Philadelphia quarterback Michael Vick at MetLife Stadium on December 19, 2010. The Eagles came back to win on the final play of the game, killing New York's playoff hopes.
Scott Cunningham/Getty Images

Suddenly, after two playoff wins, it mattered less what the Giants had done during the regular season than how they were playing at the moment. And they looked like one of the hottest teams in football.

"I think we're a dangerous team," Coughlin said.

That feeling was permeating the players.

"This team knows how to win on the road," said defensive end Justin Tuck. "It seems like right now it's our time."

Many observers believed that San Francisco was the team of destiny in 2011. Revamped and rejuvenated under new head coach Jim Harbaugh, the 13–3 49ers had their best season in years and went on to upset the New Orleans Saints in the playoffs. It was the Giants-49ers in the NFC Championship Game for the right to advance to the Super Bowl.

Manning, who had thrown for 330 yards and three touchdowns against the Packers, continued his sterling postseason run by throwing for 316 yards and two touchdowns against the 49ers. Victor Cruz caught 10 passes for 142 yards.

Still, it took a 31-yard field goal by Lawrence Tynes in overtime for the Giants to prevail, 20–17, and finish off San Francisco.

Victor Cruz does his trademark touchdown dance after scoring the game-winning touchdown against the Miami Dolphins on October 30, 2011.
John Iacono/Sports Illustrated/ Getty Images

Eli Manning led the Giants to a convincing 37–20 win over the 15–1 Packers in the NFC Divisional playoff game at Lambeau Field on January 15, 2012.
Jamie Squire/Getty Images

And it took a fumble recovery to provide the Giants and Tynes with the opportunity.

"It's amazing," Tynes said. "I had dreams about this last night. It was from 42 [yards], not 31, but I was so nervous today before the game just anticipating this kind of game. I'm usually pretty cool, but there was something about tonight where I knew I was going to have to make a kick."

Long forgotten was the mediocre 7–7 standing with two weeks left in the season. The Giants won those last two regular-season games when they had to and then ratcheted up their play to single-handedly polish off just about every one of the top teams in the NFC. They manhandled Atlanta, surpassed Green Bay, and outlasted San Francisco. It was a hard road to the Super Bowl, and a road it was, as Coughlin matched Tom Landry's record of seven career playoff wins on the road.

"It's just been a tremendous effort by all of us, man," Cruz said.

No one was going to argue with that, as the Giants readied for an unexpected Super Bowl appearance.

Kicker Lawrence Tynes (9) and the rest of the Giants celebrate Tynes' game-winning 31-yard field goal against the San Francisco 49ers in overtime of the NFC Championship Game, sending New York to the Super Bowl.
Peter Read Miller/Sports Illustrated/Getty Images

2000s NEW YORK GIANTS YEAR BY YEAR

Year	Record
2000	12–4
2001	7–9
2002	10–6
2003	4–12
2004	6–10
2005	11–5
2006	8–8
2007	10–6
2008	12–4
2009	8–8
2010	10–6
2011	9–7

SUPER BOWL XLVI

In theory, the New York Giants were underdogs leading up to their Super Bowl clash with the New England Patriots in Indianapolis on February 5, 2012, but at no time during the proceedings did they act like it.

After a slow start, this was a peaking-at-the-right-time team that felt it was the finest football team on the planet. Rallying in the waning weeks of the regular season, believing in a defense that was earning kudos for its ferocity and in a quarterback who had been overshadowed by the best gunslingers in a throwers' league, the Giants came to Lucas Oil Stadium for the Super Bowl brimming with New York bravado.

The Giants were riding a five-game winning streak and the arm of Eli Manning. Previously best-known as the younger brother of Peyton and son of Archie, the 31-year-old Eli had matured into what he himself described as "an elite quarterback."

Most of the football world viewed the game as a rematch of Super Bowl XLII from four years earlier, when the Giants upset the undefeated Patriots in Arizona. But considerably less than half of the Giants roster remained from that championship squad. Manning and coach Tom Coughlin, however, were the key connections between the two games.

Not only was Manning coming off his best season statistically (4,933 yards and 29 touchdowns), but he had the swagger, the style, and the results, leading eight fourth-quarter comeback victories during the year. Manning led the league in intangibles and was showing that he was the type of quarterback who could carry a team on his shoulders to a Super Bowl crown. He was still playing while the more heralded Drew Brees and Aaron Rodgers were watching on TV.

There had also been a transformation in the perception of Manning among hard-to-impress New Yorkers. They now believed he was the best quarterback in the whole world, and that Coughlin, whom only weeks earlier the fans were prepared to throw under the bus to Times Square, was the best coach in the whole world. The game might be in Indianapolis, but it felt like Broadway.

Manning is business-like, not a braggart, and despite the nonstop attention from a massive media contingent, he did not say anything inflammatory on media day. He was confident about the Giants' passing game even if the Patriots were 15–3 and winners of 10 straight games.

The Giants were buoyed by a regular-season 24–20 win over New England, too, a highlight on their 12–7 record and something that led the New York defense to downplay the likelihood of Patriots quarterback Tom Brady beating them.

"It's not like he is God," said young defensive star Jason Pierre-Paul. "Anybody can be rattled. Tom Brady is a great quarterback, but at the end of the day, he's just a quarterback."

Defenders like Pierre-Paul, Justin Tuck, and Osi Umenyiora were used to having their way with offensive lines and did not think Brady's protectors would annoy them any more than other teams' guards and tackles.

When experts examined the match-ups, they looked at the Patriots' erratic secondary against the Giants' receiving core of Victor Cruz, Hakeem Nicks, and Mario Manningham. All votes gave the advantage to the Giants. "Whoever they try to take away," Manning said, "other guys will get open. When things get tough, you get our best performance."

Cruz caught 82 passes for a team-record 1,536 yards during the regular season. Nicks caught 76 passes for 1,192 yards. Manningham had only 39 receptions, but he averaged 13.4 yards per catch.

"I feel it starts with us as an offense," said Manningham, who received relatively little pre-game fanfare compared to Cruz and Nicks. "We know how good we are. We know how we can go out and make plays, and we know our potential."

In preparation for the big game, the Giants stuck to a favorite pre-game routine and had 16 pizzas flown to Indianapolis from the same Umberto's in New Hyde Park, Long Island, where they would get takeout after each Friday practice during the season. The pizzas received a police escort to LaGuardia Airport before being loaded on a flight to Indiana, kept warm with special packaging. Reportedly, the pizzas were devoured in 10 minutes upon arrival.

Once the game started, with a record 111.3 million Americans watching on television, Manning had top billing. A safety on the Patriots' first play on offense was followed by a 78-yard, Manning-led drive to give New York an early 9–0 lead. The Patriots took a 10–9 lead at the half and were up 17–15 after three quarters. New England could not convert another score, however, as the Giants intercepted Brady on an under-thrown ball early in the fourth, stymying the Patriots' effort to maintain possession.

The Giants got the ball back still trailing by two with 3 minutes, 46 seconds on the clock. Starting on their own 12-yard-line, the game was clearly in Manning's hands. Tension mounted among the 68,658 fans in attendance as Manning moved his team downfield and the Patriots desperately tried to halt the Giants advance.

Manning was masterful. He completed six of seven pass attempts for 74 yards on the drive while milking the clock to set up Lawrence Tynes for a gimme field goal. Instead, to ensure that they got the ball back with enough time on the clock, the Patriots defense gave Ahmad Bradshaw a clear path to the end zone to score on a six-yard run. As Manning yelled, "Don't score!" Bradshaw attempted to go against his instincts and fall down at the one-yard line, but he couldn't pull it off and tumbled across the goal line to put the Giants up 21–17.

The magical play on the drive was a 38-yard completion from Manning to Manningham, who sliced between two defenders, grabbed the ball, and ballet-like kept both feet in bounds as he was hit along the left sideline. It was the perfect pitch and catch. The play was only slightly less miraculous, but no less significant, than the one four years earlier when David Tyree trapped a Manning toss against his helmet on the winning drive of Super Bowl XLII.

"Good thing I wear size 11," Manningham said, referring to his shoes. "If I wore 11½, I would have been out of bounds."

That's how close it was.

The Giants could not complete the two-point conversion, so the lead remained at four points as Brady looked to engineer a Patriots comeback with 57 seconds to go. He couldn't do it. His final pass was a Hail Mary into the end zone that fell just out of the reach of tight end Rob Gronkowski. It was close enough to give Giants fans heart palpitations, though.

Instead, New York got to celebrate. Manning and Coughlin claimed their second Super Bowl victory together and the fourth in team history. The quarterback was named MVP of the game for the second time, despite Nicks' 10 catches for 109 yards. Manning completed 30 of 40 passes for 296 yards, with a 2-yard touchdown throw to Cruz.

"This isn't about one person," Manning said. "This is about a team coming together. It's been a wild game, a wild season."

After the first 14 games of the season, fans had been wondering why the Giants were underachieving and if Coughlin should be sent into exile. Instead, he ended the year acclaimed as the right coach for a team that captured its second championship on his watch.

The Patriots competed in their fifth Super Bowl of the 2000s with three wins. They were trying to move closer to the Pittsburgh Steelers' record six championships and the Dallas Cowboys' and San Francisco 49ers' five. Instead, they were surpassed by the Giants.

"What I was concerned with was these guys making their own history," Coughlin said of his Giants. "This is such a wonderful thing, these guys carving their own history."

Giant fans appreciated the authorship of history. New York practically invented the championship parade, and about one million fans turned out to fete the Giants through Manhattan's Canyon of Heroes as tons of blue and white confetti fell from the sky. Fans yelled "Let's go Giants" as players hoisted the Lombardi Trophy. Soon afterward, the Giants conducted a second celebration at MetLife Stadium in East Rutherford, New Jersey, attracting 30,000 people.

During a New York ceremony following the parade, each member of the team was given a key to the city, and Coughlin revealed he had spoken to President Barack Obama about resilience.

"All things are possible for those who believe," Coughlin said.

Eli Manning earned his second Super Bowl MVP Award, and a place among the game's greats, by leading the Giants to victory over the New England Patriots in Super Bowl XLVI on February 5, 2012.
Jamie Squire/Getty Images

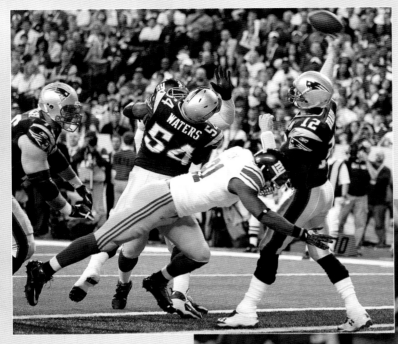

Justin Tuck's pressure on Tom Brady during New England's first play from scrimmage forced an intentional grounding penalty and provided the first points of the game with a safety.
Mark Cornelison/Lexington Herald-Leader/MCT/Getty Images

Mario Manningham made one of the greatest catches in Super Bowl history when he pulled in this sideline grab against Patriot defenders Patrick Chung (25) and Sterling Moore (29) during the fourth quarter.
John W. McDonough/Sports Illustrated/Getty Images

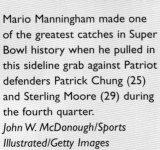

The New England defense gave running back Ahmad Bradshaw a clear path to the end zone late in the game. Bradshaw tried to pull up in order to allow more time to run off the clock, but his momentum, and instincts, pushed him over the goal line for the go-ahead touchdown.
Rob Carr/Getty Images

New England's Bill Belichick is considered one of the game's greatest coaches, but Tom Coughlin has got the better of him twice when it matters most. The two opposing coaches hugged at midfield after the Giants wrapped up the win.
Ezra Shaw/Getty Images

BIBLIOGRAPHY

Books

Barber, Tiki, with Gil Reavill, *Tiki: My Life in the Game and Beyond,* Simon Spotlight Entertainment, New York, 2007

Benson, Michael, *The Good, The Bad & The Ugly, New York Giants,* Triumph Books, Chicago, 2007.

Bowden, Mark, *The Best Game Ever,* Atlantic Monthly Press, New York, 2008.

Callahan, Tom, *The GM,* Crown Publishers, New York, 2007.

DeVito, Carlo, *Wellington: The Maras, The Giants, and the City of New York,* Triumph Books, Chicago, 2006.

Eisen, Michael, *New York Giants Stadium Stories,* The Globe Pequot Press, Guilford, Connecticut, 2005.

Gifford, Frank, with Harry Waters, *The Whole Ten Yards,* Random House, New York, 1993.

Greenberg, Murray, *Passing Game: Benny Friedman and the Transformation of Football,* Public Affairs, New York, 2008.

Grier, Roosevelt, with Dennis Baker, *Rosey: The Gentle Giant,* Honor Books, Tulsa, Oklahoma, 1986.

Herndon, Booton, *Football's Greatest Quarterbacks,* Bartholomew House, New York, 1961.

Huff, Sam, with Leonard Shapiro, *Tough Stuff,* St. Martin's Press, New York, 1988.

Izenberg, Jerry, *New York Giants: 75 Years,* Tehabi Books, Del Mar, California, 1999.

Maxymuk, John, *The 50 Greatest Plays in New York Giants Football History,* Triumph Books, Chicago, 2008.

Miller, Stuart, *Where Have All Our Giants Gone?* Taylor Trade, Lanham, Maryland, 2005.

New York Daily News, Blue Miracle: New York Giants Super Bowl Champions, Sports Publishing LLC, Champaign, Illinois, 2008.

New York Giants, staff, 2008 Media Guide.

NFL, *Total Football II: The Official Encyclopedia of the National Football League,* HarperCollins, New York, 1999.

Palmer, Ken, *Game of My Life, New York Giants,* Sports Publishing LLC, Champaign, Illinois, 2007.

Schwartz, Paul, *Tales From the New York Giants Sideline,* Sports Publishing LLC, Champaign, Illinois, 2004.

Strahan, Michael, with Jay Glazer, *Inside the Helmet,* Gotham Books, New York, 2007.

Summerall, Pat, *Summerall On and Off the Air,* Nelson Books, Nashville, Tennessee, 2006.

Taylor, Lawrence, with Steve Serby, *LT: Over the Edge,* HarperTorch, New York, 2003.

Tittle, Y.A., with Don Smith, *I Pass,* Franklin Watts, New York, 1964.

Tunnell, Emlen, with William Gleason, *Footsteps of a Giant,* Doubleday and Co., 1966.

Vacchiano, Ralph, *Eli Manning: The Making of a Quarterback,* Skyhorse Publishing, New York, 2008.

Whittingham, Richard, *Giants in Their Own Words,* Contemporary Books, Chicago, 1992.

Whittingham, Richard, *What Giants They Were,* Triumph Books, Chicago, 2000.

Whittingham, Richard, *Illustrated History of the New York Giants,* Triumph Books, Chicago, 2005.

Personal Interviews

David Diehl, Brandon Jacobs, Sam Madison, Antonio Pierce, Amani Toomer.

Press Conferences

Tom Coughlin, Eli Manning.

Web Sites

ESPN.com

NFL.com

Magazines

Collier's

Football Digest

Giants Insider

Liberty

Look

NFL Game Day programs

Pro Football Weekly

Sports Illustrated

Sport Magazine

The Sporting News

Film

The Complete History of the New York Giants, NFL Films, 2004.

Archives

Pro Football Hall of Fame Library, Canton, Ohio.

APPENDIX
NEW YORK GIANTS RECORD BOOK
(through 2011 season; regular seasons only)

SERVICE

Most Seasons, Player
- 15 Michael Strahan (1993–2007)
- 15 Phil Simms (1979–93)
- 15 Mel Hein (1931–45)
- 14 George Martin (1975–88)
- 14 Joe Morrison (1959–72)
- 14 Charlie Conerly (1948–61)
- 13 Howard Cross (1989–2001)
- 13 Lawrence Taylor (1981–93)
- 13 Harry Carson (1976–88)
- 13 Greg Larson (1961–73)
- 13 Jim Katcavage (1956–68)
- 13 Rosey Brown (1953–65)

Most Games Played, Career
- 216 Michael Strahan (1993–2007)
- 207 Howard Cross (1989–2001)
- 201 George Martin (1975–88)
- 184 Lawrence Taylor (1981–93)
- 184 Joe Morrison (1959–72)
- 179 Greg Larson (1961–73)
- 174 Amani Toomer (1996–2007)
- 173 Keith Hamilton (1992–2003)
- 173 Harry Carson (1976–88)
- 170 Mel Hein (1931–45)

Most Seasons, Head Coach
- 23 Steve Owen (1931–53)
- 8 Tom Coughlin (2004–11)
- 8 Bill Parcells (1983–90)
- 8 Allie Sherman (1961–68)
- 7 Jim Fassel (1994–2003)

Most Wins, Head Coach
- 151 Steve Owen (1931–53)
- 77 Bill Parcells (1983–90)
- 74 Tom Coughlin (2004–11)
- 58 Jim Fassel (1994–2003)
- 57 Allie Sherman (1961–68)

SCORING

Most Points, Career
- 646 Pete Gogolak, 1966–74 (268-pat, 126-fg)
- 526 Brad Daluiso, 1993–2000 (157-pat, 123-fg)
- 484 Frank Gifford, 1952–64 (78-td, 10-pat, 2 fg)
- 482 Joe Danelo, 1976–82 (170-pat, 104-fg)
- 441 Lawrence Tynes, 2007–11 (174-pat, 89-fg)

Most Points, Season
- 148 Jay Feely, 2005 (43-pat, 35 fg)
- 143 John Carney, 2008 (38-pat, 35-fg)
- 127 Ali Haji-Sheikh, 1983 (22-pat, 35-fg)
- 126 Lawrence Tynes, 2009 (45-pat, 27-fg)
- 126 Joe Morris, 1985 (21-tds)

Most Points, Rookie Season
- 127 Ali Haji-Sheikh, 1983 (22-pat, 35-fg)
- 108 Matt Bryant, 2002 (30-pat, 26-fg)

Most Points, Game
- 24 Rodney Hampton, vs. New Orleans, Sept. 24, 1995
- 24 Earnest Gray, at St. Louis, Sept. 7, 1980
- 24 Ron Johnson, at Philadelphia, Oct. 2, 1972

Most Consecutive Games Scoring
- 61 Pete Gogolak (1969–73)
- 57 Ben Agajanian (1949, 54–57)
- 47 Raul Allegre (1986–91)

TOUCHDOWNS

Most Seasons Leading League
- 2 Bill Paschal (1943 tied, 1944 tied)
- 1 Joe Morris (1985)
- 1 Homer Jones (1967)
- 1 Gene Roberts (1949)

Most Touchdowns, Career
- 78 Frank Gifford (1952–64)
- 68 Tiki Barber (1997–2006)

- 65 Joe Morrison (1959–72)
- 60 Brandon Jacobs (2005–11)
- 58 Amani Toomer (1996–2008)

Most Touchdowns, Season
- 21 Joe Morris (1985)
- 17 Gene Roberts (1949)
- 15 Brandon Jacobs (2008)
- 15 Tiki Barber (2004)
- 15 Joe Morris (1986)

Most Touchdowns, Rookie Season
- 12 Bill Paschal (1943)

Most Touchdowns, Game
- 4 Rodney Hampton, vs. New Orleans, Sept. 24, 1995
- 4 Earnest Gray, at St. Louis, Sept. 7, 1980
- 4 Ron Johnson, at Philadelphia, Oct. 2, 1972

Most Consecutive Games Scoring Touchdowns
- 10 Frank Gifford (1957–58)
- 7 Tiki Barber (2004)
- 7 Kyle Rote (1959–60)
- 7 Bill Paschal (1944)
- 7 Plaxico Burress (2007)

POINTS AFTER TOUCHDOWN

Most Seasons Leading League
- 1 Don Chandler (1963)
- 1 Pat Summerall (1961)
- 1 Ward Cuff (1938)

Most Points After Touchdown Attempted, Career
- 277 Pete Gogolak (1966–74)
- 176 Lawrence Tynes (2007–11)
- 176 Joe Danelo (1976–83)
- 159 Ben Agajanian (1949, 54–57)
- 159 Brad Daluiso (1993–2000)

Most Points After Touchdown Attempted, Season
56 Don Chandler (1963)
48 Don Chandler (1962)
46 Pat Summerall (1961)
45 Lawrence Tynes (2009)
43 Lawrence Tynes (2011)
43 Lawrence Tynes (2010)
43 Jay Feely (2005)

Most Points After Touchdown without a Miss, Game
8 Pete Gogolak, vs. Philadelphia, Nov. 26, 1972
7 by many players

Most Points After Touchdown, Career
268 Pete Gogolak (1966–74)
174 Lawrence Tynes (2007–11)
170 Joe Danelo (1976–82)
157 Brad Daluiso (1993–2000)
157 Ben Agajanian (1949, 54–57)

Most Points After Touchdown, Season
52 Don Chandler (1963)
47 Don Chandler (1962)
46 Pat Summerall (1961)
45 Lawrence Tynes (2009)
43 Lawrence Tynes (2011)
43 Lawrence Tynes (2010)
43 Jay Feely (2005)

Most Points After Touchdown, Game
8 Pete Gogolak, vs. Philadelphia, Nov. 26, 1972
7 on 7 occasions, most recently by
   Lawrence Tynes, at Washington, Dec. 21, 2009

Most Consecutive Points After Touchdown
160 Lawrence Tynes (Oct. 21, 2007–Jan. 1, 2011)
126 Pat Summerall (Oct. 26, 1958–Dec. 17, 1961)
104 Pete Gogolak (Dec. 17, 1967–Sept. 17, 1972)

Most Points After Touchdown (No Misses), Season
46 Pat Summerall (1961)
45 Lawrence Tynes (2009)
43 Lawrence Tynes (2011)
43 Lawrence Tynes (2010)
43 Jay Feely (2005)

FIELD GOALS

Most Seasons Leading League
3 Ward Cuff (1938 tied, 1939, 1943 tied)
1 Ali Haji-Sheikh (1983)
1 Pat Summerall (1959)
1 Ken Strong (1944)

Most Field Goals Attempted, Career
219 Pete Gogolak (1966–74)
176 Joe Danelo (1976–82)
160 Brad Daluiso (1993–2000)
112 Pat Summerall (1958–61)
107 Lawrence Tynes (2007–11)

Most Field Goals Attempted, Season
42 Jay Feely (2005)
42 Ali Haji-Sheikh (1983)
41 Pete Gogolak (1970)
38 John Carney (2008)

38 Joe Danelo (1981)

Most Field Goals Attempted, Game
6 on 6 occasions, most recently by
   Jay Feely, vs. Washington, Oct. 30, 2005

Most Field Goals, Career
126 Pete Gogolak (1966–74)
123 Brad Daluiso (1993–2000)
104 Joe Danelo (1976–82)
89 Lawrence Tynes (2007–11)
77 Raul Allegre (1986–91)

Most Field Goals, Season
35 John Carney (2008)
35 Jay Feely (2005)
35 Ali Haji-Sheikh (1983)
27 Lawrence Tynes (2009)
26 Matt Bryant (2002)

Most Field Goals, Game
6 Joe Danelo, at Seattle, Oct. 18, 1981
5 Jay Feely, vs. Washington, Oct. 30, 2005
5 Steve Christie, at Cincinnati, Dec. 26, 2004
5 Raul Allegre, at Minnesota, Nov. 16, 1986
5 Eric Shubert, at Tampa Bay, Nov. 3, 1985
5 Ali Haji-Sheikj, at Washington, Dec. 17, 1983

Most Consecutive Games Kicking Field Goals
18 Joe Danelo (1977–79)
15 Lawrence Tynes (2009)
15 Jay Feely (2005)
15 Raul Allegre (1987–89)
15 Ali Haji-Sheikh (1983)

Longest Field Goal (yards)
56 Ali Haji-Sheikh, at Detroit, Nov. 7, 1983
56 Ali Haji-Sheikh, vs. Green Bay, Sept. 26, 1983
55 Joe Danelo, vs. New Orleans, Sept. 20, 1981

Highest Field Goal Percentage, Career (min. 50 attempts)
84.1 Jay Feely, 58-69 (2005–06)
83.2 Lawrence Tynes, 89-107 (2007–11)
76.9 Brad Daluiso, 123-160 (1993–2000)
75.3 Matt Bahr, 55-73 (1990–92)
74.8 Raul Allegre, 77-103 (1986–91)

Highest Field Goal Percentage, Season (min. 14 attempts)
88.9 Brad Daluiso, 24-27 (1996)
85.7 Cary Blanchard, 18-21 (1999)
85.2 Lawrence Tynes, 23-37 (2007)
85.2 Jay Feely, 23-27 (2006)
83.3 Jay Feely, 35-42 (2005)
83.3 Ali Haji-Sheikh, 35-42 (1983)

Most Field Goals, 50 or More Yards, Career
9 Joe Danelo (1976–82)
6 Brad Daluiso (1993–2000)
3 Lawrence Tynes (2007–11)
3 Jay Feely (2005)
3 Steve Christie (2004)
3 Raul Allegre (1986–91)
3 Ali Haji-Sheikh (1983–85)

Most Field Goals, 50 or More Yards, Season
3 Jay Feely (2005)
3 Steve Christie (2004)
3 Joe Danelo (1981)
2 Lawrence Tynes (2010)
2 Morten Andersen (2001)
2 Brad Daluiso (1995)
2 Raul Allegre (1987)
2 Ali Haji-Sheikh (1983)
2 Joe Danelo (1980)
2 Joe Danelo (1978)

SAFETIES

Most Safeties, Career
3 Jim Katcavage (1956–68)
2 Leonard Marshall (1983–92)

Most Safeties, Season/Game
1 on 26 occasions, most recently by
   Chris Canty, at Jets, Dec. 24, 2011

ALL-PURPOSE YARDS

Most All-Purpose Yards, Career
17,359 Tiki Barber (1997–2006)
10,344 Amani Toomer (1996–2007)
9,862 Frank Gifford (1952–64)
8,750 Rodney Hampton (1990–97)

Most All-Purpose Yards, Season
2,390 Tiki Barber (2005)
2,127 Tiki Barber (2006)
2,096 Tiki Barber (2004)
2,085 Tiki Barber (2000)
1,989 Tiki Barber (2002)

Most All-Purpose Yards, Game
279 Joe Scott, vs. LA Rams, Nov. 14, 1948
276 Tiki Barber, vs. Philadelphia, Dec. 28, 2002
269 Del Shofner, vs. Washington, Oct. 28, 1962

RUSHING

Most Seasons Leading League
2 Bill Paschal (1943, 1944)
1 Eddie Price (1951)
1 Tuffy Leemans (1936)

Most Attempts, Career
2,217 Tiki Barber (1997–2006)
1,824 Rodney Hampton (1990–97)
1,318 Joe Morris (1982–89)
1,196 Alex Webster (1955–64)
1,078 Brandon Jacobs (2007–11)

Most Attempts, Season
357 Tiki Barber (2005)
341 Joe Morris (1986)
327 Rodney Hampton (1994)
327 Tiki Barber (2006)
325 Ottis Anderson (1989)

Most Attempts, Game
43 Butch Woolfolk, at Philadelphia, Nov, 20, 1983
41 Rodney Hampton vs. LA Rams, Sept. 19, 1993
38 Joe Montgomery, vs. Jets, Dec. 5, 1999
38 Harry Newman, vs. Green Bay, Nov. 11, 1934

36   Joe Morris, vs. Pittsburgh, Dec. 21, 1985
36   Ron Johnson, at Philadelphia, Oct. 2, 1972

Most Yards Gained, Career
10,449 Tiki Barber (1997–2006)
6,897   Rodney Hampton (1990–97)
5,296   Joe Morris (1982–89)
4,849   Brandon Jacobs (2007–11)
4,638   Alex Webster (1955–64)

Most Yards Gained, Season
1,860   Tiki Barber (2005)
1,662   Tiki Barber (2006)
1,518   Tiki Barber (2004)
1,516   Joe Morris (1986)
1,387   Tiki Barber (2002)
1,336   Joe Morris (1986)
1,235   Ahmad Bradshaw (2010)
1,216   Tiki Barber (2003)
1,182   Rodney Hampton (1995)
1,182   Ron Johnson (1972)

Most Yards Gained, Game
234   Tiki Barber, at Washington, Dec. 30, 2006
220   Tiki Barber, vs. Kansas City, Dec. 17, 2005
218   Gene Roberts, vs. Chi. Cardinals, Nov. 12, 1950
206   Tiki Barber, at Washington, Oct. 30, 2005
203   Tiki Barber, at Oakland, Dec. 31, 2005
203   Tiki Barber, vs. Philadelphia, Dec. 28, 2001

Most Games, 100 or More Yards Rushing, Career
38   Tiki Barber (1997–2006)
19   Joe Morris (1982–89)
17   Rodney Hampton (1990–97)
11   Eddie Price (1950–55)
10   Ron Johnson (1970–75)

Most Games, 100 or More Yards Rushing, Season
9   Tiki Barber (2004)
8   Tiki Barber (2005)
8   Tiki Barber (2006)
8   Joe Morris (1985)
5   Brandon Jacobs (2007)
5   Rodney Hampton (1993)

Longest Run from Scrimmage
95   Tiki Barber, at Oakland, Dec. 31, 2005
91   Hap Moran, vs. Green Bay, Nov. 23, 1930
88   Ahmad Bradshaw, at Buffalo, Dec. 23, 2007
80   Eddie Price, at Philadelphia, Dec. 9, 1951
79   Frank Gifford, vs. Washington, Nov. 29, 1959

Highest Average Gain, Career (min. 500 attempts)
4.71   Tiki Barber, 1997–2006 (2,217-10,449)
4.60   Ahmad Bradshaw, 2007–11 (700-3,217)
4.50   Brandon Jacobs, 2005–11 (1,078-4,849)
4.30   Frank Gifford, 1952–64 (840-3,609)
4.14   Mel Triplett, 1955–60 (553-2,289)

Highest Average Gain, Season (qualifiers)
5.60   Brandon Jacobs, 2010 (147-823)
5.58   Eddie Price, 1950 (126-703)
5.21   Tiki Barber, 2005 (357-1,860
5.21   Tiki Barber, 2001 (166-865)
5.15   Frank Gifford, 1956 (156-819)

Eli Manning rifles the ball over the middle, trying to hit receiver Amani Toomer in a game against the Cincinnati Bengals. *Joe Epstein/Star Ledger/Corbis*

Highest Average Gain, Game (min. 10 attempts)
13.30   Frank Reagan, vs. LA Rams, Dec. 1, 1946 (10-133)
12.23   Tuffy Leemans, vs. Green Bay, Nov. 20, 1938 (13-159)
11.43   Ernie Kay, at Washington, Oct. 1, 1967 (14-160)

Most Rushing Touchdowns, Career
56   Brandon Jacobs (2007–11)
55   Tiki Barber (1997–2006)
49   Rodney Hampton (1990–97)
48   Joe Morris (1982–89)
39   Alex Webster (1955–64)

Most Rushing Touchdowns, Season
21   Joe Morris (1985)
15   Brandon Jacobs (2008)
14   Rodney Hampton (1992)
14   Ottis Andersen (1989)
14   Joe Morris (1986)

Most Rushing Touchdowns, Game
4   Rodney Hampton, vs. New Orleans, Sept. 24, 1995
3   on 16 occasions

Most Consecutive Games Rushing for Touchdowns
7   Bill Paschal (1944)
6   Joe Morris (1985–86)
5   Tiki Barber (2002)
5   Rodney Hampton (1991)
5   Ottis Anderson (1989)
5   Bill Gaiters (1961)

PASSING

Most Seasons Leading League
2   Ed Danowski (1935, 1938)
1   Phil Simms (1990)
1   Norm Snead (1972)
1   Y.A. Tittle (1952)
1   Charlie Conerly (1959)
1   Harry Newman (1933)

Most Passes Attempted, Career
4,647   Phil Simms (1979–93)
3,921   Eli Manning (2004–11)
2,833   Charlie Conerly (1948–61)
2,473   Kerry Collins (1999–2003)
1,898   Fran Tarkenton (1967–71)

Most Passes Attempted, Season
589 Eli Manning (2011)
568 Kerry Collins (2001)
557 Eli Manning (2005)
545 Kerry Collins (2002)
539 Eli Manning (2010)
533 Phil Simms (1984)
529 Eli Manning (2007)
529 Kerry Collins (2000)
522 Eli Manning (2006)
509 Eli Manning (2009)
500 Kerry Collins (2003)

Most Passes Attempted, Game
62 Phil Simms, at Cincinnati, Oct. 13, 1985
59 Kerry Collins, at New England, Oct. 12, 2003
59 Kerry Collins, vs. Green Bay, Jan. 6, 2002
53 Eli Manning, vs. Washington, Dec. 16, 2007
53 Eli Manning, at Seattle, Nov. 27, 2005
53 Charlie Conerly, at Pittsburgh, Dec. 5, 1948

Most Passes Completed, Career
2,576 Phil Simms (1979–93)
2,291 Eli Manning (2004–11)
1,447 Kerry Collins (1999–2003)
1,418 Charlie Conerly (1948–61)
1,051 Fran Tarkenton (1967–71)

Most Passes Completed, Season
359 Eli Manning (2011)
339 Eli Manning (2010)
335 Kerry Collins (2002)
327 Kerry Collins (2001)
317 Eli Manning (2009)
311 Kerry Collins (2000)
301 Eli Manning (2006)

Most Passes Completed, Game
40 Phil Simms, at Cincinnati, Oct. 13, 1985
36 Kerry Collins, vs. Green Bay, Jan. 6, 2002
36 Charlie Conerly, at Pittsburgh, Dec. 5, 1948
35 Kerry Collins, at New England, Oct. 12, 2003
34 Eli Manning, vs. Tennessee, Sept. 26, 2010

Most Consecutive Passes Completed
13 Kerry Collins, at Phil., Sept. 10, 2000; at Bears, Sept. 17, 2000 (spanned 2 games)
13 Phil Simms, at Cincinnati, Oct. 13, 1985
12 Eli Manning, at Atlanta, Oct. 15, 2007
12 Y.A. Tittle, vs. Washington, Oct. 28, 1962

Highest Completion Percentage, Career (min. 1,000 attempts)
58.51 Kerry Collins, 1999–2003 (1,447-2,473)
58.43 Eli Manning, 2004–11 (2,291-3,921)
55.89 Y.A. Tittle, 1961–64 (731-1,308)
55.43 Phil Simms, 1979–93 (2,576-4,647)
55.37 Fran Tarkenton, 1967–71 (1,051-1,898)

Highest Completion Percentage, Season (qualifiers)
62.89 Eli Manning, 2010 (339-539)
62.81 Kurt Warner, 2004 (174-277)
62.81 Jeff Hostetler, 1991 (179-285)
62.28 Eli Manning, 2009 (317-509)
61.75 Phil Simms, 1993 (247-400)

Highest Completion Percentage, Game (min/ 20 attempts)
84.61 Kerry Collins, at St. Louis, Sept. 15, 2002 (22-26)
82.34 Jeff Hostetler, at Dallas, Sept. 29, 1991 (28-34)
80.95 Phil Simms, at Indianapolis, Nov. 5, 1990 (17-21)
80.95 Phil Simms, vs. St. Louis, Oct. 25, 1987 (17-21)
80.77 Phil Simms, vs. Green Bay, Dec. 19, 1987 (21-26)

Most Yards Passing, Career
33,462 Phil Simms (1979–93)
27,579 Eli Manning (2004–07)
19,488 Charlie Conerly (1948–61)
16,875 Kerry Collins (1999–2003)
13,905 Fran Tarkenton (1967–71)

Most Yards Passing, Season
4,933 Eli Manning (2011)
4,073 Kerry Collins (2002)
4,044 Phil Simms (1984)
4,021 Eli Manning (2009)
4,002 Eli Manning (2010)
3,829 Phil Simms (1985)
3,764 Kerry Collins (2001)
3,762 Eli Manning (2005)
3,487 Phil Simms (1986)
3,359 Phil Simms (1988)

Most Yards Passing, Game
513 Phil Simms, at Cincinnati, Oct. 13, 1985
505 Y.A. Tittle, vs. Washington, Oct. 28, 1962
432 Phil Simms, vs. Dallas, Oct. 6, 1985
420 Eli Manning, vs. Seattle, Oct. 9, 2011
409 Phil Simms, vs. Philadelphia, Sept. 2, 1984

Most Games, 300 or More Yards Passing, Career
22 Eli Manning (2004–11)
21 Phil Simms (1979–93)
17 Kerry Collins (1999–2003)
9 Y.A. Tittle (1961–64)

Most Games, 300 or More Yards Passing, Season
8 Eli Manning (2011)
5 Kerry Collins (2001)
4 Eli Manning (2010)
4 Kerry Collins (2002)
4 Phil Simms (1986)
4 Phil Simms (1984)

Longest Pass Completion (in yards)
99 Eli Manning (to Victor Cruz), at Jets, Dec. 24, 2011
98 Earl Morrall (to Homer Jones), at Pittsburgh, Sept. 11, 1966
94 Norm Snead (to Rich Houston), vs. Dallas, Sept. 24, 1972
89 Earl Morrall (to Homer Jones), vs. Philadelphia, Oct. 17, 1965
88 Frank Reagan (to George Franck), vs. Washington, Oct. 12, 1947

Most Touchdown Passes, Career
199 Phil Simms (1979–93)
185 Eli Manning (2004–11)
173 Charlie Conerly (1948–61)
103 Fran Tarkenton (1967–71)
96 Y.A. Tittle (1961–64)

Most Touchdown Passes, Season
36 Y.A. Tittle (1963)
33 Y.A. Tittle (1962)
31 Eli Manning (2010)
29 Eli Manning (2011)
29 Fran Tarkenton (1967)

Most Touchdown Passes, Game
7 Y.A. Tittle, vs. Washington, Oct. 28, 1962
6 Y.A. Tittle, vs. Dallas, Dec. 16, 1962
5 Phil Simms, at St. Louis, Sept. 7, 1980
5 Fran Tarkenton, vs. St. Louis, Oct. 25, 1970
4 on many occasions

Most Consecutive Games Touchdown Passes
15 Y.A. Tittle (1962–64)
12 Eli Manning (2005–06)
12 Eli Manning (2004–05)
10 Eli Manning (2007)
10 Phil Simms (1988–89)
10 Phil Simms (1986–87)
10 Charlie Conerly (1948–49)

Lowest Percentage Passes Had Intercepted, Career (min. 1,000 attempts)
2.8 Kerry Collins, 1999–2003 (70 int., 2,473 att.)
3.3 Eli Manning, 2004–11 (129 int., 3,921 att.)
3.4 Phil Simms, 1979–93 (157 int., 4,647 att.)
3.5 Dave Brown, 1992–97 (49 int., 1,391 att.)
3.8 Fran Tarkenton, 1967–71 (72 int., 1,898 att.)

Lowest Percentage Passes Had Intercepted, Season
1.3 Phil Simms, 1990 (4 int., 311 att.)
1.4 Kurt Warner, 2004 (4 int., 277 att.)
1.4 Jeff Hostetler, 1991 (4 int., 285 att.)
2.0 Fran Tarkenton, 1969 (8 int., 409 att.)

Fewest Passes Had Intercepted, Game (most attempts)
0 Scott Brunner, vs. St. Louis, Dec. 26, 1982 (51 att.)
0 Phil Simms, at LA Rams, Sept. 30, 1984 (48 att.)
0 Kerry Collins, vs. Seattle, Dec. 23, 2003 (47 att.)
0 Dave Brown, vs. Baltimore, Sept. 14, 1997 (46 att.)
0 Fran Tarkenton, at Dallas, Oct. 11, 1971 (46 att.)

Most Passes Had Intercepted, Career
167 Charlie Conerly (1949–61)
157 Phil Simms (1979–93)
129 Eli Manning (2004–11)
72 Fran Tarkenton (1967–71)
70 Kerry Collins (1999–2003)

Most Passes Had Intercepted, Season
25 Elli Manning (2010)
25 Charlie Conerly (1953)
25 Frank Filchock (1946)
23 Joe Pisarcik (1978)
22 Phil Simms (1986)
22 Scott Brunner (1983)
22 Norm Snead (1973)
22 Y.A. Tittle (1964)
22 Charlie Conerly (1951)

Most Passes Had Intercepted, Game
5 Jeff Rutledge, at New Orleans, Nov. 22, 1987

5 Charlie Conerly, vs. Detroit, Dec. 13, 1953
5 Charlie Conerly, vs. Chi. Cardinals, Oct. 14, 1951
5 Frank Filchock, at Washington, Oct. 13, 1946
5 Harry Newman, at Portsmouth, Sept. 24, 1933

PASS RECEPTIONS

Most Seasons Leading League
1 Earnest Gray (1983)
1 Bob Tucker (1971)
1 Tod Goodwin (1935)

Most Pass Receptions, Career
668 Amani Toomer (1996–2008)
586 Tiki Barber (1997–2005)
395 Joe Morrison (1952–72)
371 Jeremy Shockey (2002–07)
368 Ike Hillard (1997–1003)
367 Frank Gifford (1952–64)

Most Pass Receptions, Season
107 Steve Smith (2009)
82 Victor Cruz (2011)
82 Amani Toomer (2002)
79 Hakeem Nicks (2010)
79 Amani Toomer (1999)
78 Amani Toomer (2000)
78 Earnest Gray (1983)
76 Hakeem Nicks (2010)
76 Plaxico Burress (2005)
74 Jeremy Shockey (2002)

Most Pass Receptions, Game
13 Tiki Barber, at Dallas, Jan. 2, 2000
12 Hakeem Nicks, at Houston, Oct. 10, 2010
12 Mark Bavaro, at Cincinnati, Oct. 13, 1985
12 Jeremy Shockey, vs. Dallas, Nov. 11, 2007
12 Amani Toomer, at Philadelphia, Sept. 17, 2006

Most Consecutive Games, Pass Reception
98 Amani Toomer (1998–2004)
83 Jeremy Shockey (2002–07)
68 Ike Hillard (1997–2002)
47 Chris Calloway (1996–98)
45 David Meggett (1989–92)

Most Yards Gained, Career
9,497 Amani Toomer (1996–2008)
5,434 Frank Gifford (1952–64)
5,183 Tiki Barber (1997–2006)
4,993 Joe Morrison (1959–72)
4,845 Homer Jones (1964–69)

Most Yards Gained, Season
1,536 Victor Cruz (2011)
1,343 Amani Toomer (2002)
1,220 Steve Smith (2009)
1,214 Plaxico Burress (2005)
1,209 Homer Jones (1967)
1,192 Hakeem Nicks (2011)
1,183 Amani Toomer (1999)
1,181 Del Shofner (1963)
1,139 Earnest Gray (1983)
1,133 Del Shofner (1962)

Most Yards Gained, Game
269 Del Shofner, vs. Washington, Oct. 28, 1962
212 Gene Roberts, at Green Bay, Nov. 13, 1949
204 Plaxico Burress, vs. St. Louis, Oct. 2, 2005
204 Amani Toomer, vs. Indianapolis, Dec. 22, 2002
201 Gene Roberts, vs. Bears, Oct. 23, 1949

Longest Pass Reception (in yards)
99 Victor Cruz (from Eli Manning, at Jets, Dec. 24, 2011
98 Homer Jones (from Earl Morrall), at Pittsburgh, Sept. 11, 1966
94 Rich Houston (from Norm Snead), vs. Dallas, Sept. 24, 1972
89 Homer Jones (from Earl Morrall), vs. Philadelphia, Oct. 17, 1965
88 George Franck (from Frank Reagan), at Washington, Oct. 12, 1947

Highest Average Gain, Career (min. 200 receptions)
22.6 Homer Jones, 1964–69 (214-4,845) *NFL record
18.1 Del Shofner, 1961–67 (239-4,315)
17.2 Aaron Thomas, 1962–70 (247-4,253)

Highest Average Gain, Season (qualifiers)
24.7 Homer Jones, 1967 (49-1,209)
23.5 Homer Jones, 1968 (45-1,057)
21.8 Homer Jones, 1966 (48-1,044)

Highest Average Gain, Game (min. 4 receptions)
50.3 Gene Roberts, vs. Bears, Oct. 23, 1949 (4-201)
49.0 Homer Jones, at Washington, Oct. 1, 1967 (4-196)
37.5 Frank Liebel, vs. Detroit, Nov. 18, 1945 (4-150)

Most Touchdowns, Career
54 Amani Toomer (1996–2008)
48 Kyle Rote (1951–61)
47 Joe Morrison (1959–71)
43 Frank Gifford (1952–64)
35 Homer Jones (1964–69)
35 Aaron Thomas (1962–70)
35 Del Shofner (1961–67)

Most Touchdowns, Season
13 Homer Jones (1967)
12 Plaxico Burress (2007)
12 Del Shofner (1962)
11 Hakeem Nicks (2011)
11 Del Shofner (1961)

Most Touchdowns, Game
4 Earnest Gray, at St. Louis, Sept. 7, 1980

Most Consecutive Games, Touchdown Reception
7 Kyle Rote (1949–50)
6 Plaxico Burress (2007)
5 Chris Calloway (1997–98)
5 Bobby Johnson (1984–85)
5 Aaron Thomas (1967)
5 Joe Morrison (1966)
5 Homer Jones (1966)
5 Del Shofner (1963)
5 Frank Liebel (1945)

INTERCEPTIONS

Most Seasons Leading League
2 Dick Lynch (1961, 1963)

Most Interceptions By, Career
74 Emlen Tunnell (1948–58)
52 Jimmy Patton (1955–66)
41 Spider Lockhart (1965–75)
35 Willie Williams (1965–73)
35 Dick Lynch (1959–65)

Most Interceptions By, Season
11 Jimmy Patton (1958)
11 Otto Schnellbacher (1951)
10 Willie Williams (1968)
10 Frank Reagan (1947)
10 Emlen Tunnell (1939)

Most Interceptions by, Game
3 on 18 occasions

Most Consecutive Games, Interceptions By
7 Tom Landry (1950–51)
6 Willie Williams (1968)
5 Spider Lockhart (1969–70)
5 Emlen Tunnell (1954–55)

Most Return Yards, Career
1,240 Emlen Tunnell (1948–58)
712 Jimmy Patton (1955–66)
574 Terry Kinard (1983–89)
568 Dick Lynch (1959–66)
475 Spider Lockhart (1965–75)

Most Return Yards, Season
251 Dick Lynch (1963)
251 Emlen Tunnell (1949)
203 Frank Reagan (1947)
195 Erich Barnes (1961)
194 Otto Schnellbacher (1951)

Most Return Yards, Game
109 Ward Cuff, at Philadelphia, Sept. 13, 1941
104 George Cheverko, at Washington, Oct. 3, 1948
102 Erich Barnes, at Dallas, Oct. 15, 1961

Longest Gain (in yards)
102 Erich Barnes, at Dallas, Oct. 15, 1961 (TD)
101 Henry Carr, at LA Rams, Nov. 13, 1966 (TD)
97 Lawrence Taylor, at Detroit, Nov. 25, 1982 (TD)
96 Kevin Dockery, at Dallas, Oct. 23, 2006
96 Ward Cuff, vs. Washington, Dec. 4, 1938 (TD)

Most Touchdowns, Career
4 Jason Sehorn (1994–2002)
4 Dick Lynch (1959–66)
4 Emlen Tunnell (1948–58)
3 George Martin (1975–86)
3 Spider Lockhart (1965–72)
3 Jerry Hillebrand (1963–66)
3 Erich Barnes (1961–64)
3 Tom Landry (1950–55)

New York Giants' end Michael Strahan sacks Green Bay Packers' quarterback Brett Favre late in the fourth quarter on January 6, 2002, to set a new NFL single-season sack record of 22.5.
Reuters/Ray Stubblebine Reuters/Corbis

Most Touchdowns, Season
   3   Dick Lynch (1963)

Most Consecutive Games, Touchdowns
   2   Spider Lockhart, at Phila., Sept. 22;
        vs. Washington, Sept. 29, 1968
   2   Dick Lynch, vs. Cleveland, Oct. 13; vs. Dallas,
        Oct. 20, 1963
   2   Tom Landry, at Cleveland, Oct. 28; vs. NY Yanks,
        Nov. 4, 1951

PUNTING

Most Seasons Leading League
   2   Sean Landeta (1986, 1990)
   2   Dave Jennings (1979, 1980)
   1   Don Chandler (1957)

Most Punts, Career
   931   Dave Jennings (1974–84)
   526   Sean Landeta (1985–93)
   525   Don Chandler (1956–64)
   513   Jeff Feagles (2003–2009)
   380   Brad Maynard (1997–2000)

Most Punts, Season
   111   Brad Maynard (1997)
   104   Dave Jennings (1979)
   102   Mike Horan (1996)
   101   Brad Maynard (1998)
   100   Dave Jennings (1977)

Most Punts, Game
   14   Carl Kinschef, at Detroit, Nov. 7, 1943

   13   Brad Maynard, at Washington, Nov. 23, 1997
   12   Brad Maynard, at Tampa Bay, Sept, 12, 1999

Most Yards, Career
38,792 Dave Jennings (1974–84)
23,019 Don Chandler (1956–64)
22,806 Sean Landeta (1985–93)
21,161 Jeff Feagles (2003–2009)
15,958 Brad Maynard (1997–2000)

Most Yards, Season
   4,566   Brad Maynard (1998)
   4,531   Brad Maynard (1997)
   4,445   Dave Jennings (1979)
   4,289   Mike Horan (1996)
   4,211   Dave Jennings (1980)

Most Yards, Game
   583   Carl Kinscherf, at Detroit, Nov. 7, 1943 (14 punts)
   537   Brad Maynard, at Washington, Nov. 23, 1997
           (13 punts)
   526   Brad Maynard, at Tampa Bay, Sept. 12, 1999
           (12 punts)

Longest Punt
   90   Rodney Williams, at Denver, Sept. 10, 2001
   74   Don Chandler, at Dallas, Oct. 11, 1964
   74   Len Younce, vs. Bears, Nov. 14, 1943
   73   Dave Jennings, vs. Houston, Dec. 5, 1982
   72   Dave Jennings, vs. Dallas, Nov. 4, 1979
   72   Len Younce, at Brooklyn Tigers, Oct. 15, 1944
   72   Carl Kinscherf, at Philadelphia-Pittsburgh,
           Oct. 9, 1943

Highest Average, Career (min. 150 punts)
   43.8   Don Chandler, 1956–64 (525 punts)
   43.4   Sean Landeta, 1985–93 (526 punts)
   42.1   Mike Horan, 1993–96 (303 punts)
   42.0   Brad Maynard, 1997–2000 (380 punts)
   41.7   Dave Jennings, 1974–84 (931 punts)

Highest Average Season (min. 35 punts)
   46.6   Don Chandler, 1959 (55 punts)
   45.7   Steve Weatherford, 2011 (82 punts)
   45.6   Don Chandler, 1964 (73 punts)
   45.2   Brad Maynard, 1998 (101 punts)
   44.9   Don Chandler, 1963 (59 punts)

Highest Average, Game (min. 4 punts)
   55.4   Brad Maynard, at Tennessee, Oct. 1, 2000 (5 punts)
   55.3   Dave Jennings, vs. Houston, Dec. 5, 1982 (4 punts)
   55.1   Rodney Williams, at Denver, Sept. 10, 2001
           (8 punts)
   54.1   Don Chandler, at Cleveland, Oct. 11, 1959
           (8 punts)
   54.0   Dave Jennings, at Dallas, Oct. 5, 1980 (5 punts)

Most Inside the 20, Career
   170   Dave Jennings (1974–84)
   141   Sean Landeta (1985–93)
   132   Jeff Feagles (2003–2009)

Most Inside the 20, Season
   33   Brad Maynard (1998)
   33   Brad Maynard (1997)
   32   Mike Horan (1996)
   31   Jeff Feagles (2003)
   31   Brad Maynard (1999)

Most Inside the 20, Game
   6   Jeff Feagles, vs. Carolina, Dec. 10, 2006
   6   Brad Maynard, vs. Tampa Bay, Sept. 12, 1999
   5   Brad Maynard, vs. Oakland, Sept. 13, 1998
   5   Dave Jennings, vs. St. Louis, Oct. 24, 1983 (OT)

PUNT RETURNS

Most Punt Returns, Career
   261   Emlen Tunnell (1948–58)
   213   Phil McConkey (1984–88)
   202   David Meggett (1989–94)
   122   Tiki Barber (1998–2002)
   109   Amani Toomer (1996–2001)

Most Punt Returns, Season
   53   Phil McConkey (1985)
   52   Leon Bright (1981)
   47   Chad Morton (2005)
   47   Amani Toomer (1997)
   46   David Meggett (1989)
   46   Phil McConkey (1984)

Most Punt Returns, Game
   9   Phil McConkey, vs. Philadelphia, Dec. 6, 1987
   9   Pete Shaw, at Philadelphia, Nov. 20, 1983
   9   Leon Bright, vs. Philadelphia, Dec. 11, 1982

Most Fair Catches, Career
   84   Phil McConkey (1984–88)

80　David Meggett (1989–94)
61　Spider Lockhart (1965–75)

Most Fair Catches, Season
25　Phil McConkey (1988)
22　Amani Toomer (1998)
20　Tiki Barber (2000)
20　David Meggett (1993)

Fewest Fair Catches, Season
0　Leon Bright (52 returns, 1981)

Most Fair Catches, Game
6　R.W. McQuarters, at Atlanta, Oct. 15, 2007
5　Amani Toomer, at Dallas, Sept. 8, 1996
5　Phil McConkey, vs. Philadelphia, Nov. 20, 1988

Most Punt Return Yards, Career
2,230　David Meggett (1989–94)
2,214　Emlen Tunnell (1948–58)
1,708　Phil McConkey (1984–88)
1,181　Tiki Barber (1997–2001)
1,060　Amani Toomer (1996–2001)

Mot Punt Return Yards, Season
582　David Meggett (1989)
506　Tiki Barber (1999)
489　Emlen Tunnell (1951)
467　David Meggett (1990)
455　Amani Toomer (1997)

Most Punt Return Yards, Game
147　Emlen Tunnell, vs. Chi. Cardinals, Oct. 14, 1951
143　Leon Bright, vs. Philadelphia, Dec. 11, 1982
123　Tiki Barber, vs. Dallas, Oct. 18, 1999
114　David Meggett, at New Orleans, Dec. 20, 1993
113　Amani Toomer, vs. Buffalo, Sept. 1, 1996

Longest Punt Return
87　Amani Toomer, vs. Buffalo, Sept. 1, 1996 (TD)
85　Tiki Barber, vs. Dallas, Oct. 18, 1999 (TD)
83　Eddie Dove, at Philadelphia, Sept. 29, 1963
81　Bosh Pritchard, at Chi. Cardinals, Nov. 25, 1951
81　Emlen Tunnell, vs. Chi. Cardinals, Oct. 14, 1951

Highest Average Return, Career (min. 30 returns)
12.1　Ward Cuff, 1941–45 (35 returns)
12.0　Domenik Hixon, 2007–11 (44 returns)
11.0　David Meggett, 1989–94 (202 returns)
9.7　Tiki Barber, 1998–2002 (122 returns)
9.7　Amani Toomer, 1996–2001 (109 returns)

Highest Average Return, Season (qualifiers)
16.6　Amani Toomer, 1996 (18 returns)
15.5　Merle Hapes, 1942 (11 returns)
15.1　Domenik Hixon, 2009 (17 returns)
14.9　George Franck, 1941 (13 returns)
14.4　Emlen Tunnell, 1951 (34 returns)

Highest Average Return, Game (3 Returns)
36.8　Emlen Tunnell, vs. Chi. Cardinals, Oct. 24, 1951
(4 returns)
35.3　Emlen Tunnell, vs. Washington, Dec. 7, 1952
(3 returns)
32.7　David Meggett, vs. Seattle, Nov. 19, 1989 (3 returns)

31.0　Emlen Tunnell, vs. Washington, Oct. 7, 1951
(3 returns)

Most Touchdowns, Career
6　David Meggett (1989–94)
5　Emlen Tunnell (1948–58)
3　Amani Toomer (1996–2001)

Most Touchdowns, Season
3　Emlen Tunnell (1951)
2　Amani Toomer (1996)
2　David Meggett (1994)

Most Touchdowns, Game
1　on 24 occasions

KICKOFF RETURNS

Most Seasons Leading League
1　David Meggett (1990)
1　Joe Scott (1948)
1　Clarence Childs (1964)

Most Kickoff Returns, Career
146　David Meggett (1989–94)
126　Clarence Childs (1964–67)
84　David Patten (1997–99)
71　Willie Ponder (2003–05)
68　Domenik Hixon (2007–11)

Most Kickoff Returns, Season
57　Domenik Hixon (2009)
55　Brian Mitchell (2003)
43　David Patten (1998)
41　Hershel Walker (1995)
39　Ahmad Bradshaw (2008)

Most Kickoff Returns, Game
8　Ahmad Bradshaw, vs. Minnesota, Nov. 25, 2007
8　Willie Ponder, vs. Pittsburgh, Dec. 18, 2004
8　Brian Mitchell, vs. Dallas, Sept. 15, 2003

Most Kickoff Return Yards, Career
3,163　Clarence Childs (1964–67)
2,989　David Meggett (1989–94)
1,872　Willie Ponder (2003–05)
1,768　Rocky Thompson (1971–73)
1,724　David Patten (1997–99)

Most Kickoff Return Yards, Season
1,291　Domenik Hixon, (2009)
1,117　Brian Mitchell (2003)
987　Clarence Childs (1964)
967　Willie Ponder (2004)
947　Rocky Thompson (1971)

Most Kickoff Return Yards, Game
259　Willie Ponder, vs. Pittsburgh, Dec. 18, 2004
230　Domenik Hixon, at New Orleans,
Oct. 18, 2009
230　Domenik Hixon, vs. New England,
Dec. 29, 2007
207　Joe Scott, vs. LA Rams, Nov. 14, 1948
198　Rocky Thompson, at Detroit, Sept. 17, 1972

Longest Kickoff Return
100　Clarence Childs, vs. Minnesota, Dec. 6, 1964
100　Emlen Tunnell, vs. NY Yanks, Nov. 4, 1951
99　Joe Scott, vs. LA Rams, Nov. 14, 1948
98　Jimmy Patton, vs. Washington, Oct. 30, 1955

Highest Average Return, Career (min. 40 returns)
27.2　Rocky Thompson, 1971–73 (65 returns)
27.2　Joe Scott, 1948–53 (54 returns)
26.4　Willie Ponder, 2003–05 (71 returns)
26.4　Emlen Tunnell, 1948–58 (46 returns)
25.1　Clarence Childs, 1964–67 (126 returns)

Highest Average Return, Season (qualifiers)
31.6　John Salscheider, 1949 (15 returns)
30.2　John Counts, 1962 (26 returns)
29.0　Clarence Childs, 1964 (34 returns)
28.5　Joe Scott, 1948 (20 returns)
28.3　Rocky Thompson, 1972 (29 returns)

Highest Average Return, Game (min. 3 returns)
60.0　Domenic Hixon, at Arizona, Nov. 23, 2008
(3 returns)
51.8　Joe Scott, vs. LA Rams, Nov. 14, 1948
(4 returns)
50.3　Ronnie Blye, at Pittsburgh, Sept. 15, 1968
(3 returns)
49.5　Rocky Thompson, at Detroit, Sept. 17, 1972
(4 returns)

Most Touchdowns, Career
2　Willie Ponder (2003–05)
2　Rocky Thompson (1971–73)
2　Clarence Childs (1964–67)

Most Touchdowns, Season
1　on 17 occasions

Most Touchdowns, Game
1　on 17 occasions

FUMBLES

Most Fumbles, Career
93　Phil Simms (1979–93)
61　Kerry Collins (1999–2003)
54　Charlie Conerly (1948–61)
53　Tiki Barber (1997–2006)
48　Frank Gifford (1952–64)

Most Fumbles, Season
23　Kerry Collins (2001)
16　Phil Simms (1985)
13　Eli Manning (2009)
13　Eli Manning (2007)
12　Kurt Warner (2004)
12　Kerry Collins (2003)

Most Fumbles, Game
5　Eli Manning, at Buffalo, Dec. 23, 2007
5　Charlie Conerly, vs. San Francisco, Dec. 1, 1957
4　Y.A. Tittle, at Philadelphia, Sept. 13, 1964

OWN RECOVERIES
Most Recovered, Career
  28 Phil Simms (1979–93)
  26 Charlie Conerly (1948–61)
  25 Tiki Barber (1997–2006)

Most Recovered, Season
   7 Kerry Collins (2001)
   6 Tiki Barber (2001)
   6 Jeff Hostetler (`99`)

Most Recovered, Game
   3 Eli Manning, at Buffalo, Dec. 23, 2007
   3 Tiki Barber, at Philadelphia, Oct. 29, 2000
   3 Jeff Hostetler, vs. Phoenix, Oct. 21, 1990

FUMBLES RECOVERED
Most Recovered, Career
  19 Jim Katcavage (1956–68)
  15 Michael Strahan (1993–2007)
  15 George Martin (1975–88)
  14 Harry Carson (1976–88)
  13 Keith Hamilton (1992–2002)
  13 Cliff Livingston (1954–61)

Most Recovered, Season
   5 Ernie Jones (1978)
   5 Ray Poole (1950)

Most Recovered, Game
   2 by many players

FUMBLE RETURNS
Longest Fumble Return (in yards)
  87 Keith Hamilton, at Kansas City, Sept. 10, 1995
  81 Andy Headen, vs. Dallas, Sept. 9, 1984 (TD)
  75 Osi Umenyiora, vs. San Francisco, Oct. 21, 2007 (TD)
  72 Wendell Harris, at Pittsburgh, Sept. 11, 1966 (TD)
  71 Roy Hilton, vs. Dallas, Oct. 27, 1974 (TD)

Most Touchdowns, Career
   3 Osi Umenyiora (2003–11)
   2 Kenny Holmes (2001–03)
   2 Tito Wooten (1994–98)
   2 George Martin (1975–88)
   2 Sam Huff (1956–63)
   2 Tom Landry (1949–55)
   2 Al DeRogatis (1949–52)
   2 Doc Alexander (1925–27)

Most Touchdowns, Season
   2 George Martin (1981)

Most Touchdowns, game
   1 by many players

QUARTERBACK SACKS (since 1982)
Most Sacks, Career
141.5 Michael Strahan (1993–2007)
132.5 Lawrence Taylor (1982–93)
 79.5 Leonard Marshall (1983–92)

 63.0 Keith Hamilton (1992–2003)
 46.0 George Martin (1982–88)

Most Sacks, Season
 22.5 Michael Strahan (2001)
 20.5 Lawrence Taylor (1986)
 18.5 Michael Strahan (2003)
 16.5 Jason Pierre-Paul (2011)
 15.5 Lawrence Taylor (1988)
 15.5 Leonard Marshall (1985)
 15.0 Michael Strahan (1998)
 15.0 Lawrence Taylor (1989)
 14.5 Osi Umenyiora (2005)
 14.0 Michael Strahan (1997)

Most Sacks, Game
  6.0 Osi Umenyiora, vs. Philadelphia, Sept. 30, 2007
  4.5 Pepper Johnson, at Tampa Bay, Nov. 24, 1991
  4.0 Michael Strahan, at St. Louis, Oct. 14, 2001
  4.0 Lawrence Taylor, vs. Philadelphia, Oct. 12, 1986
  4.0 Lawrence Taylor, vs. Tampa Bay, Sept. 23, 1984
  3.5 Michael Strahan, at Philadelphia, Dec. 30, 2001
  3.5 Leonard Marshall, vs. Philadelphia, Sept. 8, 1985

TEAM RECORDS: OFFENSE

SCORING
Most Points, Season
 448 in 1963
 427 in 2008
 422 in 2005
 402 in 2009
 399 in 1985

Most Points, Game
  62 vs. Philadelphia, Nov. 26, 1972
  56 vs. Philadelphia, Oct. 15, 1933
  55 vs. Green Bay, Dec. 20, 1986
  55 at Baltimore, Nov. 19, 1950

Fewest Points, Season
  79 in 1928
  93 in 1932
 115 in 1936
 122 in 1925
 128 in 1937

Most Touchdowns, Season
  57 in 1963
  49 in 1967
  49 in 1962
  48 in 2010
  48 in 1985

Most Touchdowns, Game
   8 vs. Philadelphia, Nov. 26, 1972
   8 at Baltimore, Nov. 19, 1950
   8 vs. Philadelphia, Oct. 15, 1933
   7 vs. Green Bay, Dec. 20, 1986
   7 vs. St. Louis, Dec. 7, 1969
   7 vs. Washington, Oct. 28, 1962
   7 vs. Washington, Nov. 5, 1961
   7 vs. NY Yanks, Dec. 3, 1951

   7 vs. Chi. Cardinals, Nov. 12, 1950
   7 at Green Bay, Nov. 21, 1948
   7 vs. Cleveland Rams, Nov. 16, 1941

Fewest Touchdowns, Season
  12 in 1928
  14 in 1932
  15 in 1937

Most Touchdowns Rushing, Season
  27 in 1930
  24 in 1985
  21 in 1950
  20 in 1992
  19 in 2008

Most Touchdowns Rushing, Game
   6 at Baltimore, Nov. 19, 1950
   5 vs. New Orleans, Sept. 24, 1995
   5 at Chi. Cardinals, Sept. 28, 1958
   5 vs. Philadelphia, Oct. 15, 19333

Fewest Touchdowns Rushing, Season
   3 in 1932
   4 in 1996
   4 in 1987
   4 in 1937
   4 in 1936

Most Touchdowns Passing, Season
  39 in 1963
  35 in 1962
  33 in 1967
  31 in 2010
  29 in 2011

Most Touchdowns Passing, Game
   7 vs. Washington, Oct. 28, 1962
   6 vs. Dallas, Dec. 16, 1962
   5 at St. Louis, Sept. 7, 1980
   5 vs. St. Louis, Oct 25, 1970

Fewest Touchdowns Passing, Season
   0 in 1928
   4 in 1926
   5 in 1934

Most Touchdowns on Returns, Season
  10 in 1951
   6 in 2007
   6 in 1996
   6 in 1963
   6 in 1961
   6 in 1949
   6 in 1948
   6 in 1947
   6 in 1944

Most Points After Touchdown, Season
  52 in 1963
  47 in 2010
  47 in 1962
  46 in 1961

Fewest Points After Touchdown, Season
4 in 1928
7 in 1932
8 in 1925

Most Points After Touchdown, Game
8 vs. Philadelphia, Nov. 26, 1972
8 vs. Philadelphia, Oct. 15, 1933
7 vs. Green Bay, Dec. 20, 1986
7 vs. St. Louis, Dec. 7, 1969
7 vs. Washington, Oct. 28, 1962
7 vs. Washington, Nov. 5, 1961
7 at Baltimore, Nov. 19, 1950
7 at Green Bay, Nov. 21, 1948
7 vs. Cleveland Rams, Nov. 16, 1941

Most Field Goals Attempted, Season
42 in 2005
42 in 1983
41 in 1970
39 in 2008
38 in 1989
38 in 1981

Most Field Goals Attempted, Game
6 vs. Washington, Oct. 30, 2005
6 at Minnesota, Nov. 16, 1986
6 at Washington, Dec. 17, 1983
6 at Seattle, Oct. 18, 1981
6 at Philadelphia, Nov. 14, 1954

Most Field Goals Made, Season
36 in 2008
35 in 2005
35 in 1983
29 in 1989
26 in 2002
26 in 1993
26 in 1986

Most Field Goals Made, Game
6 at Seattle, Oct. 18, 1981
5 vs. Washington, Oct. 30, 2005
5 at Cincinnati, Dec. 26, 2004
5 at Minnesota, Nov. 16, 1986
5 vs. Tampa Bay, Nov. 3, 1985
5 at Washington, Dec. 17, 1983

Fewest Field Goals Made, Season
0 in 1932
1 in 1948
1 in 1936
1 in 1931
1 in 1930
1 in 1928
1 in 1926

Highest Field Goal Percentage, Season
92.3 in 2008
88.9 in 1996
85.2 in 2007
85.2 in 2006
84.4 in 2009

Most Safeties, Season
3 in 1927
2 accomplished in 8 seasons

Most Safeties, Game
2 vs. Washington, Nov. 5, 1961
2 at Pittsburgh, Sept. 17, 1950

FIRST DOWNS

Most First Downs, Season
356 in 1985
338 in 2008
331 in 2011
331 in 2010
324 in 1986

Most First Downs, Game
34 at Cincinnati, Oct. 13, 1985
33 vs. St. Louis, Dec. 7, 1969
31 vs. New Orleans, Sept. 24, 1995
31 at Pittsburgh, Dec. 5, 1948
30 at Seattle, Nov. 7, 2010

Most First Downs Rushing, Season
138 in 1985
130 in 2008
127 in 1993
127 in 1986
125 in 1970

Most First Downs Rushing, Game
19 at Baltimore, Nov. 19, 1950
18 at New Orleans, Oct. 27, 1985
18 at Philadelphia, Dec. 15, 1957

Most First Downs Passing, Season
216 in 2011
198 in 1984
197 in 1999
195 in 2002
195 in 2000

Most First Downs Passing, Game
29 at Cincinnati, Oct. 13, 1985
22 vs. St. Louis, Dec. 7, 1969
22 at Washington, Oct. 1, 1961
22 at Pittsburgh, Dec. 5, 1948

Most First Downs by Penalty, Season
36 in 1997
35 in 2007
34 in 2005
33 in 2004
32 in 2008

Most First Downs by Penalty, Game
6 vs. Cincinnati, Oct. 26, 1997
6 vs. Baltimore, Sept. 14, 1997
6 vs. Atlanta, Nov. 11, 1979
6 at Washington, Nov. 27, 1966
6 at Philadelphia, Oct. 5, 1957

NET YARDS

Most Yards Gained, Season
6,161 in 2011
6,085 in 2010
5,884 in 1985
5,856 in 2009
5,787 in 2005

Most Yards Gained, Game
609 vs. NY Yanks, Dec. 3, 1950
602 vs. Washington, Oct. 28, 1962
568 vs. San Francisco, Nov. 17, 1963

RUSHING

Most Rushing Attempts, Season
581 in 1985
580 in 1978
567 in 1934

Most Rushing Attempts, Game
61 at Philadelphia, Oct. 3, 1937
60 at Philadelphia, Nov. 20, 1983
60 vs. St. Louis, Dec. 4, 1977

Fewest Rushing Attempts, Season
244 in 1982
316 in 1945
362 in 1948

Most Yards Rushing, Season
2,518 in 2008
2,451 in 1985
2,336 in 1950

Most Yards Rushing, Game
423 at Baltimore, Nov. 19, 1950
377 vs. NY Yanks, Dec. 3, 1950
351 vs. Washington, Nov. 29, 1959

Fewest Yards Rushing, Season
769 in 1945
842 in 1982
1,049 in 1953

PASSING

Most Passes Attempted, Season
616 in 2003
602 in 1999
589 in 2011

Most Passes Attempted, Game
62 at Cincinnati, Oct. 13, 1985
59 vs. New England, Oct. 12, 2003
59 vs. Green Bay, Jan. 6, 2002
54 vs. Philadelphia, Nov. 22, 1992
53 vs. Washington, Dec. 16, 207
53 at Seattle, Nov. 27, 2005
53 vs. Dallas, Sept. 21, 1998
53 at Pittsburgh, Dec. 5, 1948

Fewest Passes Attempted, Season
125 in 1944
148 in 1942

149   in 1943
149   in 1934

Most Passes Completed, Season
359   in 2011
350   in 1999
339   in 2010

Most Passes Completed, Game
40   at Cincinnati, Oct. 13, 1985
36   vs. Green Bay, Jan. 6, 2002
36   at Pittsburgh, Dec. 5, 1948
35   at New England, Oct. 12, 2003
32   at Washington, Oct. 28, 001

Fewest Passes Completed, Season
47   in 1944
63   in 1943
64   in 1934

Highest Completion Percentage, Season
62.9   in 2010
62.4   in 2009
61.6   in 2002

Most Yards Gained (net), Season
4,734   in 2011
4,019   in 2009
3,951   in 2002

Most Yards Gained (Net) Passing, Game
505   vs. Washington, Oct. 28, 1962
443   at Cincinnati, Oct. 13, 1985
403   vs. Dallas, Oct. 6, 1985
401   vs. Cleveland, Dec. 6, 1959
400   at Dallas, Dec. 11, 2011

Most Passes Had Intercepted, Season
34   in 1953
31   in 1966
31   in 1983

Most Passes Had Intercepted, Game
7   at Pittsburgh, Nov. 30, 1952
5   many times

Fewest Passes Had Intercepted, Season
5   in 1990
8   in 1991
8   in 1969

PUNTING
Most Punts, Season
112   in 1997
104   in 1979
102   in 1976

Most Punts, Game
15   at Bears, Nov. 17, 1935
14   at Detroit, Nov. 7, 1943
14   at Brooklyn, Nov. 26, 1936

Fewest Punts, Season
55   in 1987
55   in 1984

55   in 1983
55   in 1953

Most Yards Punting, Season
4,566   in 1998
4,531   in 1997
4,445   in 1979

Most Yards Punting, Game
607   at Detroit, Sept. 23, 1934
602   at Brooklyn, Nov. 26, 1936
597   at Bears, Nov. 17, 1935
583   at Detroit, Nov. 7, 1943
537   at Washington, Nov. 23, 1997

PUNT RETURNS
Most Yards Gained, Season
717   in 1941
675   in 1951
626   in 1938

Most Yards Gained, Game
149   vs. Chi. Cardinals, Oct. 14, 1951
143   vs. Philadelphia, Dec. 11, 1982
123   vs. Dallas, Oct. 18, 1999

Highest Return Average (in yards), Season
15.3   in 1941
14.1   in 1951
13.3   in 1943

KICKOFF RETURNS
Most Returns, Season
80   in 1966
73   in 1994
72   in 2003

Most Returns, Game
12   at Washington, Nov. 27, 1966
10   vs. Chi. Cardinals, Oct. 17, 1948
9   at Dallas, Sept. 18, 1966
9   at Pittsburgh, Nov. 30, 1952

Most Yards Gained, Season
1,688   in 1964
1,658   in 2004
1,616   in 1966

Most Yards Gained, Game
274   at Washington, Nov. 27, 1966
263   vs. LA Rams, Nov. 14, 1948
259   vs. Pittsburgh, Dec. 18, 2004
236   at Cleveland, Dec. 4. 1966

Highest Return Average (in yards), Season
27.4   in 1944
26.3   in 1953
26.0   in 1946

FUMBLES
Most Fumbles, Season
49   in 1960
44   in 1975
44   in 1964

Most Fumbles, Game
9   at Buffalo, Oct. 20, 1975
8   vs. San Francisco, Dec. 1, 1957
7   vs. Philadelphia, Dec. 28, 2002
7   vs. Philadelphia, Oct. 18, 1964
7   vs. Washington, Nov. 5, 1950

Most Own Fumbles Recovered, Season
23   in 1960
21   in 1981
21   in 1975
21   in 1964

Most Own Fumbles Recovered, Game
6   at Buffalo, Oct. 20, 1974
5   vs. Dallas, Oct. 27, 1974
5   vs. Philadelphia, Oct. 18, 1964
5   vs. Washington, Nov. 5, 1950
5   at Philadelphia Nov. 3, 1946
5   vs. Pittsburgh, Oct. 21, 1945

Most Opponents' Fumbles Recovered, Season
27   in 1950
26   in 1946
23   in 1980

Most Opponents' Fumbles Recovered, Game
6   at Pittsburgh, Sept. 17, 1950
5   at Dallas, Oct. 11, 1971

PENALTIES
Most Penalties, Season
143   in 2005
127   in 2003
124   in 1998

Most Penalties, Game
17   at Washington, Oct. 9, 1949
17   vs. Boston Yankees, Nov. 28, 1948
16   at Seattle, Nov. 27, 2005

Most Yards Penalized, Season
1,115   in 2005
1,090   in 2003

Most Yards Penalized, Game
177   at Washington, Oct. 9, 1949
175   vs. Boston, Oct. 19, 1947
150   at Minnesota, Nov. 19, 2001
150   at Detroit, Nov. 2, 1947

TEAM RECORDS: DEFENSE

SCORING
Fewest Points Allowed, Season
20   in 1927
51   in 1926
67   in 1925

Fewest Points Allowed, Game
0   many times

Most Points Allowed, Season
501   in 1966

427 in 2009
425 in 1980
400 in 2011

Most Points Allowed, Game
  72 at Washington, Nov. 27, 1966
  63 at Pittsburgh, Nov. 30, 1952
  63 vs. Chi. Cardinals, Oct. 17, 1948

Fewest Touchdowns Allowed, Season
  3 in 1927
  7 in 1926
  8 in 1925

Most Touchdowns Allowed, Season
  66 in 1966
  55 in 1980
  54 in 1948

Most Touchdowns Allowed, Game
  10 at Washington, Nov. 27, 1966
  9 at Pittsburgh, Nov. 30, 1952
  9 vs. Chi. Cardinals, Oct. 17, 1948

Most Points After Touchdown Allowed, Season
  63 in 1966
  52 in 1948
  51 in 1980

Most Points After Touchdown Allowed, Game
  9 vs. Washington, Nov. 27, 1966
  9 vs. Pittsburgh, Nov. 30, 1952
  9 vs. Chi. Cardinals, Oct. 17, 1948

Most Field Goals Allowed, Season
  29 in 1994
  29 in 1991
  28 in 2003
  28 in 1995

Most Field Goals Allowed, Game
  7 vs. Dallas, Sept. 15, 2003
  5 at Dallas, Dec. 17, 1995

Most Safeties by Opponent, Season
  3 in 1984
  2 in 1965

FIRST DOWNS
Fewest First Downs Allowed, Season
  104 in 1938
  106 in 1937
  116 in 1941

Fewest First Downs Allowed, Game
  1 at Pittsburgh, Sept. 20, 1933
  2 at Philadelphia, Oct. 3, 1937
  2 vs. Bklyn. Dodgers, Oct. 14, 1934

Most First Downs Allowed, Season
  338 in 2011
  336 in 1980
  335 in 1995

Most First Downs Allowed, Game
  38 at LA Rams, Nov. 13, 1966
  32 vs. Dallas, Sept. 10, 1978
  31 at New Orleans, Nov. 28, 2011
  31 vs. Tennessee, Dec. 1, 2002
  31 at San Diego, Oct. 19, 1980

Fewest Rushing First Downs Allowed, Season
  55 in 1982
  58 in 1938
  59 in 1937

Most Rushing First Downs Allowed, Season
  156 in 1980
  155 in 1978
  137 in 1975

Most Rushing First Downs Allowed, Game
  19 at Buffalo, Nov. 26, 1978
  19 vs. Green Bay, Oct. 22, 1967
  17 vs. St. Louis, Dec. 12, 1976

Fewest Passing First Downs Allowed, Season
  41 in 1937
  43 in 1938
  47 in 1941

Most Passing First Downs Allowed, Season
  195 in 1997
  189 in 2006
  189 in 2005

Most Passing First Downs Allowed, Game
  23 at San Diego, Oct. 19, 1980
  22 vs. St. Louis, Oct. 2, 2005
  21 vs. Tennessee, Dec. 1, 2002

NET YARDS
Fewest Yards Allowed, Season
2,029 in 1938
2,054 in 1935
2,169 in 1937

Fewest Yards Allowed, Game
  48 at Bklyn. Dodgers, Oct. 17, 1943
  62 at Pittsburgh, Sept. 20, 1933
  66 vs. Pittsburgh, Dec. 8, 1935

Most Yards Allowed, Season
6,022 in 2011
5,752 in 1980
5,479 in 2006

Most Yards Allowed, Game
  682 vs. Chi. Bears, Nov. 14, 1943
  577 at New Orleans, Nov. 28, 2011
  572 at LA Rams, Nov. 13, 1966

RUSHING
Fewest Attempts, Opponent, Season
  301 in 1982
  350 in 1986
  359 in 2000

Fewest Attempts, Opponent, Game
  7 at Houston, Dec. 8, 1985
  9 at Philadelphia, Nov. 20, 1983
  9 at Philadelphia, Oct. 3, 1937

Most Attempts, Opponent, Season
  640 in 1978
  618 in 1979
  584 in 1980

Most Attempts, Opponent, Game
  60 at Washington, Dec. 9, 1945
  58 at Washington, Nov. 18, 1956
  58 at Philadelphia, Oct. 4, 1947

Fewest Yards Allowed, Season
  913 in 1951
  977 in 1940
1,000 in 1944

Fewest Yards Allowed, Game
  -24 at Bklyn. Dodgers, Oct. 17, 1943
  -1 vs. Chi. Cardinals, Oct. 18, 1953
  6 at Cleveland, Nov. 6, 1960

Most Yards Allowed, Season
2,656 in 1978
2,507 in 1980
2,452 in 1979

Most Yards Allowed, Game
  420 at Boston (Redskins), Oct. 8, 1933
  366 at Buffalo, Nov. 26, 1978
  341 at Detroit, Nov. 15, 1936

Fewest Rushing Touchdowns Allowed, Season
  1 in 1927
  2 in 1944
  3 in 1938
  3 in 1926

Most Rushing Touchdowns Allowed, Season
  31 in 1980
  25 in 1978
  25 in 1948

Most Rushing Touchdowns Allowed, Game
  5 at Buffalo, Nov. 26, 1978
  5 vs. Green Bay, Oct. 22, 1967

PASSING
Fewest Attempts, Opponent, Season
  149 in 1963
  182 in 1937
  184 in 1934

Fewest Attempts, Opponent, Game
  3 at Detroit, Sept. 23, 1934
  4 vs. Bklyn. Dodgers, Dec. 7, 1941

Most Attempts, Opponent, Season
  596 in 1997
  589 in 2011
  587 in 1986

Most Attempts, Opponent, Game
62 vs. St. Louis, Oct. 2, 2005
61 at Carolina, Dec. 10, 2006
60 at Washington, Nov. 23, 1997

Fewest Completions Allowed, Season
54 in 1934
60 in 1936
62 in 1933

Fewest Completions Allowed, Game
0 at Washington, Dec. 11, 1960
1 many times

Most Completions Allowed, Season
361 in 2011
334 in 1986
333 in 2006

Most Completions Allowed, Game
40 vs. St. Louis, Oct. 2, 2005
35 vs. St. Louis, Sept. 7, 2003
34 vs. Carolina, Dec. 10, 2006
34 vs. Dallas, Oct. 5, 1997
34 vs. Chi. Bears, Oct. 23, 1949

Fewest Yards Allowed (Net), Season
744 in 1934
809 in 1933
914 in 1938

Fewest Yards Allowed (Net), Game
-13 at Philadelphia, Dec. 11, 1977
-6 at Washington, Dec. 11, 1960
0 at Chi. Cardinals, Nov. 22, 1959

Most Yards Allowed (Net), Season
4,082 in 2011

3,649 in 2006
3,616 in 1997

Most Yards Allowed (Net), Game
488 vs. Chi. Bears, Nov. 14, 1943
460 at Philadelphia, Nov. 8, 1953
456 at San Diego, Oct. 19, 1980

Fewest Touchdowns Allowed, Season
2 in 1927
3 in 1944
3 in 1939

Most Touchdowns Allowed, Season
36 in 1966
31 in 2009
28 in 2004
28 in 1964

Most Touchdowns Allowed, Game
7 vs. Chi. Bears, Nov. 14, 1943
6 vs. Cleveland, Dec. 12, 1964

INTERCEPTIONS

Most Interceptions Made, Season
41 in 1951
39 in 1948
35 in 1939

Most Interceptions Made, Game
8 at NY Yanks, Dec. 16, 1951
8 at Green Bay, Nov. 21, 1948
7 vs. Washington, Dec. 8, 1963

Fewest Interceptions Made, Season
10 in 2003
11 in 2002
12 in 1991

12 in 1982
12 in 1977
12 in 1976

Most Return Yards, Season
569 in 1941
561 in 1948
549 in 1944

Most Return Yards, Game
144 at Philadelphia, Sept. 13, 1941
138 at Dallas, Oct. 15, 1961
137 at Washington, Oct. 29, 1995

Fewest Return Yards, Season
62 in 1976
91 in 1974
93 in 2002

Most Returns for Touchdown, Season
5 in 1963

Most Returns for Touchdown, Game
2 at Buffalo, Dec. 23, 2007
2 at Detroit, Oct. 27, 1996
2 vs. Washington, Dec. 8, 1963
2 vs. Washington, Dec. 4, 1938

SACKS

Most Sacks, Season
68 in 1968
59 in 1986
55 in 1987
54 in 1998
54 in 1997

Giants defenders come together during pre-game warm-ups against the Dallas Cowboys.
Andy Mills/Star Ledger/Corbis

INDEX